Published by Limited Means Productions

Copyright © 2013 Glenn Young
All rights reserved.
ISBN-10: 1492714615
ISBN-13: 978-1492714613
LCCN: 2013919245

Photo credits

All photos taken by Glenn Young except where noted

- Cover Photo
  Pamukkale, Turkey

- Copyright page
  Roadside shot in Cappadocia, Turkey

- Back cover
  Head shot of Glenn Young is Carmel, California shot taken by a sister

- Preface
  Sam Wolf inside the Blue Mosque, Istanbul, Turkey

- Seeing the Political Historically Page
  The Lion's Gate at Hattusa, Turkey

- Relatively Modern Times
  Skyline of Seattle, Washington taken from east of Lake Washington.

- The Personal as Historical Page
  Catal Huyuk excavation, south central Turkey – shot taken by L.P. Glenn's traveling companion

NO SENSE OF HISTORY

OR

WHY WE HAVE SUCH A HARD TIME UNDERSTANDING THE PRESENT AND THE POTENTIAL FUTURE

Political, personal and historical essays from the last decade or so

That incorporates history –
(Which few seem to know; or want to know)
and the
conflicts between modernism and
religious fundamentalism
(which few seem to understand).

Glenn Young
MPA, amateur historian and general outlier

Table of Contents	Page
Acknowledgements	iii
Preface	vii

Introduction:
- Section I: History, Modernism, Religion and the Constant Battle through Time 1
- Section 2 Comment on Religious Impact on Overviews of Historical Characters or; the Battle of the Super Heroes 21

Part I - Seeing the Political Historically

Section 1- Setting the Stage

1) Where Did This Fantasy of the US Being a Progressive Country Come From? 33
2) Comments on the American Experience – A problem in Understanding History 42
3) Cincinnatus Reconsidered – The Real Inspiration of the Founding Fathers 51
4) Two Essays on Time
   A) What Year Is This? - How the Designation of This Year as 2013 Disrespects Most of the Cultures of the World. 63
   B) When Did This Modern World Start? 87
5) Is South Carolina the Most Important State in US History? 105
6) What is the Second Most Important Date in the History of African Americans? 130

Section 2 – Relatively Modern Times   Page

1) American Christian Fundamentalist –
   Is America Being Taken Over By People
   Suffering From a Form of Mental Illness?   149
2) The Real Peace Dividend   179
3) Israel for Sicily   184
4) Iraqi Democracy less like the American
   Constitutional Era, More like
   Southern Reconstruction   204
5) Would We Have Our Constitution
   in the Age of Mass Media?   213
6) American Response to the Economic
   Crisis – No Sense of History   216
7) Drones and the Theories of
   General War   252
8) May Day, Boston and Our History of Terror   260
9) Ten Things I learned about Religion   268
10) A Heaven for Democracy   290

Part II - Seeing the Personal Historically

1) How I Almost Met Bill Gates and
   Almost Changed the World   321
2) The Pope and the Great American Bird   332
3) *I Almost Cut My Hair* – Revised –
   Censored Version   348
4) On the Passing of a Comrade   356

Acknowledgements

In one of my favorite Bob Dylan songs, *Tom Thumb Blues* he talked of desperate situations where he was alone and without support: (copyright laws prevent a direct quote of the specific lines.) For many years, these images, along with similar stories told in his song I am the *Lonesome Hobo* capsulized how

I saw my life for a good many years; isolated, friendless, highly dysfunctional, with no one there to help to even "con." However, over time I learned to view things a bit more optimistically. And in writing the acknowledgements for this book I have to recognize that I had lots of people with me all along, whether I tried to bluff them or not, they were there.

All of them figured into this effort of conceiving and then writing these essays, whether they recognized it or not. The list is extensive and will be limited by reason and space. Also, while there is a difference between acknowledgement and thanking, in this case, let the word acknowledgment stand in for both terms.

First I need to acknowledge my siblings who, despite our vast differences on the concepts of religion, continued to love me (well most of them did). Sometimes, for periods of my life they were the only ones who did say the word love to me. They were also the first ones with whom I argued about most of the themes in these essays. They taught me skills in how to argue points.

I also have to acknowledge my siblings' children, and their children, and an ex-brother-in-law who have given me something that I lacked through much of my life, a positive sense of family. And my friend Lorie and her child Tutu gave me the surrogate daughter and grandchild I needed.

And my good friend Helene, who made sure the positive passages of my life were not only celebrated but celebrated well. I need to also acknowledge my daughter, whose unwillingness to accept anything but quality, forced me to become a far better person than I once was. With all of these there was somewhat of a safe place to explore ideas.

I also need to acknowledge (in a reverse time sequence) my long-time friend and lover Janet, who allowed me to ramble on about ideas that have found themselves in many of these essays. She listened and replied with wisdom. In addition, I need to speak of a lover before her, named Temmie, who, as with so many others with dyslexia who rely on someone to edit them, was the main editor of my college writing. In my mid-thirties, she had to teach me how to write in a coherent and academic fashion almost from scratch.

And as is traditional with most dyslexics who are identified later in life, there is the teacher, for me Dee, who finally taught me, between my thirty and thirty-third years of life, how to read and understand what the words meant. She had me start with the basics of letter-sound relationship and worked with me for months having me just air-drawing letters and saying the sound. It was a tedious task made possible by her skills.

There is also my partner of many years, Carol, who when I was first spot diagnosed as having dyslexia, did everything I should have done to start the rehabilitation process, but was too frozen to do. It was her, not me, who arranged for me to be formally diagnosed, found Dee, and made sure I went to the classes and did my "homework;" and did not ridicule me in the least as I used Scrabble to slowly expand the ability to spell word that consisted of more than four letters. A Dylan quote about family and friends could go well here, but once again I am stopped by copyright laws.

In addition there is now A.T. who has shown extensive tolerance and knowledge in working with me as my current editor. The few errors that may be found in this version of the book are her fault, but the thousands of errors that no longer exist are also her doing. Of course the errors are really my issue … since the final copy is mine, and she did not do the final proofing, but … like a good editor she can take the blame.

Lastly, there is the long parade of various people of all types who I've meet and who impacted me by their personalities and their knowledge. Of the multitudes of options of stories to tell here there is one that should be told. In 1968, I spent a week hanging out at the old Industrial Workers of the World (IWW) headquarters in Chicago.

The few ancient "Wobblies" that remained there were thrilled that a young "fellow worker" not only remembered them, but was willing to listen for hours on end as they told the history of labor, from their viewpoint. To me it was my college-level course in labor history, to them one more chance to tell stories of their glory days.

When I was getting ready to head out, to hitch-hike back to San Francisco, one of the old men took me aside and shook my hand. As he did, this veteran of the fight for labor justice, who went to jail rather than fight in WWI, and who later actual volunteered to fight in the International Brigades against Franco in Spain, this man who had become a hero to me, placed a single dollar bill there, and offered me his hope for a good trip home. "Stay out of Utah" he said in a reference to the execution of Joe Hill in that state, some fifty years before (1916).

That man's giving of what was surely a large percent of his monthly pension, helped me to understand what life-long commitment meant, what love of and learning from history meant, and taught me to always give back to others. These essays are one more effort on my part to keep history alive and to give back to those who gave so much for me.

Glenn Young, September 2013

Preface

In *No Sense of History*, my Great Uncle Glenn Young, my father's uncle, through his essays explores the links between the past, present, and future;, and the consequences that history has on the present day. He breaks through barriers: exploring the details of humanities good and not-so-good past, and forms astonishing conclusions about our own modern world.

Why do we indeed have such a hard time understanding the past, present and the potential future? Is it the declining standards of education? Or is it rather the lack of a need to understand such things in our society's culture? Maybe it is even because most people don't feel the necessity to connect to and understand our potential future, simply because they don't see how it relates to them. Whatever the answer is, I can say for certain that it is not because too many people are like my Great Uncle Glenn. Not only does Glenn Young have the great gift of being able to connect history to our present and future, but he also is fantastic at sharing his knowledge with others.

For several years, it was my family's tradition that, right when school let out for the summer, my father, Glenn and I would take a road trip across America. However, in the summer of 2012, when I was thirteen, Glenn offered a new option for that's year's travel. He asked my parents if he could take me to Turkey. And after much conversation they agreed to the trip.

So, Glenn and I went on a trip to Turkey, with the primary goal of seeing the artifacts of long gone cultures that exist there. However, I soon learned through conversation with Glenn that, although those cultures may have faded away thousands of years ago, they are by no means long gone.

This was Glenn's greatest lesson to me: that all societies leave a trace of themselves in our modern world, and that the place we live in today could have been entirely different if not for the events of the distant past.

One of the first places we visited in Turkey was the Hagia Sofia mosque in Istanbul. I had just seen the Blue Mosque less than a mile away: a place of astonishing beauty and history, and had expected something of the same nature when I entered the Hagia Sofia. How wrong I was! Inside this mosque, along with the Muslim religious writing and symbols, there were undeniably Christian paintings on the walls as well. On any given wall, next to some beautiful Islamic calligraphy, you could see a picture of Jesus Christ!

At first, I was very befuddled at this. However, my Great Uncle Glenn soon explained that the Hagia Sofia was once, in fact, a church. Before the Turks took over Istanbul in 1453, it was called Constantinople, and was the capital of the Eastern Orthodox Byzantine Empire. When the Ottoman Empire conquered the city, they decided to use the church for a new mosque.

However, instead of destroying the Christian artwork, they kept it, and merely added on the Muslim ones alongside it. Not only does this serve as an excellent reminder of religious tolerance, but it also shows a piece of living history. Although both the Byzantines and the Ottomans eventually fell, the cultures both live on within the Hagia Sofia and you can see a remnant of the religious tolerance of the Ottomans every time you look within this church. The Hagia Sofia can be taken as a metaphor for the modern and future world in many ways, and it was my Great Uncle Glenn who helped me see this.

Throughout our trip, Glenn Young showed me some of the most exquisite historical sites from the very first civilizations.

We travelled around Turkey for almost two weeks, not nearly enough time, but my understanding of the world deepened hugely during that short trip. I learned that history textbooks often present the past in a false, Westernized way.

This is not true with Glenn Young's writings and conceptions in the slightest. Many people present the rise as Christianity as being inevitable. However, Glenn taught me that this was hardly so, as in a remote site in Eastern Turkey, as I walked slowly down a dark cave that was a "Mithraic" holy site. Mithraism was a religion with Persian origins that is not unlike Zoroastrianism.

I learned that, during the time that Constantine legalized Christianity, there were far more Mithraists than Christians in the Roman Empire. It is entirely possible that Mithraism could take taken whole of the empire rather than Christianity, which would have completely changed the course of history.

In another desolate location in Eastern Turkey, only twenty miles from the Syrian border (something my parents were not thrilled about me going there), we went to a place called Göbekli Tepe. At first, it didn't seem any different from the other historical sites we had travelled to. However, Glenn started telling me the story of the place and how it is currently believed that it is over 12,000 years old! The settlement was definitely permanent, which means that civilization had begun far earlier than we knew. These people built advanced structures and seemed to have a religion, as well as beautiful stone carvings of animals. The fact that such a society existed in that time period calls into question everything we know about history, and could change how we look at all civilizations that followed it.

It was impossible not to feel a sense of awe as Glenn explained this to me, and I felt like everything that I learned in school could be drawn into question.

In conclusion, my Great Uncle presents history in a completely unbiased way, relying on facts, not cultural myths, crossing barriers that others have not dared to. He questions our religion, culture, and society by looking back into the past, and many of his conclusions, wild as they seem, may well be correct. If you want to hear what seems like revolutionary new theories that link almost every known society in the history to the present and to each other, while presenting fascinating new conclusions, you should learn from Glenn Young. Since you will most likely never have the chance to travel with him like I did, the essays in this book give you a chance to get a little of what I did on my trip to Turkey.

Samuel Wolf, September 2013
Seattle, Washington

No Sense of History

INTRODUCTION

History, Modernism, Religion and the Constant Battle through Time

Part I – Me

In late 1989, as I propped myself up in my bed and watched the incredible events of the people of East Germany and West Germany destroying the famous Berlin Wall, I turned to my companion of the time and asked her; "So, OK now that Communism is toast, what will be the next Hegelian shift?" She always accused me of having the strangest pillow talk of any man she ever knew and suspected she suspected would ever know. I would imagine she was right in her assumption. Perhaps it's because most people have no sense of history and are not willing to talk about history, in bed or anywhere else.

However, at that time, with a little frustration in her manner, and what appeared to be a challenging tone, she did ask me what the new conflict would be, and I said to her, "the modern world against religious fundamentalism of all kinds." Bad pillow talk for sure, but my projection of the time seems to have been accurate; and something few people would have foreseen (besides few people thinking or speaking of events unfolding in terms of Hegel.) She thought my projections were odd, strange, and most likely off- base (a polite way of saying wrong and crazy), as did most people I told at the time. But then again, few people in general really have a sense of history that I have developed, over the time. I, and most of the rest of the world, then and now, simply operate from a differing base of knowledge.

In fact, many people I have known, in many locations and over the years times, thought I had odd, strange, and off- base (wrong) takes on most things current (or current at the time of my commenting on them), or on my projections of the future, and, even more so, in my explanations of the past.

And like Cassandra, it seems when my projections turned out to be true, few remembered my offerings. So here we sit, the two of us in bed, at the beginnings of the new world-wide struggle between modernism and fundamentalism, at the beginnings of a new Hegelian shift, and it seemed to me that only a few knew what I knew and almost no one other than my lover knew that I knew that it was happening.

I often thought of my writings on things not thought by about by others or not analyzed as I had analyzed the events, as lonely isolated tomes; or as I would say to myself, great political essays unread by others. Therefore when I wrote on events as they occurred of on viewing the past, I again felt as if almost no one knew what I was saying. Now I try to adjust for that by complying some of these thoughts, somewhat out of time and context.

The essays included in this book, which are by no means all focused on the rise of fundamentalism, actually contain few projections or predictions, but focus more on the background base of knowledge that I used to make these projections. I've tried to provide insights as to why I see the current world and the potential future so differently (strange and odd, but not wrong) from how others see it. I don't really assume that I know the future (since so many unforeseen events can impact the timeline). But, I do think that ignoring the past makes our vision of the now and of the future hazy at best

At this point in the introduction I can write with vehemence on the importance of knowing and understanding history, especially from a non-biased point of view. However so many have done so in the past, I will avoid repetition here. After all these essays are supposed to be focused on my odd take on things ... and there is nothing odd about promoting the study and understanding of history. It's not just that cliché "we are condemned to re-live the past", it's also my fear that without an understanding of history, we would not even be aware that we are doing so.

Unlike most people, I have had the privilege of the time, inclination and resources to independently study history, and to visit historical sites, etc. I have been able to (again independently) talk to leading historians and archeologist as just a person, not someone looking for a grade, or a grant, or a position, nor as a competitor. I do look upon these life events as truly a privilege; and it has provided me with that sense of history so few are able to develop.

- This is one of the unifying points of the essays presented in this book – I have a different perspective than most, based on my study and understanding of history, and on my multicultural research and experiences.

These essays incorporate some comments of my on the present, and, with some of my projections about the future, through a prism created (or perhaps distorted) and my knowledge of the past.

Perhaps through my experience in opposition to the Viet Nam War and decades of work against social injustice, I have learned in my study of history to not accept the "official story," but to look at as many sides to the events as possible (winners, losers, neutrals, etc.). I also have learned to find my own takes on any give topic based on looking at multiple competing views. In addition, I determined that while there is a great deal of propaganda and distortions presented on any given event, "truths" are not common.

I have often quoted Bob Dylan's *Gates of Eden* about defining and finding "truth" (copyright laws prevent the direct quote) to underscore that sense. So I hope the readers can find some "truth" in my essays, making them something not common.

Therefore, while I do not in any way claim to know it all or to fully reach "truths," I do claim, based on these experiences to know a great deal more than the vast majority in the field of history, as limited as that field may be in knowing how to functioning this world. And I do claim that my understanding of the present and the potential future is based on these facts that few seem to have in their realm of knowledge.

My wonderful great nephew, also a lover of history, thinks of me as a "history savant." I do not claim such a status. What I do have is the gift or curse of good memory of over fifty years of serious reading and evaluations of history, and, on occasion, the time to really do some serious thinking about what I have read. In addition, due to limiting barriers that others may have (such as a need to compete in academia or be dependent upon my writing for wealth, I can make connections in evaluation of events that so many others can or will not do.

In an interview I saw many years ago, Joseph Campbell said that after college, he went "up-state" and read for five years. At the time, I was so envious that Campbell had the resources to be able to do such a thing. During the following years, I tried to do what I could to read as much as I could, but life often interfered. ... Then I had a severe illness that forced me to retire but then allowed me a somewhat similar experience to Campbell (actually closer to ten years of relatively undisturbed reading time). I am not claiming to be anything near a

Campbell, but I did have, like him, extensive time to read and did take advantage of it to the degree my health would allow.

As mentioned, I'm not forced to survive in the restraint of an academic setting or depending upon income from my historic studies. Therefore, I see myself as not just an enthusiastic amateur, but as a "free thinker" who is able to make the connections that few are able to see or dare to see and write about without potential social and economic loss. I therefore have been free to write about the connections of multicultural, trans-time and space events (for example how events occurring in different locations in different times actually are related and impact each other. One really well-accepted example of this is how the Huns failed to take China and therefore moved west.

As noted most historians are not allowed to too far from their smokestack due to the risk of professional ridicule. I really do not have much fear or concern about ridicule from others. How much more shameful can the ridicule be beyond your lover trashing your ideas in your own bed?

My view of people as mostly having no sense of history is in no way a statement against the capacity or intelligence of people. It is a statement on how few in this culture are provided with a chance or are encouraged to have a desire to know the past: other than the convenient overview offered by schools and the cultural myths presented to us to help maintain a sense of a national identity.

- In most things technological and most things musical etc., I am a "very limited" person.

So, my view of most peoples' statements on history or current events even, is somewhat akin to a musicians' view of my evaluation of hip hop or Mozart; I can make comments that sound rational to me but are, well close to idiotic to someone with a solid foundation in the field. I've been told by professional historians who have read some of my works that I definitely "think like a historian." My essays are that – examples of thinking out of the box like a historian, often uninfluenced by the norms and demands of the current society.

Part II - How These Essays Differ From Others

As a quick review of what has been stated, the reader will find that these essays differ from others since I tend not to be limited by restraints of others. The four ones I can discuss here, and a key to understanding my essays, are:

- Professional requirements ... both in writing style
- and in limiting of focus
- Religious demands
- Cultural Chauvinism
- Monetary needs

Therefore, what I can address is somewhat different than most political and historical writers. I am writing without need for acceptance from an audience of the narrow band of academics and historians, but, well, towards anyone and everyone interested in looking for solutions in this modern world.

I can write in a flowing fashion without footnotes, because I answer to no one but my readers (and myself). I can cover a wide range of issues, because I am not pigeonholed by political or cultural restraints.

I direct these essays to people who see this world filled with both old thoughts and beliefs and new concepts and innovations, all of which are in great conflict, and who cannot understand why no solutions offered tend to work. My contention is that the solutions offered lack historical foundations, and broad cultural respect. This theme runs through all of these essays.

- While the essays are primarily serious, unlike most serious historians, I do attempt to follow the directive of the one of the bad guys in the original Manchurian Candidate when he commented that one should always use a little humor in all situations (again copyright laws prevent direct quote).

The reader will find that some of these essays are highly focused, and some cover a wide range of time and issues; some are concrete in approach and some seem farfetched in premise and conclusion (purposely). The uniting force is that all of the essays return to history, mostly not well known or understood history, to provide the basis for the observations and conclusions.

Part III - Restraints Avoided

One of the recurring themes in my essays and other writings is that people in this culture (as well as perhaps all other cultures), rely too much on their religious background for any historical base they may have. Much of what most individuals' understanding of the "Ancient World" is based mainly on the Bible, if they are Christian or Jewish, or the Koran, if Muslim, or many sacred books if they are Hindu, and a vast number of ancient writings of China, if they are Chinese.

I would state without concern that almost all the history presented in these books are myths, or greatly impacted by myth, especially the "foundations stories" of the culture.

- So many of the things believed to be historic facts based on religious stories are in fact not supported by modern historical research and archeology.

This projection is especially true of the "Abrahamic" religions of Christianity, Judaism and, to a far lesser degree, Islam. Even the fact-based sacred histories of India and China are now so filled with legends and religious diversions, that the actual life stories of the people who gave these cultures their morals and norms are undependable, at best.

While there is much more evidence to support the existence of the Buddha or Lord Kong (Confucius) and especially Mohammad, than there is for Jesus or Moses, what becomes problematical is when cultures add "stories" to support the divinity or superiority of the foundation person; these stories become necessary to justify others following the new prophet, teacher, reformer, god, etc. And then these stories become ingrained into belief and require acceptance, and then become official history of the culture that cannot be challenged.

Unfortunately in this world, myth is far too often forced upon people as history.

- An essay in the introduction section addresses some of this issue of religious history versus the actual provable history, looking at the lives and times of David and Achilles.

I once worked on a project to redesign the US citizenship test, to update it and make it more relevant to current day life. In this process I sat through a series of noted people who gave the team their perspectives on what should or should not be changed in the exam. I was more than shocked when the noted historian on the panel stated that in his mind it was more important that immigrants to the US should know the "myths" of America far more than the "history" of America.

Needless to say, I disagreed then as I do now.

Our myths are as often as untrue as the myths of religions, and our American myths have greatly altered our American history and the choices we make as a nation.

- One of the essays (on the US being a progressive country) takes on some of these issues

In addition, mostly people see history from their cultural perspective --- their "peoples' history" therefore most writings on history become American Chauvinist, or Western Chauvinist or Sino Chauvinist or African-American Chauvinist or Euro-Centrist or Turkish-Centrist, or Russian-Centrist and so on and so on depending a great deal on where the writer or story-teller was born. There is an old saying, "where you stand depends upon where you sit." This is never more-true than in the focus of historic studies as conducted in this world.

For the most part, most peoples, even peoples from small nations, see themselves as "the motivating force in history," and view history that way, through that prism. This theme of chauvinistic views is woven through my essays, and, in direct and indirect means, I attempt to show how it impacts our ability to work with others in a productive fashion.

So if we look at World War II as an example --- or the Great Patriotic War as it is called in Russia, we in the West tend to study the Battle of Britain, Normandy invasion, the Battle of the Bulge and the Italian Campaign, and the Russians tend to study the Battles of Stalingrad and Leningrad, and the taking of Berlin. We in the West think we were the essential force that beat the Nazis, and in Russia, they're positive it was they who did so.

- An example of how small nations may oversee their importance, look at the early 1970's Albanian claims to leadership of the world communist movement.

For cultural, political and academic reasons this division and limited focus is somewhat natural.

But it so constrains the ability to gain agreements and respect; to see the other's point of view, so to speak. This tendency of focus is reflected in the history written and taught in each country.

- For a real eye opening experience visit the Military History Museum in Istanbul, and see the Turkic view of people like Tamerlane or Attila the Hun: very different from the "West's.

I try to transcend this type of chauvinism, as much as I can. Several of the essays approach this chauvinistic bias (the one on Israel, and those dealing with determining the passage of time, and the determination of the "ages" and the one looking at African-American history).

Also, there are very few "generalist" historians. For academic and social reasons, even the best historians find the "niche" and become experts in their areas, and may append their area to a narrow band of other history around their time. But few historians attempt to know "all history" on a far thinner level and look to bridge those various histories into connecting and related sense. Most of my essays attempt to assess the events from a broad perspective rather than the traditional smokestack method of history. Historically speaking, few historians write grand theories and fewer still write in a cross-cultural viewpoint.

In addition, from the beginning of historical writing, most of the products have been in one form or another, propaganda. Non-biased, detached, authentic history is a very recent development. And it is often difficult to find that style among the continued outpouring of propaganda, especially right wing and religious presentations, masked as history. I try and determine the bias and the propaganda in all historical sources before I incorporate its findings into my views.

Even those great works such as Gibbon's *Decline and Fall of the Roman Empire*, pointedly focused on the Western Roman Empire and gave a false conception to the world that the fall of the West was the fall of the Empire.

In the modern West, 476 AD became a mandatory date, for us to learn as the end of the Empire, when this declaration had no factual connection to how the people of the time viewed the events. Gibbon was writing propaganda as a cautionary tale for the English Empire in his tales of the end of the Roman Empire; therefore he wrote to support his view.

Propaganda can and often does backfire and ends up being used in later times for other purposes. For example, consider how Tacitus writing in 117 CE/AD made one offhand statement on the fire of Rome that took place in 64 CE/AD, noting that there were "immense multitudes" of Christians in Rome at the time of the fire and how Nero put the blame on them. Tacitus was attempting to attack Nero (whom he hated) and to attack the Christians, who were just becoming a "problem" in his time. (Tacitus may have in fact coin the term "Christians.") He considered them both (Nero and Christians) incredibly foolish.

However, the Christians, once they gained more power, some two hundred years later seized upon the Tacitus statement to show that there were huge numbers of Christians in Rome only some thirty years after the Crucifixion. They used this one statement, unsupported and unmentioned by all the other historians writing at the time, as propaganda to support their writings about Paul and Peter as being correct and as support evidence that Christianity spread quickly and successfully right away.

Modern historians know these claims of Tacitus to be unlikely; but, the Christian propagandists of the time were very successful. So, today most people in the US know about Nero throwing Christians to the lions (which is never even stated by Tacitus, and is not supported by any other history of the time), and think that Christians were greatly persecuted under Nero, which did not happen. And that Christianity did spread quickly and was initially very successful, which is historically very false. So centuries later, we see this manipulation of a manipulation, this propaganda myth, as factual and as almost universally accepted "truth."

- The theme of this religious distortion of world history runs throughout most of the essays in this book.

All these constraints (religious, Chauvinism, limited view points, propaganda) so curtail our ability in the modern world to understand each other and to find solutions. We are all working from a different background of facts.

- The essay on Israel and Sicily looks at how social and political perspectives impact our view of the current world and how this view limits our options in address pressing issues.

Working with differing facts leads to failure to communicate and understand each other.

Part IV - My Point of View

I can now state why my view points are so strange and odd and wrong, to others. My views of history are, as much as I can ensure are:

- NOT based on religious evaluations or needs;
- NOT based on a cultural, political or economic premise that I am supporting or promoting; and
- NOT based on looking at single or limited events in isolation of each other.

They are based on the best history available (which of course is always changing and expanding. For a view of when history was being eliminated from public discourse, see Charles Freeman's *The Closing of the Western Mind*, 2005).

As free as I can possibly be (I hope) from these distortions, my views are based on looking at the broad view of history --- forward and back (in time) and side to side (across the world at a given time) --- linked together as part of the human experience.

While I cannot claim to be really free of these culturally induced barriers (I am a human and therefore greatly impacted by the culture all around me), I do try to at least present things purged of these factors as much as I can.

So devoid of the big four restrictions (and many others I hope), how do I see the world?

I see the world much as Hegel did, in constant conflict and in a continuous process of change. Thus, back in 1989/90, unlike some, who saw or hoped for the "end of history" with the soon-to-be-realized end of the "Communist threat" or Communist "hope" or "dream" or "terror" (based on one's perspective), I just saw the ending of one "antithesis," the process of "synthesis," and then new thesis and antithesis coming soon in its wake.

- See … right here, I am open to the charge that Hegel is a "Western Chauvinist" writer and thinker, and I am trapped in what appears to be a contradiction of claiming to not write or think from a Chauvinistic point of view.

- Well, I said I would do my best, and at least Hegel approaches things from a semi-religious and pragmatic view of history; so do I.

As we can observe from history, far too often this Hegelian process has been between religion (of all forms) and the "other." This "other" could be another religion, or it could be the then- current concept of "the modern." Hegel would give different terms than these.

The ongoing struggle could also be between two world-views that simply used religion as a tool to present and promote their views, such as the events of the Thirty Years War.

The importance of the religious aspects of that dreadful war is based on the point of view of the writers. Most Western historians put a great deal of emphasis on the religious aspect (as did the people of the time).

Hegel described this war as a conflict between the rising merchant classes (who were now Protestant), and the older nobility (who remained Catholic). Some have looked back to see the origins of German fascism in this war.

I tend to look at that war and those religious conflicts leading up to the war and following, as part of a far larger issue of the huge Hegelian "shift," with slightly less economic determinism than Hegel, where the thesis was "rule of the nobility" and the antithesis was "rule of the people." From my view, this extensive long drawn-out process took centuries and finally seemed mostly resolved with the widespread collapse of monarchy at the end of World War I and then only more or less fully resolved with the demise of the Russian Communist Empire, with the collapse most dramatically starting with the fall of the Berlin Wall.

- The essays on determining how to measure time and when the Roman Empire fell address these issues.

These extensive long draw out struggles created the new thesis of some vague form of democratic socialism as the apparent goal of almost every nation on the earth. We have our new modernism--the merging of some socialism with somewhat restrained capitalism with a democratic veneer, and greatly expanded and supported by the new technologies of the world.

And, as Hegel would predict, as soon as it was created, we have the new rebellion against it; this time in the guise of religious fundamentalism. In many ways the appeal of this new antithesis is the same as the socialist appeal against capitalism; the fundamentalists talk to those who feel powerless and unsuccessful in the new "modern world."

With socialism having failed, and since the new modernism is in part based on Social Darwinism none speak for the poor and unconnected in this world except the fundamentalists What horrible conflicts lay ahead, without insight on both sides; insights that come from history.

Seen from this point of view, the attacks against the World Trade Center, Madrid, Boston, etc. make sense.
It's clear with the study of the concepts of Hegel that at the beginning of every Hegelian shift is a long period of terror acts, perpetrated by the new antithesis. This current period of terrorism is so predictable and so "normal." We saw it in the beginning of the rise of the workers' movement against the

capitalist modernists, with assassinations of Czars, and presidents and tycoons, and bombing of mines and factories. We saw this in the destruction of the dikes in Holland by the merchant classes fighting against the Spanish nobility/monarchy; and so many other examples in history.

- The essay on the Boston bombing addresses this issue.

Obviously the concept of "the modern" changed over time and place and … well, over history. In addition, the argument of what is wrong with the modern is based on then current model of the modern, etc. Few if any people other than myself, looks at the world and historical events from this large-scale and long-term perspective.

- The essay on drones does some of this projecting.

Now, this brings us to another way I see this current world - as a world that rejects history. Again, this is only natural in that we are in a new thesis and we have a new beginning of culture, so to speak. Therefore what went before is unimportant, because it was not really part of the new. (This is most famously described in Orwell's *1984* that the rulers can and do rewrite history with his famous quote about war with Eurasia (again, copyright issues prevent full quote.) This rewrite needs to be done because what which was the past conflicts with the myths of the new antithesis.

This new culture, as with all new cultures, and the new antithesis rely on myths and images of the present, or how it is presented in the present, to avoid understanding or thinking of the past.

- What is past is not prologue in this world. In this world, or at least in what is called the developed world, what is past is unimportant and non-impacting and basically not to be thought about.

- That is past in the world where fundamentalism is appealing is their myths, and their myths are presented as the real history; a different view of the world, where the ideal is one devoid of the modern.

While these conflicting views of the past are normal and to be expected, I see this new "modern" world's avoidance of the past as dangerous, if not immensely dangerous. Many of my essays look at the inherent danger of negotiating the present without knowledge of the past, at the danger of not knowing your enemy and not even knowing yourself.

If we view the past with disdain and/or accept myths as facts, we simply cannot understand others' views of their world. In the end all we end up doing is insulting each other without understanding we do so.

I once met a far-right-wing Christian who was so angry at China for not allowing her and her group to go to that country and bring the word of God to "the billions of souls condemned to hell." I asked her what she knew of Chinese history, and how for millennia the source of almost all the revolutions in that land came from minority religious-based uprising. She of course knew nothing of this.

I asked her if she had ever heard of the Tai Ping Rebellion in which tens of millions died as a result of someone believing he was Jesus's brother, God's Chinese son, and he was bringing the better improved Chinese version of Christianity to his homeland. She had no knowledge of that either.

I asked her if she understood that Christianity was the main religion of the "sea barbarians" (what the Chinese called the

Europeans) that humiliated and destroyed China from the 1830s through the 1940s --and nearly 400 million peopled died violently in that one century.

She of course did not. But, in the end, she still saw China having no reason to keep her out, and from her view she still saw China as a horrid land it must be to live where God is prevented.

I asked her if she realized that the Chinese Communist Party was responsible for ending poverty among more people than any other organization by far in the history of the world, and she responded that "they don't allow religious freedom, how good of a place could it be?"

Both of us from the other's point of view just presented myth and perceptions to support our argument.

- We both saw each other as very wrong.

If we escalate this type of discussion to a one between nations or among groups on world wide scale and to tensions between nations and movements rather than just two individuals, we create a very dangerous world.

My essays address this danger and lack of perception and lack of opportunity for alternatives in a world ever-increasingly devoid of history and ever-increasingly dominated by all forms of religious concepts (both in the form of organized religions and in other guises). And the danger presented is not just in the land of the "others" but in our own country.

Here we can see the rise of religious all religious-based fundamentalism as an attack on the modern, as much as Islamic fundamentalism is overseas. We can see the success in this American fundamentalism as we watch our nation become a land where the facts of economics and statistics are being replaced in the public arena, once again, with the "truth" of faith and myth.

- I address this American concern in an essay on fundamentalism.

And here, I will admit that I am biased and I am writing from a biased view, despite the effort to avoid such.
While I present my facts in what appears to be liberal or progressive means, they are really being presented in a "modernist" form, in a form against fundamentalism of all forms.

For in this major struggle of the new thesis against new antithesis, I am a modernist: a modernist demanding reform of the modern, but a modernist.

- My essays tend to be against governments that embrace the old and religions that work to prevent the new, and governments that use religions for their own means.

So please do not look at these essays in the standard left-right conflict. They are not intended as such, but intend to look at the world in terms of the new Hegelian conflicts of the here and now, but, with the works perceived (or seen?) through the eyes of history.

We no longer live in a left/center/right world, but a world of conflict between modernism and fundamentalism and those wishing to participate in both the modern world and maintaining the benefits of what some see as "old time religion." With the changing of the world's conflict, old terms fade in meaning and effectiveness. Most writers of political nature have not upgraded their terminology to meet the current world. I at least attempt to do such upgrading.

Part V - One Look at the Ancient

While the essays in the main body of the text deal with relatively modern times and issues, as part of the introduction I include an essay which deals with the past of writings of the late Bronze Age that shows my views of how important history and myths of history are to current and past times. This essay comes from my book on development of religion of the West entitled *The Ba'al Theory of Christianity*.

- The essay looks at two key heroes of respective cultures: Achilles and David. As far as I can tell I may be the first to compare the two.

However, the heroes both show that the conflicts between the "modern" and "fundamentalism" are present going back to our earliest sacred writings (or what we call our earliest sacred writings).

Feel free to read this first essay or not if you find the subject matter of the past too "historic" and look to the main body of the essays for more modern issues …. But then again, by doing so you may be missing the whole point of the book.

Setting the Stage

This essay is from the series of books I wrote on the impact of the mostly forgotten religion of the Canaanites and Phoenicians on the creation of modern Western religions, particularly Christianity. This essay attempts to shows how our conceptions of the present, and, even what we consider as "true," are impacted by long-forgotten political and cultural events of the past.

This essay looks at how developing new knowledge shows that many of the people and events in the Jewish and Christian Bibles are accepted as fact simply because they are in these books, despite no modern-based research supporting these "truths." On the other hand "folk heroes" such as Achilles are offered to the modern world as legends and myths, despite the overwhelming archeological evidence of the world in which they lived. The focus here is on if either Achilles or David were factual, the issue here is on how religion still dominates so much thinking in what we consider a modern world.

Comment on Religious Impact on Overviews of Historical Characters or; the Battle of the Super Heroes

To illustrate this problem of cultural myths and history, and our current views on them, let's take a look at two "culture heroes" of two different ancient societies; the famous "Greek" from the *Iliad*, Achilles, and the famous "Jew" from the Bible, King David. (Both "Greek" and "Jew" are terms neither one of them, if they were real at all, would have associated with themselves.)

- These two heroes were relative contemporaries, from the late Bronze Age. (Achilles' exploits were dated as happening somewhere about 1100 -1200 BC and David's about 1000 BC), so there is a common time frame involved.
- Both heroes have great and powerful stories written about them in "ancient" literature that has somehow avoided destruction and made it through all the ages to us.
- Both heroes were recognized by their respective cultures for centuries as idealized, but flawed, leaders.
- Both were studied by the leaders of their peoples, as well as by the "masses" of their cultures, to help to determine "right actions," and in general helped shape the "ethos" of multiple generations of Greeks (and those emulating Greeks) and Jews (and later Christians), respectively.

However, the *Iliad* was vastly more popular for the first 1200 years of its "shelf life" (from about 800 BC to 400 AD, give or take a few hundred years). When Homer lived (if at all) is, again, open to debate. However, it is generally agreed by most current historians that the epic poem on the Trojan War first appeared among the Greeks in its current form, about 750 BC or so. It also appears that the oral tradition of Achilles was much older.

Who wrote the Bible, and when it was written, is a subject of modern controversies, but it also appears that the stories of David were well known among the Jewish tribes and in the two "Jewish" kingdoms, and were developed in some written form by about 750 BC. Again, the oral traditions of David go back a bit more … As noted the "David stories" are at least two or three hundred years less old then Achilles, but the two heroes are still in the same relative time frame, and were relatively "cultural hero rivals."

However, in the first 1200 years or so of their "cultural myth rivalry," Achilles had by far the better "press." Achilles was "universally" known, first in the Greek world, and then later throughout the Roman/Greek world. The *Iliad* went with Greek culture (Hellenism) where ever it spread. In many ways, the *Iliad* was used in the spread of Hellenism in the same way as the Bible was used to spread Christianity (although Hellenism was certainly not limited to one book).

At the time of Caesar, the *Iliad* was read and studied, and Achilles held up as either the "ideal," or as the great anti-hero. (The Romans tended to favor Hector and the Trojans since one of the foundation stories of Rome proclaimed that it was started by Trojan survivors of the war) from what today is called the British Isles, to Afghanistan and Pakistan.

Reading and study of Achilles' life, and his life choices, was "mandatory" for any "cultured" person of the time. This time period ran for some 1100 years in duration (roughly 700 BC-400 AD), with the first years being focused more on just the Greek idolization, but after Alexander, 325 BC or so, Achilles was made "universal" in his appeal.

For most of these 1100 years of Achilles' dominance, David was more of a "backwater" hero, mostly known and admired in the relatively narrow "world" of the "Jews" (again, loosely using that term). Remember, most of this time period, was a time of Jewish defeat, exile and rule by rival cultures.

Even within the Jewish community, David was not always considered a "valued person." In the Jewish writing he is portrayed as a flawed person, the seducer of women, the killer of his own son (and perhaps more than one son), and a man too filled with evil acts to build the house of the Lord, so evil that at times God condemned him to death (only to have his infant son die in his place).

And as Judaism evolved, especially during and after the Babylonian Exile, the idea of toleration of other religions, such as Ba'alism, (which David clearly did supported and is portrayed as practicing it's rites, was seen as grievous error that eventually caused the destruction of the Jewish kingdoms. So, among Jews of this time, David's flaws appear to greatly outweigh his good deeds. Even among the Jews, he was not always given the status Achilles was given within the Greek world.

The status of both David and Achilles, however, changed greatly with the rise of Christianity and the subsequent repressing of Greek (Hellenistic or "classical") culture by the new power elite (the Christian Church).

Starting roughly about 350 AD, the writings of Homer, as well as almost all other "classical" writers, were not only repressed, but soon, by 400 AD, the study of these classical writings was made a capital offence in the new "Roman Christian world."

And once in power, the new Christian elite did all they could "to eliminate the competition" of their newly won power, and the Church tried to destroy all books counter to their world views, of not only religion, but of science, math, and all other forms of "culture."

- The "Christian Emperors," in support of their new "universal religion" closed the schools of philosophy throughout the Roman world, and even ended the (1200 year old) Olympic Games.

- The rise of Christianity was the rise of the "dark ages" in the area of thought and also the "fall of Achilles" from his 1100 year reign as the "cultural ideal."

And, since within this new Christian world, the Old Testament was among the few pieces of literature allowed to be read (or told to the illiterate by priests) the rise of Christianity led also to the rise of King David to a new status of a "super hero" to all under the rule of the Christians. In the arena of an "action hero," in this new world of repressed literature, David had almost no competitors, being the "top king" in the only book allowed to relay history.

And, since the Muslims used the Old Testament as a foundation for their religion, David became a "cultural hero" in the Muslim world as well. While David did have some localized rivals (King Arthur, or Roland, for example) he was the only "universal" hero in the lands where the Bible (and the Koran) dominated the world view. So for the next 1000 years or so, while the stories of Achilles could not be completely repressed, David became the dominant "super hero."

What a sad world it would be for DC Comics, and the lovers of DC comics, if Batman was the only super hero around. In some ways this is exactly what happened for David. He was the only "action hero" around, and for young men wanting an action hero, he was the only option that could be read and talked about (without threat of death).

- His kingdom and its importance was overstated (as an understatement!), by the readers of the time.

Therefore, for most of the next 1000 years (say 500 to 1500 AD or so), David far outdid Achilles, in being a "cultural hero."

- The powers to be in the West (the Church) demanded belief in the Bible as "literal fact."

Therefore, not "believing" in King David and the "history of his time" as presented in the Bible, was a "sin" and, actually, for most of the 1000 years (and more), a sin punishable by at least ostracism, "spiritual damnation," and often torture and death.

The "Renaissance" and *the Age of Reason* brought Achilles back as a competitor for "number one" cultural icon. And, even with the revival of the studies of classical literature (during both the Renaissance and later) the reading of the *Iliad* and other writings was only "allowed" by the Church as the study of "myths" and ancient stories, rather than being allowed to be considered actual "history." The Church had to resist anything that questioned the Bible and the *Iliad* showed a different world than that of the Davidic kingdoms.

- Therefore, as early as the 5th century AD, few in the West (or at least few in the Christian sections of the West) or in the Christian/Muslim dominated areas of the world could question if David was real or not, without dire threat to themselves and their families.

The concept of the "historic David" was therefore incorporated as "history" in the West, because it was in the Bible, and the Bible could not be questioned.

Due to the expansion of the Western world through colonialism, modern technology and religious apostatizing even today, most of the history books used in the schools of these Christian/Muslim areas (and), throughout the world, hold David to be an actual historical "being," while Achilles, if anything, is considered a good story, but a mythical character.

History as taught in the West talks extensively about the David (and David's and Solomon's kingdom). Modern atlases that show the ancient world almost all include maps of the Davidic Kingdom based on what is stated in the Bible. Fundamental Christians and Jews who support the "Greater Israel" concept base their justification in the Bible's description of the extent of the Davidic kingdom (from the "Euphrates to the Nile").

Achilles, while revived from the obscurity he "suffered" during the "dark ages," for most of these 500 to700 years (the time period from the Renaissance began to the present) was relegated to "myth," if discussed at all. The *Iliad* was read in literature or "mythology" courses, if read at all.

However, by the 19th century, Achilles stories were read extensively to the "modern young man," of the middle and upper classes in Europe (to prepare him for a life of being a soldier) but Achilles was still seen as a quaint and curious character of the past. His story of being the son of a God was stressed as a myth, while Jesus being the son of God could still not be questioned. One of these children of the 19th century, Heinrich Schliemann, did grow into adulthood believing these stories to be truth, and eventually his efforts led to the finding of Troy.
(See http://library.thinkquest.org/3011/troy.htm)

Because of this "enthusiastic amateur," what we know now, despite what is presented in most Western "history" books even until the present, is there is actually far more archeological and "contemporary other-source documentation" support for the existence of Achilles, than for David.

- In fact there is basically no documentation, (other than the Bible) or any archeological evidence to support there ever existed a King David and extensive documentation of other cultures of the time make no mention of a great Jewish Kingdom around 1000 BC.

For facts supporting the existence of Achilles, we have Troy itself, with strong evidence for the sacking of the city in the relative timeframe of Homer's epic poem. We also have found the Mycenaean cities throughout Greece, and have strong evidence of their "wars of expansion."

We have extensive articles of art and weapons from the period, which fill museums around the world showing that much of what was discussed in the *Iliad* (type of weapons, type of combat, valued objects, religion, etc.) and which clearly supports Homer's written accounts. Also, tombs of the time discovered reflect the culture presented in the Homer stories. While the supposed "death mask" of King Agamemnon and "Clytemnestra's tomb" are real and dated to the relative time period of Achilles (they actually seem to be older), we cannot really prove that these artifacts are really connected to the "historic" people that the tourist industry would like us to believe, but the Lion's Gate and the tombs and the mask exist.

We also have extensive records from other cultures, including the Hittites, of their relationships with Troy, and we have these other cultures' chronicles which record worry about the Mycenaean Greeks and their warlike intentions. It is still not completely clear, but it is strongly possible that the famous "Sea People," which almost conquered Egypt, were in fact part of a renegade Mycenaean Greek group. (It is also possible that the Mycenaean Greeks were destroyed by the "Sea People"). See http://www.phoenician.org/sea_peoples.htm

While there is no direct evidence that there was an Achilles, such as a tomb with his name, there is extensive evidence that the events written about may have occurred in a fashion that is represented in the writings.

- Something happened there, at Troy, during the time period.

So while we cannot really say Achilles existed, or in fact the Trojan War, as represented in the *Iliad*, took place, there is enough evidence to say, well, "maybe" and even "possibly." Considering the evidence, the Achilles character, or someone like him clearly could have existed (stripped of all the legends – half god, protected from harm, except in the heel, etc.). The evidence from multiple sources shows the story fits the times, and the times fit the story.

- However, we have none of this type of evidence in support of David. There are no independent sources to show David was king of a united Israel, never mind a mighty king, with a relatively vast empire from the Nile to the Euphrates.
- There is no evidence in the well-kept and organized Egyptian chronicles to support this Biblical claim.
- There is nothing in the remains of the Hittites or Assyrian (nor Phoenician) writings about David or a mighty Jewish kingdom in the timeframe presented in the Bible.
- Herodotus, who seemed to have talked in great detail about everything, never mentions David, never mind the Jews (which is interesting in itself).

And perhaps most damning of all, there is simply no archeological evidence at all to support either a mighty kingdom in the time period, nor a great temple built by David's famous son, Solomon.

There are no coins bearing his name or title, (ok, just testing you since coinage was not developed for 300 years after David, and if there was a coin saying David King of Israel, it has to be a total fake), no stone writings with his name or warning of the coming of the great Jewish kingdom army, nor actually artifacts of any kind dated back to the Davidic Kingdom.

We do have one find, dated three hundred years after David, in which a king claims to be from the House of David, but that may only mean that David was a cultural icon, not a real king (comparable to the Kings of England claiming descent from King Arthur or such).

What artifacts we do have from that time period of about 1000 BC, actually show "the holy land" a relatively disorganized land dominated by other peoples and cultures than the Jews (or Hebrews or Israelites, as a more proper term for the time); but, the evidence clearly shows the "David" as portrayed in the Bible did not exist. Serious "disinterested" historians (meaning people who look at only the "facts" and don't try to prove the "cultural myths" of the Bible) seem to agree that if David existed at all, he was a minor leader of a minor group, perhaps even a group of outlaws: a Robin Hood rather than a King Richard.

This expansion of the "role" of the culture hero is nothing new. The Arthur stories start him off as king of a small Celtic land in Britain (remember the name "England" is derived from the Angles invaders of the Angles, Saxons and Jutes, so originates much later than Arthur) then, in later medieval legends, Arthur's the ruler of all of Europe. So it appears that the land under the rule of David expanded as his myth grew. Nothing really new here, except, since it was in the Bible, for centuries it was deemed true, and un-challengeable.

But the sole reason that the concept of David, and all the modern political outgrows of the myth of David, is based almost exclusively in religion. The acceptance of David as a real historical character and the rejection of Achilles as such, in the face of all the non-evidence for one verses all the extensive evidence for the other, show clearly that religion is still vastly too dominate in our culture. It also shows how difficult it is to get the religious to accept facts that conflict with their religion and there sacred books.

Glenn Young

Part I –
Seeing the Political Historically

Section 1-

The Past to the Present

Setting the Stage

A connective theme in these essays is the impact of myth on current thought. This essay takes full aim at one of the great American myths of us being the light of the world, the progressive, freedom-loving country that all others should model. Looking at things in comparison to so many other places, on so many levels, the United States has not been progressive, not freedom-loving. In fact, on so many critical social issues (slavery, women's rights, social protections, unionism, civil rights and others) we were, well, "late to the party."

Our claims of leadership in these areas tend to make our nation look arrogant and ignorant to many places and people and confuse the progressive elements at home. So many expect the US to do the right thing and are befuddled when we do not (in elections and policy). This essay gives support and justification to the views of the "other" and explains why the current trend in the US to conservatism is actually "a return to normalcy."

Where Did This Fantasy of the US Being A Progressive Country Come From?

The United States, almost from its beginnings, has been a center-right- to far-right-wing country unable to accept progressive ideas and forces except under very unusual situations. We really have been a laggard in almost every social effort in the world, and have been unable to address basic human needs in our own country, denying freedoms and opportunities to peoples for generations at a time. We should not be surprised by the ongoing efforts and actual successes of the relatively far right in the US in recent years, since in fact this is normalcy in the United States.

If we take an honest look at ourselves, we would see a nation in which the right has dominated the political agenda at almost all times; but we maintain the rhetoric that we are a nation of freedom and progressiveness.

But that's it --- it is rhetoric and an American fantasy. Somehow we maintain the illusion that the US is a progressive, liberal country. I don't know where this myth comes from; our history clearly shows this not to be the case.

Even our revolution, often held as a beacon to the world as the creation of a free republic, with equal justice for all, accepted the enslavement of 1/3 of the population of the time; never mind limiting the enfranchisement to something like 5% of the population. The revolution was a war basically of a local elite fighting against the "other" elite of England, not truly a social revolution to any progressive mindset. Our Constitution allowed for the continuation of slavery and created an oligarchy of the land-holding elite that had no direct election of the president or the senate, no income tax and virtually no controls over the lifestyle of the rich.

The rules had to be modified and changed extensively to allow for more direct participation of "the people" and to recognize the rights of what became the middle class. None of these extensions of rights were easy fights, and faced vigorous and, for a long time, successful "right wing" opposition.

For example, the vote was expanded slowly and it took wars and near revolutions and decades of struggle to allow for landless, and Blacks and women to win the vote. And up until sixty years ago, we had poll taxes, literacy tests and the "grandfather clause" and so much more that denied voting rights to so many legally entitled to it. Now, today, states again are enacting extensive legislation to "limit the franchise" – this is nothing new in American history, the right has always tried to limit the franchise, and when in power does so successfully.

In truly looking at our history we have been a nation dominated by one right-wing effort after another. These groups include, but by no way are limited to:

- Indian-hating Jacksonians,
- Emancipation-hating slave holding Southern States,
- Immigrant-hating Know Nothings,
- African-American-hating Klu Klux Klan (include Jews and Catholics here too),
- Labor-hating Liberty Committees,
- Lefty- and Jew-hating House on Un-American Activities Committee,
- Everyone-hating Joe McCarthy,
- Equal rights-hating Racist Southern Senators,
- Rationalist and science-hating Religious Right, and;

… never mind the likes of J Edgar Hoover, and Father Coughlin (who makes Rush Limbaugh look downright tame), and now Tea Baggers.

So where was this "progressive time?" Never has there truly been a progressive force that dominated the discussion in the US. At best, there were organized efforts to fight against such things as the Viet Nam War and institutionalized racism, and to fight for the right to organize unions and for women's right to vote and to choose, but the proponents always seemed to be a minority fringe, never able to win major elections or create a coherent national force: more of a social conscience rather than a real political force.

Only the People's Party of the 1870s and 80s came close to being such a force, but they were too racist and anti-urban life to really become a "progressive" force in the US. And, in the midst of the "free times of the sixties and seventies" this nation elected Richard Nixon twice.

We only act progressive when disaster strikes; it literally took our rivers catching fire and our rain turning to acid before we passed environmental legislation. And it took a near "China Syndrome" to put some kind of controls over nuclear power.

- The free distribution of land under Lincoln (the Homestead Act) only happened because the Southern politicians were not in Congress,
- The Thirteenth through Fifteenth Amendments were made a condition for rejoining the country by the "radical Republicans to the Southern states.
- The ending of selling every governmental job (with the creation of the Civil Service) only happened as tribute to the assassinated Garfield.
- The Square Deal and the New Deal, the New Frontier, and the civil rights and anti-poverty laws of the 1960s were attempts to buy off people and prevent a real social revolution from occurring.

The so-called progressive agendas have won only in times of disaster or of national trauma – the Civil War, the Great Depression, the aftermath of World War II (with seven million solders wanting to get paid off for losing the "best years of our lives"), following the assassination of Lincoln, Garfield or JFK, or when 165 American cities were burning, or on those occasions when the Republican party splits ---- Wilson and Clinton only won in three-person races; Carter barely won even with the disgrace of Nixon. Great "progressive" Teddy Roosevelt only at first became president because of McKinley's assassination, not by the will of the electorate.

And our internal and external politics and policies have almost always been --- well, not progressive.

- We ethnically cleansed the Eastern part of the nation of Native-Americans,
- We conquered half of Mexico,
- We created wars (with Spain, and Iraq) to get our colonies and pseudo-colonies.
- We supported European colonialism and even the reinstatement of colonies throughout the world after World War II, leading to endless tragedy and millions dying in anti-colonial wars.
- We had our own colonial wars and killed millions in the Philippines and Viet Nam to prevent their national independence.
- We supported endless right-wing military and monarchal dictatorships and paid for and planned huge numbers of coups against legally elected left-leaning governments
- For a century we treated the Caribbean as our private lake and intervened with our military dozens of times. We even created our own country (Panama) when we couldn't bully Columbia into giving us land for a canal.

And as far as social justice and access to core elements of what are considered "elements of a liberal society," we again lag far behind so many other "modern countries." We can simply look at our history and compare it to other nations to see how un-progressive we really were and, in fact, continue to be so.

We were the last of the "major powers" of the time to eliminate slavery (and it took a civil war to do so).

- France did so some seventy-plus years before the US, England thirty-plus years. And remember, one of the goals of the Texas revolt against Mexico in the 1830s was to reinstitute slavery, which Mexico had banned in the 1820s. (Only Brazil held on to slavery longer than the US.)

We were the last of the major powers to legalize the right to organize unions.

- We only did so in the midst of the Great Depression; Germany had done so some fifty years before, and, prior to Hitler, the Socialist party of the labor unions was the largest party in Germany. Even Spain had legalized unions decades prior to the US. The US smashed the Knights of Labor and the IWW and tried hard to smash the CIO.
- Prior to World War I, Germany and France both had state-funded unemployment and retirement pensions; it took the Great Depression to get some of this through in the US.

We clearly were not among the first major Western nations to allow women to vote.

- Women in Russia and Finland (and many other countries) could vote before the women of the United States, and;

We are the last major country in the West without some form of Universal Healthcare.

We are also the only major country in the West that allowed one-third of the country to completely disregard our basic laws concerning equal justice and the right to vote.

- We allowed Jim Crow to last almost 100 years with virtually no challenge by the central government. We not only allowed Jim Crow, but allowed tens of

thousands of outright murders of citizens to go unpunished (lynching).
- South Africa did not start apartheid until 1947; we had it in place starting in some states right after the Civil War, and fully in place in the vast majority of states, not just the South, by the late 1880s and lasting till the 1960s.

We were also the last major power in the West to enter the fight against Fascism; and only did so when we were attacked at Pearl Harbor.

- Up until that point, the vast majority of population of the US was unwilling to fight Hitler or Japan; they were willing to let the Fascists win the war.

Roosevelt broke law after law and circumnavigated many more, just to try and keep England and Russia afloat, because the majority of the people of the US were against becoming involved. Massive pro-Hitler meetings took place in the 1930s and early 40s in the US, with the (pro-Hitler) American Bund winning hundreds of thousands of members.

So I still ask: when was this progressive time in the US?

Under the New Deal, which mostly failed (since the Great Depression continued until WWII) and was mostly declared unconstitutional by the Supreme Court?

Under Kennedy/Johnson, when we got laws passed only based on the martyrdom of Kennedy, and the Guns and Butter policy of Johnson while American cities went up in flames every summer? (And it was the Courts that started the process [Brown v. Board of Education] when nothing could pass the US government with its racist Southern Senators blocking all efforts at reform).

Under Clinton, who in his third year completely caved to the Republicans on welfare reform and free trade and also declared the "era of big government is over"?

I am sorry, but as a historian, I am at a loss to see any time when the US truly had a progressive agenda that was actually in power and dominant.

Our normal state is that of a country dominated by the Right and Far Right, with occasional surges of progress in response to near total disaster, and then with equal if not more than equal reactions from the Right.

When the Progressives seem to be in power, the Right is constantly attacking and winning the battle to define the debate – since the Right has and continues to control the media in the US. So what we see in Congress now with the Tea Baggers and the right dominating is actually normalcy in the US. And on the rare occasion when the Right is not in power, they take revenge through every means they can.

- After Roosevelt, the New Dealers were purged from government
- After World War II the Anti-communist movement with its support in Congress blacklisted those who were anti-fascist
- After Roe v. Wade, we have seen clinics bombed, doctors murdered and endless right-wing-sponsored legislation attacking a right to an abortion, and
- After the progressive win of Obama, we have the endless race-based unprecedented attacks on a sitting president as the enemy of the nation and something "un-American." (Only Lincoln received such ridicule in the past, by a pro-slave and secessionist South.)

And through the Right's revenge, they often bring the nation to the point of destruction (the Civil War, the Great Depression, the violence and near revolution of the 1960s, the economic collapse of the recent times). They have and will again actually take us off the cliff at some point, and disaster will follow, and then, possibly, we will be able to have a brief period of progressive efforts that will lead to the passing of some of the real modernizations we need.

We will tend to forget the long periods of social nightmares caused by the Right and only remember that time of a brief surge of progress, which again is what is normal in the US's history. We live with our own illusion of being progressive when in fact it's the truly is a fantasy.

Setting the Stage

This essay was initial part of the introduction to a book on religious history I have developed. The premise is that most people would not be able to follow the book, simply because the information and approach to history was so different than the mass popular history taught to and incorporated as part of the American view of the world. Therefore this introductory essay was intended to show a bit of why Americans' view of history is so different then the views of most other peoples of the world. We are a privileged people devoid of tyranny and destruction. This privilege sets both us and our understanding of the past apart from the rest of the peoples of the world. We come to the table to negotiate whatever is needed with very different paradigms on the nature of the world.

Comments on the American Experience – A Problem in Understanding History

In general, the history that is presented to us, in America, perhaps not in the advance classes, but in general education is that of the linear transition from the Ancient to the Classical to the Christian world, with then a transition into modernism.

As far as the far Mediterranean, as presented the Ancient world supposedly faded into the Classical world sometime around 600 BCE, and then overwhelmed the homeland of the Ancient World between 325 BCE – 100 CE with the invasion of the Near East under Alexander, and the solidification of Roman power in that area. This time line continues with the Classical world fading into the Christian world beginning sometime in the mid-third century CE.

However, this concept is greatly tainted by the Christian and American world view. In both the books, *Religion of the Occident*, and in *The Closing of the Western Mind*, both authors argue that the concepts of liberty and freedom of thought developed by the Classical mind view lost out to the concepts of absolutism and control of the deity prevalent in the Ancient world, over nearly a 1,000 year period.

Both works state that the Europe of the Post-Roman Empire period (that which is called the Dark Ages, and the early Medieval period) looked like the world of the Ancients (with its absolute rulers, its religious domination, and its use of God as the answer to all events (God wills it!!!), and both books show how the classical world lost out in Europe, to the Ancient's world view.

The authors of these books would say that the great victories of the Greeks at Marathon and Salamis were reversed over the course of some 1000 years with the development of the absolutist Roman rulers, supported by the absolutist Christian church; or exactly the world of Persia and what the Greeks were fighting against.)

Both books generally conclude that the Europe of the 6th- 10th centuries CE looked more like Hindu India of say 1000 BCE (a major source of the Ancient world view), than any other culture in history.

- In other words, the evolution into the Christian world was actually a tremendous step backwards into the Ancient world.

As throughout world history, today, the vast majority of the world's people view history based on religious "beliefs" and not historical "facts." In the US, most persons assume that the events of history in the Bible are true to some (greater or lesser) degree. Even if we get beyond rejecting of the Eden story and the flood, most people, at least in America, think, the Exodus from Egypt took place in some form or another; that "Joshua fit the battle of Jericho;" and that David and Solomon were mighty kings.

These same people think that Nero fed the Christians to the lions, and that Christianity saved the soul of the Roman Empire, and that Christianity has been the true religion that brought enlightenment and freedom foe the oppressed.

And despite the mounting evidence that the history outlined above is not supported by archeological and other sources, most American people still accept them as "facts" because it was taught to them through religion and also in fact through public schools. Even with the development of non-church based schools, or public education, in the West, much of what was taught in the new school systems had to be accepted and approved by the various churches, and the history taught mostly conformed to religious dogma. When facts did not fit the Bible and are taught in schools, extensive battles ensued and still rage (Darwinism, the age of the earth, etc.)

In addition, more or less, the concept of the "White Man's Burden" still prevails in the minds of most Americans today if in somewhat different forms, such as "bring Democracy to the world." Perhaps we should say that the "White Man's Burden" has evolved to the "American Burden." The belief in some form of "manifest destiny" though somewhat dated, still prevails in this country, as most people (or at least most politically active people) in this country still think of the US as the old Christian view of the "shining city on the hill," or, the only hope for human kind.

Most Americans see the world as almost predetermined and continual in the process. We tend not to be a cynical people, but one that think "right will prevail", and events will occur to assure continuation and progress. This concept of predetermination and progress is actually, strangely enough, manifested in the fact that some 40% of Americans think that the second coming of Jesus will occur in their lifetimes, and that the end of the world as we know it will come about as described in the Bible.

No Sense of History

Perhaps it's because so many people in the United States are religious and believers in the eventual triumph of good over evil, (no matter how devastating this triumph, as described in "Revelations" will be for most people) that we as a people have a very distorted view of world history. We tend to see things as a chain of events always progressing, with perhaps a few bumps along the road, but always progressing towards the enviable positive outcome. We also see the history through religious eyes, and base our perception of the present on the religious stories of the past.

We as a people tend to gloss over the "bad points in history" and only look at the "good" (which is perhaps a normal process). However, by doing so we miss what really happened in history, and perhaps more importantly, why it really happened. This ignorance of "real history" leads to us failing to properly project how others in the world will react to our actions

Take for example the Crusades. If Americans know anything about the Crusades, it is that the "wonderful" Christian knights, driven by divine spirit, were able to gain control of the "Holy Land" back from the Muslim infidels, who had been preventing Christian pilgrims from going to pray at the holy places in the area. So we gloss over the bad points, which are many, when it comes to the Crusades; we know little of:

- The history of religious intolerance in the West and that the Muslims actually were among the most tolerant of rulers in so far as religion went.
- The Crusaders slaughtering Jews and Eastern Orthodox Christians, and almost everyone the encountered along the way that were not Roman Catholic, and
- When they finally reached Jerusalem, and took the city, they killed almost all the inhabitants, regardless of age and religions.

Since we look at the history from the European Christian perspective, we think of the Crusades as the foundation for the Renaissance, since the Crusaders learnt so much from going East, but we know so little of the;

- The devastating impact the Crusades had on the overall history of culture, and especially on the political entity that the Crusades were originally intended to help, the Byzantine Empire (the remnants of the Roman Empire), and how the fourth Crusade did what no Muslim army had be able to do, take and sack Constantinople, and to establish for sixty years a Latin Empire in its place.
- The Crusades, by destroying Byzantium, actually helped to unlock the door to Europe, which enabled the Ottoman Turks to occupy the Balkans for close to 500 years, and almost led to the complete conquest of Europe by the Muslim Turks.
- This Latin takeover and there rule of terror solidified the schism between the East and West Churches that still exists.

And since we don't really know history, and missed what really happened, we cannot really understand what others perspectives are concerning the present; the average American may know the Crusades failed and see them as a noble effort of noble knights, but they fail to understand that the Muslim successful resistance to the Crusades over a one hundred and fifty year period continues to play out in current world politics. The Muslims see their history of resistance to the Crusaders as a model for today, including giving the Muslims a historical basis for supporting "terror" as a means to resist.

- Bin Laden models himself after the founder of the sect know in English as "the Assassin" who during the Crusading period, was able to use "suicide" attacks against leaders of both the Muslim and Christian sides to force political and military confrontations.

In addition, we simple do not get that the people of the region see the Crusades as a precursor to modern day European Imperialism, and view Israel, and the invasion of Iraq as just a continuation of a war that has been raging for over 1600 years.

- We, in America, simply do not understand that the Crusades mostly had little to do with religion, but were mainly a pretext for the younger nobility of Europe, who could not gain land in the Europe to establish their own fiefdoms and kingdoms in new lands away from their older siblings.

Clearly in the minds of the current residents of the area, events look the same now as they did then. But we don't get this ... because we don't "get history."

A few years ago a movie was released call *The Kingdom of Heaven* which showed the Crusading period far closer to reality than any other cinematic effort. Although the story line was "Hollywoodized" to include a love story that never took place, the main story line of the Christians losing control of Jerusalem to the Islamic forces was fairly accurate (leaving out that the Christians actually paid a huge ransom to get all the people safely out of Jerusalem). The movie mainly made the Christians, or at least the Christian knights, the bad guys, and, Muslims, under Saladin, if not the good guys, at least the far more noble guys.

The movie had everything going for it; great action, Orlando Bloom, etc. and it bombed, at least in the US, at the box office. I would project the failure was due to that fact that the Christians lose, and Saladin (played by an actor who looked amazingly like Bin Laden,) enters Jerusalem in triumph, replacing Christian signage with Muslim ones (while showing respect for the Christian imagery). In a time of "war on terror," and in the rise of Christian fundamentalism, this movie never really had a chance.

Almost at the same time another movie came out called *Passion of the Christ* created by Mel Gibson. The movie had almost "nothing" going for it, in so far as a film that generally appeals to Americans. It had no super stars, no major action, and was spoken in relatively dead languages, which required subtitles (something most Americans hate). It also has a long scene of torture done in gruesome realism (ok, maybe it had that going for it).

This movie based on a very strict reading of the Bible, on the last day of the life of Christ, despite mixed reviews, and protests for its anti-Semitic bias broke all kinds of box office records. It almost became a mandatory event for fundamentalist Christians to go and see how "Christ died for our sins." And, it appears, the more gruesome the death the more that it seems to appeal to those types of Christian.

Unfortunately, this response to the *Kingdom of Heaven* and *Passion of the Christ* is typical to the Americans response to history in general. We as a people do not want to know much that goes counter to our world view. And our world view is greatly tainted by our own positive experiences, as a people, and our own national views on (the Christian) religion. To greatly generalize this American view is to say;

- The general feeling of the traditional American is to mainly forget about the past, and to more forward, into the wilderness or into the future, (and not with the irony intended in the song title from Bob Dylan) *With God on Our Side*.

However, this world view is primarily an American view, not shared by most peoples of the world. Unlike the history of the United States, most of the rest of the peoples of the world have known chaos and despotism as the norm throughout their history. If there was ever a "rise" of a people or nation, it was surely followed by a great fall.

No Sense of History

Throughout history, we see time and again, that which was a rich and stable society wiped away and often expunged from existence. If there was a recovery, it could take generations and before the return of stability and growth. Often the return of stability was at a cost of elimination of freedoms and a great demand for conformity, or stimulated by foreign wars.

For the history of humanity, in general, until very modern times, the statement of Hobbs that life was "nasty, brutish and short" was mostly, if not nearly completely, true; perhaps except for the American, and at times the Chinese, Persian and Indian experience, and for the hundred years or so of the "Pax Romana," those living in the Roman Empire.

- For most of the peoples, and history of the world, nothing seemed inevitable except chaos and destruction, and tyranny of one form or another. (Our cynical view of "death and taxes" is something so very mild compared to others experiences.)

What is clearly different from American history and that of most of the peoples of the world is that the US to date:

- Has never been destroyed or occupied (except for the Southern states in the civil war), its peoples sent off into servitude, nor has it experienced the collapse of its ecological systems, its central government, nor has it lived through periods of great plagues.

The concept of the "end of the world is near" in America is more a punch line of a joke, rather than the practical real experiences of peoples of the Ancient and Classical world

The "end of time" was not only near, it came for the Jews losing to the Babylonians, and the Romans (three times), and the end of the world came for the peoples of the numerous beautiful cities that were through the Roman Empire destroyed by German, or Hunnic invaders. The end of the world did come for 1/3 to 1/2 of the population of Europe who died during the Black Death. And on and on to the present day; for the peoples in cities that were exterminated and cultures and peoples enslaved and driven from history, the world did in fact end, for them.

This living with the dread of the end, and a seemingly inability to fend off the end, greatly shaped the view of the people under threat, and also the view of those remnants who did survived to build a world over again.

In these "endings" we lost not only people, and art, but great knowledge of what was known and what had been known. Culture is not always maintained, and as we study history, we find not a direct line of advancement, but a hodgepodge of loops and currents leading all over the place, with great deal of knowledge gained and then lost again. Therefore, we see great periods of time where study and knowledge is fostered and developed, only to see that knowledge lost and forgotten for centuries. Then for some unknown reason, safety, and the pursuit of knowledge, begins again.

A modern American, who has never tasted these types of historical events of extensive disasters and social collapse, and basically ignorant of the events of the history of the world, simply cannot relate to the fears of other peoples. But it is important for American readers to understand what a great privilege and oddity the history to date of the United States has been in comparison with the history of the world. This is not to say that the privilege will continue, but as long as it does, the American's perspective of world history is greatly tainted.

Setting the Stage

In political power struggles, history is often rewritten to be used by the side out of power or having just gained power. We are seeing this process take place in the United States now as the right wing tries to claim the mantle of the "Founding Fathers" to support their cultural and political power grabs. One of the key tools they are using is the claim that the "Founding Fathers" were true Christians and that the writers of the Declaration of Independence and the Constitution used the Bible and the conceptions of Christianity as the core principles for the creation of the Republic. In other words, the United States is and has always been a "Christian nation." This essay refutes that premise and brings to modern readers a reminder of who the Founding Fathers really idolized: a defender of the Roman Republic.

Cincinnatus Reconsidered

While the controversy as to the influence of religion on the development of the US government rages - were we founded on Christian principles or not; whether the founders were religious people or not- there is little doubt that the US Founding Fathers were well versed in classical literature (which few of us are today). Therefore, from a historical viewpoint the debate over influences should hinge on whether the Founding Fathers' real "heroes" and inspirations came more from Roman and Greek literature than from Jewish and Christian stories.

In looking at the outcomes of their efforts, it is clear, if we don't project the politics and religion of today retrospectively, that our government was created by leaders looking to the classics for guidance far more than the Bible. This realistic, historic view of the influences of the Founding Fathers can present a counter to the Christian argument, but can also give us a foundation for fighting to end the rise of the imperial president and the current threat to the freedom of American citizens.

In fact the two points (the imperial president and the treat to freedom) are greatly connected: But first, as a brief overview of how we know the Classical influence was greater than the Christian influence, just consider that they, Madison, Jefferson, Washington, Franklin, et al.

- created a Republic greatly influenced by the Roman model, not a kingship modeled after the Biblical governments;
- created a two-house legislature to create policy, to advise and consent; they did not institutionalize a national prophet to guide our nation's soul and demand conformity; and
- imposed no restrictions on the practice of religion; they did not impose a state religion where failure to comply could result in ostracism or death (as proposed in both the New and Old Testaments).

It is also clear that the founders were more influenced by the role model of the Roman Republic rather than during the imperial period. The Republic hero that most appealed to founders accepted power only when absolutely needed and resigned power at the earliest possible time (and returned to his plow). His name, so well-known among our early leaders and mostly forgotten now, was Cincinnatus: the inspiration for the name of the city of Cincinnati and the nearly forgotten Cincinnatus Societies, once so popular in the US.

- In time of terrible crisis, with military threats all around, Cincinnatus was granted, as within the Roman constitution, dictatorial powers.

He soon won great victories and stabilized the situation. He was wildly honored and loved by the Romans, and at that point when all the power could have been his, he gave up his dictatorship and returned to his life as a "gentleman farmer" ---- he returned to the plow.

- Therefore the motto of the Cincinnatus Society is "Omnia reliquit servare rempublicam" ("He relinquished everything to save the Republic").

When formed, the organization included almost every Founding Father. (Unfortunately, like the Roman Republic and most of our Founding Fathers, the Society seemed to favor an oligarchic approach to government and was criticized for laying the foundation for a new American "nobility.") See http://en.wikipedia.org/wiki/Society_of_the_Cincinnati

Cincinnatus's model of giving up power when danger passed was an ideal that went a long way in both the creation of the form and the power of the presidency in the United States Constitution and in practice by those who have held the office. George Washington was modeling Cincinnatus when he rejected the idea of a US kingship or even military dictatorship when he stated that he "did not fight to rid us of George III, only to replace him with George I."

- In fact, at the time Washington was hailed as an "American Cincinnatus."

Washington's act of rejecting power won through the glory of the battlefield shocked the world and inspired many to believe that a new world was truly in the making; but it was Washington and the other classically trained Founding Fathers who were really seeking to re-create an older world forgotten, the Roman Republic. The eventual Constitution and so many of our federal buildings and national symbols come not from the Bible but from what the Founding Fathers knew of Ancient Rome.

The actions of Cincinnatus, again not much remembered today, were far more important to the writers of the Constitution than the acts of Peter, or commandments of Moses or the sermons of Jesus. The Founding Fathers did not create a theocracy where all were responsible to follow the absolute rules and dictates of a distant (or even a close) god, but a Republic where power was not vested in the supernatural but in "men" (a term of the time), and the men had limited powers and limited time to wield the powers. And when extraordinary events occur and there is need for a man to have greater power, the man was responsible for giving up that power when the crisis had passed.

- You find no such system anywhere in the Christian worldview, and only limited occurrences in the Old Testament (the time period covered in the Book of Judges).

From this point of view, what we have seen in US history is a playing out of the ideals of Cincinnatus and the ideas that can be called the absolutism of both the Christians (one way to salvation) and the absolutism of the Imperial Roman model of empire and dictatorship. Fortunately for the US and the world, for the most part the Cincinnatus model (generally) seems to have been a motivating force in how the United States has dealt with the world throughout its history. For unlike any other world power in history, the United States has seldom sought empire and control of other lands through conquests or promulgated ideas based on conformity to an absolute ideal. And when pushed into war, after the crisis passed, the US wanted to just "return to normalcy" or "return to the plow."

However, throughout the course of US history there has been a struggle for the American soul between those who saw Cincinnatus as their model and those who saw others from Classical times and later (Alexander, Caesar, Napoleon, an unquestionable and perfect God/ Christ, etc.) as their ideal. In looking at our history, at times we can see the rhetoric and actions of the lovers of absolutist gods and emperors dominating (Manifest Destiny, 54/40 or fight) and actions of conquests taken, (the ill-conceived efforts to take Canada; the Mexican, Spanish and Iraq wars; and taking land from the Native Americans).

Far too often these lovers of empire also infused their justification with rhetoric on the value of their form of Christianity and justified conquest on bringing the "good news" to others. The ideals and even the name of Cincinnatus were masked at the times when the absolutists dominated.

We can, however, see the influence of Cincinnatus most obviously at the end of the two World Wars, where the US was among the grand winners and sought neither power nor lands.

Instead of the impulse for empire dominating, the US (though Wilson's 14 Points and Roosevelt's United Nations and other efforts) at both times, as Cincinnatus of old, rejected the "imperial robes" and instead sought to "return to the plow." Instead of demanding (extensive) money and land, the US promoted the concepts of a united world free of terror and tyranny with self-determination for all people as the cornerstone of a concept of international liberty. (At least on paper and in public policy, this was what was sought.)

Throughout the Cold War the rhetoric (not always supported by action) was about the United States as the leader of free peoples united in defense of liberty, not as one empire versus another. And again, in 1990, when the "evil empire" fell, and the crisis had passed, the United States sought not to absorb the pieces into a new empire but sought means to give up power. We wanted the "peace dividend" not pieces of the action. Even with the name and ideal of Cincinnatus mostly forgotten, the concepts seemed to continue.

It was this difference in action from any other super power in the world's history that may prove to be the most successful tactic in achieving our national goals of a peaceful and free world. It was not the vengeful god of the Old Testament or the "good news" of the New Testament that was the impulse for creation of US policy towards the world and rejection of Empire, it was the impulse to return to the plow, the impulse towards "governments instituted among men deriving their just powers from the consent of the governed," it was the model of ancient Rome and Cincinnatus that seems to be the (by far) greater influence than the realities of the Christian religion, with its long history of attacking and killing those who did not agreeing with them.

Again, there is no doubt there were diversions from the course, and ill-conceived actions when the lovers of empire dominated and allowed for the reestablishment of the Western empires throughout Asia after World War II, and supported repressive regimes during the Cold War.

And there is no doubt that the involvement of the US in a number of wars and military actions from 1950 to 1990 (from Korea to supporting the insurgent efforts against the Russians in Afghanistan) greatly drove the US towards the concept of "the imperial presidency." And there is no doubt that all of these events costs millions of lives and extensive "treasure" and allowed for repression of the aspirations of millions of people.

It will be the role of historians to determine which of these two approaches actions (fitting into the Cincinnatus model, or desire for empire), more fully responded to the crises that have, and will be, face the United States. Future historians will determine if, in the future, as in the past, the ideals of the Cincinnatus model was continued and eventually win out again, despite the sense in the present that the imperialist and religious absolutist are winning the internal struggle for that thing I have called the American soul.

Things looked worse in periods of US history before, and the American tendency towards Cincinnatus eventually won out.

What is different now is that the crisis of the "War on Terror" or the "struggle against Islamist fundamentalist" is seen in terms of decades-long struggles, with no declared description of what is "victory" or in other words, the end of the crisis. So rather there being a set time frame for the need of "dictatorial powers" for example six months the time allowed for dictatorship in the Roman Constitution or till the end of a "declared events, such as with the beginning and ending, of World War II we seem to be in a crisis without end.

We really saw the rise of the imperial presidency during the open ended "Cold War" years. We see the continued expansion of it in this new open period of endless war against a non-nation state. In both these times, end of the crisis is never defined. Without an "end point" it is unclear when power can be returned. We now live in the world where extensive videoing of movements and security screenings of phone calls and e-mails are now "normal" and mostly accepted; something almost unthinkable some fifteen years ago. These were powers granted for a "crisis", and if the crisis never ends, the powers are never "given up."

If the "crisis" worsens and more powers granted, will they ever be returned? George Orwell addressed how states can respond to the impact of unending war in the novel 1984. In that Orwellian future, Cincinnatus will become a "non-person" someone who never existed.

However, throughout all this time, the concept of the US not wanting power and being a reluctant leader and ruler, and of a nation wanting to give up this responsibility of rule was mostly maintained by virtually every president and most leaders (again with noted exceptions). It was this Cincinnatus concept of the US that was principally admired and respected by the peoples of the world.

It was not the call to create a Christian world, or to bring "all the world to Christ" that preserved the world from the tyranny, but the willingness by the US to reject power and support republican values of self-determination and equal justice and rejection of absolutism and promoting limits on the powers of government that has led to the current world: one mostly free of war and one where there are now more nations that, at least on paper, profess to be a republic than any other time in history.

We have passed through a terrible time, from the beginning of the World War I till now, that has been horrendous in its destruction yet ultimately beneficial in its outcome. In large part these outcomes:

- the fall of colonialism,
- the fall of Communism,
- the failure of Fascism and Nazism,
- the end of despotic rule of kings and emperors,

Some of the positives that came out of these struggles included by no way limited to:

- the liberation of women,
- the gaining of the rights of minority populations in countries,
- the access to education, and
- the access to power by the "commons" of the world through the rise of republics

All these positive changes in the world were made possible by the willingness of America address a given crisis but then to return "to the plow" and refuse to take power over the world (with some major blunders and, at times, some real slowness in action). These changes in the world came about in large part by the admiration and inspiration found in Cincinnatus by our founders and their successors and the long term modeling of policy based on this inspiration.

(It should be noted that in a 2013 trip to South Africa President Obama, heaped praise on President Mandela for not just leading his nation to a peaceful transition to democratic rule, but also for his knowledge and willingness to walk away from power when the goals were reached. President Obama was indirectly calling President Mandela his nation's Cincinnatus.)

If, on the other hand, we look at the various options offered in both scripture and the rhetorical interpretation of by many Christians, the justification and demand for expansion and empire was almost pushed (in the name of civilization and spreading Christianity) throughout American history by many of their leaders, as well as at critical times, a demand for passivism and non-resistance to aggression came from many of the leading Christian thinkers.

Thankfully for the United States and the world, the Founding Fathers (so aware of the evils of religion when involved in the state) were not all that inspired by the teachings of Jesus or how the Christians had presented those teachings), when it came to founding a government.

Even with the wars of the last quarter century (Iraq I and II and Afghanistan), that could be argued fits into the imperial aspirations the words and the actions of the US were framed in the same concepts of liberation and not conquest, and creating freedom and not homogeny.

The wars were fought at least according to policy, to defeat tyrants and protect the world from those who would use terrorism as a tactic to create disorder and despair and a tyrannical rule of a religious oligarch. Again, at least in the eyes of many, there was a crisis and with the crisis came the need to defend the "republic." Again, history will show what actions fit the impulse for empire or that constitute true defense of the Republic.

However, with the death of Bin Laden and the rise of Arab democratic demands, and with what looks like the ending of the current "war on terrorism," comes the question: is the US now willing to again "return to the plow"?

- Can the US once again back away from the impulse towards empire and imperial rule?
- Can the rulers of the US give up the powers that were granted in time of crisis created by 9/11 and other events and empowered through the Patriot Act?

Now we can look at the debate of how influential Christian models were on the Founding Fathers with a new understanding. The facts show that the Founding Fathers saw in religion a form of tyranny and absolutism, and in Cincinnatus they found the ideals of service to people without reward. It is clear that the founders of the nation were not focused on Biblical prophecy or the need to create the "shining city on the hill" but on the need to limit the powers of the rulers in peace and in crisis, and when the crisis ends, the returning of powers to the people.

So, why is there this push by so many to rewrite history to show the founders to be good Christians and motivated by the Ten Commandments? Since the premise is so false, the basis for the claims must be seen as a means to re-write the truth for an uneducated public; one with no sense of history little understanding of so much of American history, and of course little knowledge of Cincinnatus, for some purpose.
One obvious reason for making the US a Christian nation is to build the case for more war with Islam. If we are a Christian nation we must in (in their minds) be a natural enemy of Muslim nations. There the war must continue until Islam itself is defeated (a war without end).

With this claim of the need for ongoing war, and ongoing crisis, comes the claim to ongoing dictatorship or use of dictatorial methods (to address the crisis). Their logic follows that with the crisis comes the justification of torture and secret courts and warrantless wire taps and indefinite imprisonment without charges, and the president being empowered to kill citizens without a process of the courts. All these and more are being done in the name of a "current crisis" of the "war on terror." And, of course the actions are justified to protect the good and innocent Christians ... from "them." As the wars in countries end, there is a need by those who want to continue to dominate through fear, to maintain the crisis, somehow.

So the silly statements by what appear to be ignorant religious nuts are in fact something far more serious and are laying a foundation for a less free and more imperial America and a continuing crisis. Since the statements mostly go unchallenged in the current Christian dominated media environment, the statements become left as more or less unchallenged facts. And of course the result of these unchallenged statements is that Cincinnatus comes closer to becoming a non-person.

We cannot tolerate leaving the concept of this being a Christian country unchallenged. We must engage the debate even when the statements are so silly. If the public debate on the future of America is framed in the ideals of the Ten Commandments and the impulse of the religious right forces to "give unto Caesar" then there is little room for alternatives, since the debate is based on the Christian values so long used to support the concepts of tyranny and of empire.

Therefore, it is time to remind the country of the real views of the Founding Fathers, and of their love for the ideal of Cincinnatus and the necessity of returning to the plow. We need to accept the debate in the US about the influences on the Founding Fathers. We need to make this a land where both the leaders the people are once again versed in "classical history," we need to be telling the story of Cincinnatus and how our founders found inspiration in him on the virtues of government far more than Jesus and Moses. It is time for Cincinnatus reconsidered.

And by this reconsideration, here we will find the historical justification for asking our leaders to back away from the centralization of power and the actions of dictators and allowing the US to return to a state of more freedom. Here we find the justification to combat the supposed morals of the Christian right with the real historical tendency of the US to want to "return to the plow."

Two Essays about Time

First Essay

Setting the Stage

In this essay the theme of religion dominating modern times far more than it should focuses on the issue of how we measure the passage of time. It ascribes the general world-wide acceptance of the Christian, actually the Western Christian, conception of the year in which we live to Western military dominance and colonialism. Here, we review the creation of this "timeline" and reveal the "timeline" of other cultures, showing the wide variety of conceptualizations of time that differ from our dominant measurement. In addition, it offers a solution to the measurement of time that attempts to respect other cultures and their sense of history, by once again "resetting the clock."

What Year Is This?

Or - How the Designation of This Year as 2013 Disrespects Most of the Cultures of the World.

Part I – Conflict and "Compromise"

The world is in a process of recovering from centuries of Western imperialism and colonialism. The underlying forces that enabled this world dominance included such concepts as racism and cultural chauvinism. As we move back towards a world less dominated by ideology to one more dominated by conflicting cultures, and as we move into a world that is less dominated by one culture over another, we see a reversion to a world where cultures are competing (as opposed to nation states or ideologies in competition).

In such a world, we need to consider ways to lessen tensions between cultures; which includes the West showing more respect to the cultures we so dominated for centuries. One (not likely considered) way to show this willingness to accept others as more equal in a world of more equals is a simple matter of time, or actually, the designating of time; specifically what we call the year we are living in.

The fact that we call this year 2013 and expect the rest of the world to also agree to this time designation is a remnant of Western domination and shows little respect to the religious and cultural differences of other countries. The only reason that this is year 2013 throughout the world is because the West tried, with a great deal of success, to impose its values, worldview and religion on the rest of the world. And we know, in fact, that 2013 is a Western Christian religious view of time, and actually only one of many competing concepts of measuring years developed in the West, with all of them based on a narrow interpretation of one book in the Western Christian religion. Yet on the surface of things, the year 2013 is now the "common era."

There is acceptance of this Western domination by the likes of Kofi Annan Former United Nations Secretary-General who stated that:

The Christian calendar no longer belongs exclusively to Christians. People of all faiths have taken to using it simply as a matter of convenience. There is so much interaction between people of different faiths and cultures - different civilizations, if you like - that some shared way of reckoning time is a necessity. And so the Christian era has become the Common Era.

Perhaps it is time to revisit this concept of "year designation" and really separate "church from state" and West domination over others. Perhaps it is really time for a new understanding of what is a "Common Era" and create a new measurement that respects all cultures and peoples and steps back from a Western Christian world domination of time designation. Can we try and find a means of stating the year that is functional and respects all cultures and truly reflects an event that all can agree that altered the state of the world?" Can we find one event that was truly so significant to (almost) all cultures that it ushered in a new era?

Yes, this changing of the designation of the year could be very inconvenient for many. However, it was inconvenient when the Western world, over some three hundred years, changed "time" to move away from the Julian to the Georgian calendar.

It was also very inconvenient, when other cultures, faced with the imperialist ventures of the West, were forced to measure time based on Western religion traditions, rather than their traditional approaches. It was inconvenient for "a time;" but sometimes and for both political and scientific reasons change was needed and no matter how inconvenient, (over time) it was accomplished. And as we move into a new type of world, perhaps it really is time for a change on time.

While the premise of the Mr. Annan's statement is true (in a truly connected world, some form of shared agreement on "year" is needed); but do we really have to accept the Christian concept as imposed on so many? Numerous people staunchly resist this concept of dating, especially among the 1.2.billion Muslims.

The people of multiple Muslim nations resist the concept of this being 2013 CE and, true to their faith, maintain the traditional dating of the Muslim world (this being 1434 AH). Although also Muslims, the Iranians have a slightly different concept of the year; based on their traditions the year is 1392 SH.

While mainly accepting of the "Christian" year, the 1.4 billion Chinese have a traditional dating system that is different from the West, as do the 1.2 billion Hindus, who generally accept the Common Era dating (in large part due to British rule for some 175 years), but have their own conception of the year that they see as more realistic, based in their very ancient counting procedures.

So, while the Christian/Common Era year is accepted now by most, it can and is a source of cultural conflicts that are used to make an "anti-Western" or "Anti-Christian" point. There are those who are against all that is "Western," including the year, and make political points with their people by showing Western cultural indifference created by imposing a "Christian counting" system on their culture. There are those who are against Christianity and it being imposed on their culture, including the concept of the Common Era being based on an event with positive significance only to Christians.

Accepting the clear need for a common frame of reference for the current and future years, can we actually come up with a new way of counting the passage of time that can be accepted throughout the world and be seen as non-chauvinistic by all of the major cultures? Can we help to lessen tensions between cultures by eliminating an unneeded cultural preference that is in constant use, that being the Christian year?

Before trying to answer these questions, first perhaps it is best to understand why the "Western World" says its 2013 AD or

CE and how this designation came about. Also, we should know "what year it is" in other cultures to look at their frame of reference. Then perhaps we can consider some alternative ways of counting the years that are offensive to none (or almost none.)

Part II - Why 2013?

The commonly held view of the current world is that this is the year 2013 CE with CE meaning "common era" or "Christian era" or even the "common/Christian era." Not too long ago this year would have been referred to with an even more overt Christian term, 2013 AD or Anno Domini "(the year of our Lord," based on the assumed year of the birth of Christ, but actually set based on the assumed year of the conception of the Christ).

This change of from AD to CE supports the premise for the need to respect other culture's conception of time in our multiple-religion world. This political shift started, over the past fifty or so years as non-Christian historians complained about the designation of time. Therefore with the AD to CE shift, the West still tried to maintain its dominance by not changing the counting of years but by making the terminology of the measuring of the years less "Christian" by talking about the "common era" (CE), rather than the year of "our lord." (AD)

- In addition, my call to restart or change how we count the years is not all that new, it has occurred multiple times even in the Christian world.

The idea of measuring time from some event around Christ (conception, birth, death, rising, etc.) was not initially the way that the passing of years was even measured by the Christians; it was developed some five hundred years into the "Christian

Era." The early Christians either used the traditional Roman way of stating the years, or used the Jewish system.

- The Romans used two ways of designating the years, those being either from the founding of Rome (definitely their significant event) or (more commonly) by stating the name of the Counsel of Rome as the year. (The Counsels served one-year terms so each year was named for the Counsel.)

- The Jews also used two means in ancient times; a date determined through interpretation of the book of Genesis for the creation of the Earth, and also the years of the reign of a king (for example, in the tenth year of King Herod, and so on).

So in both Roman and Jewish cultures (and many other cultures), each year had multiple numbers attached to its designation.

And the baseline for starting the year count changed frequently in ancient and early medieval times. The "cause" of the change, or reset, was something that occurred that seemed significant to the people at the time. The imperial Greeks, Alexander's successors, started measuring time in ages or epochs. They reset the count based on the life of Alexander the Great or the Alexandrian era. To them, Alexander's conquest of Persia was definitely the significant event of their time, and the new world order flowed from that event.

The resetting of time based on a new dynasty or some major event was traditional in much of the ancient world, once there was a rise of monarchs. Each monarch tended to see themselves as the significant event and the cause of the beginning of a new era. Therefore, in much of the world, there have been frequent restarts of counting the years as one ruler came and went and one dynasty rose or fell.

This tradition of resetting time based on significant events played out in the conquered territories of the Greeks long after the Greek presence faded into a distant memory. The declaration of "eras" in Persia (Iran) was somewhat frequent in the successor states to Alexander and even continued at the beginning of Muslim rule.

This tradition explains why Iran (and Afghanistan) see this year as 1392 (of the Yazdgerdi era – one of the last Iranian rulers before the Muslim conquest) and not 1434 (AH), or after the Hijra, or the time Mohammed left Mecca for Medina, the significant point in the Muslim world view, and the reset point for almost all Muslims.

There were variations on how to count the years in many of the great cultures of the world. Like the Romans and Jews, the Chinese too had a duel system of counting years, based on monarchs and dynasties but each year was also named according to their twelve house astrological system. Therefore, dates in ancient Chinese writings are stated as something like "the second year of the tiger in the rule of such and such."

Despite Western efforts to change this approach, the Chinese maintained their system as the official stating of time until the founding of the Republic in 1912. We in the West most often come in contact with this dating system on the table mats at most Chinese restaurants; it seems trivial to us, but remains highly important to so many of the 1.4 billion Chinese in the world.

It obvious that the significant event to Christians is the life of the "person" they call Christ. As such it would seem common and traditional to do a time reset based on some moment in his life or for his death. However, this idea was not at all prevalent in the early Christian movement; it took centuries for the idea of such a reset to even be offered as a viable concept. The idea of measuring the passing of years based on Christ was first proposed by a Christian monk named Dionysius Exiguus in what now is called the year 525 (CE). And contrary to what is often stated, he did not establish his new baseline, or significant event, based on the year of the birth of the Christ, but on what he thought was the year of the conception of Christ, the "announcement."

It took some time for even Dionysius to start to use the idea and he first employs the system in his "new" year of 532 CE, or AD. Prior to this we see that the "early" Christians had mainly just used the existing Roman and Jewish year systems to talk about the time. Perhaps the first set of followers of Christ didn't feel the need to do a reset, since many of the very early Christians felt the end of days would come imminently and the second coming of Christ would happen in their lifetime.

However, since Christ did not return, and the world continued, the Christians of the late Roman Empire (in the West) did start a reset of the year, and did begin to use the term AD, around the year that we call 315 CE. The significant event that they saw as a reason for reset was not Christ or the second coming, but survival of an attack on the community. The initial meaning of AD was Anno Diocletiani, or the years after Diocletian's repressions (303-311 CE) and the issue of the Edict of Milan of 313 CE.

The late-Roman-Empire Christians saw this event (the last great time of martyrs) and the official acceptance of Christianity as a legitimate religion as their significant event; significant enough to begin a "new era." They saw this ending of repression and their toleration by the Roman state as the true point at which the years should be counted.

So Dionysius really didn't even "coin the phrase" AD; he simply changed an already existing designated use of AD to better fit his conception of how years should be measured. His saw the need for a new baseline (Christ's conception) because he felt that the existing designation of years was based on a "negative" and secular event, not a holy and divine act (the impregnation of Mary.) He simply (perhaps for the sake of convenience) changed the designation of "D" from referring to a temporal Roman lord to referring to his spiritual "Lord."

- In his time, Dionysius simply reset the year he was living in from 247 AD (the year after the repressions) to 532 AD, basically by logic and a stroke of a pen.

That must have been confusing and difficult for many people of the time.

Part of this confusion and difficulty of jumping some 285 years in designation may explain why initially Dionysius's new option of measurement did not take hold quickly. The new "AD" was not generally accepted at first, even in the West. Most still clung to the traditional Roman dating system (as the Roman world fell apart), while the "traditional Christians" still mostly used their original meaning of AD and counted the years as they had done for nearly three centuries.

In addition, Dionysius projected his concept for a reset some fifty years after the "collapse" of the Roman West, and the rise of the German successor states (which mainly used years of the king for their designation of the year). With all the wars and instability of the time the internal controversy between the Christians on the year of Christ's birth seemed relatively unimportant.

To most Christians at the time, based on the chaos and destruction, (again) the end of the world was near and surely (again) the "Second Coming was at hand." The suffering people of the time were more anxious about when Christ would come back to stop the rule of the "pagans" and "barbarians," rather than being concerned about how long ago Christ was born or died or rose ... in some time past. However, (at least for the survivors of the time), the issues of "time" did continue, and how to mark the passing of the time became an issue again later.

After the initial chaos in the West, when much of what was Rome faded away, there were slowly some efforts to reset culture again, and there were now openings for change (since so much had been forgotten or lost). The old (Roman) use of counting time faded and only a few people even were concerned with such concepts.

Some two hundred years after the monk Dionysius, we see his concept of AD coming into use; the English historian, the Venerable Bede, one of the leading "intellectuals" of his time, used the "new" AD in the 8th Century and set time based on the "announcement of Christ" in his history of England.

With Bede's writing, Dionysius's concept finally gained a wider acceptance (by what passed for the intellectuals of the time, mainly the monks of the Catholic Church). However, it would take another seven hundred years for all the Catholic countries to use Dionysus's counting designation (Portugal being the last to accept it in 1422 AD, or what they then starting calling 1422 AD). So, even in the West, AD was a relatively controversial means of marking time, almost until the time of Columbus.

However, in Eastern Christianity the concept of "AD" was rejected completely by the Eastern Orthodox Church. The

Byzantine Empire and Eastern Orthodox Church, as with Jewish tradition, tracked time from what they saw as the creation of the earth or Anno Mundi (AM), "the year of the world". An Eastern monk, Annianus of Alexandria, traced the creation back to precisely March 25th in what today we would call the year 5509 BC (or before Christ or before the Common Era, or Before the Common/Christian Era). So even in the Christian Church there has never been agreement on AD/BC.

The Eastern (Greek) Empire long before Dionysius or Bede already had had an internal fight over time (and almost every other aspect of the Christian religion), since much of the Greek world used the first Olympiad (776 BCE, or BC) as a reckoning of years (as opposed to the founding of Rome in the West). The Emperor Theodosius banned the Olympic Games (in 396 CE or AD) since the games, dedicated to the God Zeus, came to be considered as "anti-Christian."

He and successor emperors imposed their single brand of Christianity and a single set of rules (including how the years were counted) on their territories, with much resistance from the populace. Therefore, the East saw the new attempt of dating as proposed by Dionysius or later by Bede as a refight of something already done, and something very costly and would have none of it.

So for the Eastern Church, and the lands controlled by the Byzantines, the Dionysius year of AD 532 was the year 6541 AM (with the extra year being added for the lack of year zero in the new Western System). To the Byzantines there seemed no greater significant act than the creation of the world. With the chaos of the routine coming and going of dynasties and of wars and of plagues, they never saw any reason for a reset.

In addition, for many in the West, even with the fall of the Empire, the real event that marked the dividing point in history was the founding of Rome. Therefore 532 AD would have been considered as 1315 AUC (the Latin designation for "after the founding of the city"). So if Byzantine year (AM) count had in fact become universal, as opposed to the AD approach, we'd be currently living in the year 7521 AM (with the New Year still occurring on Mach 25th). And if the Roman tradition was kept we'd be in fact living in 2766 AUC.

In addition, when the Western Protestants got hold of the translation of the Bible in the vernacular, they tried to determine the year of the creation on their own, and came up with a different date than the Eastern Church. Bishop Usher, in the 17th century determined that the date of creation was actually 4004 BC. Therefore, according to this Christian tradition of scholarship, the year is not 7521 AM but 6017 AM, and if the fundamentalist Christians gain extensive control, we may soon find ourselves referring to years based on this count.

Actually, to add a bit to the confusion, besides what year it was, agreement on the day to mark the beginning of the "new year" was a point of controversy for much of Western history as well. For many centuries January 1, March 25th, September 1st and some other dates competed for the honor. In some places there was both a civil and a religious New Year celebration (often January 1 and March 25th) allowing for two traditions to maintain themselves side by side, and perhaps to give people more holidays as well. Over a very long period of time in Europe (16th to the 20th century) January won out with the acceptance of the Georgian Calendar which replaced the Julian system.

The British Empire, including the American colonies, did not accept the new counting system (Georgian) until 1752 AD, with Russia only doing so after the revolution in 1918 AD. Spain, Holland and the Holy Roman Empire moved much quicker to adapt the changes, doing so in the 1580s, leaving much of

Europe in disagreement for almost two hundred years regarding what year it was, never mind when to celebrate the new year.

The British, in order to get the new counting process in place, actually had one year (1753 CE or AD) in which they eliminated months, starting the year on January 1 and jumping the very next day to March 25th eliminating all of January, February and most of March from that year. (If you ever see a document dated March 1st 1752 you know it's a forgery.) This must have been truly inconvenient for many.

So, for many centuries throughout Europe (Eastern and Western) there was little agreement on what year it was or even when the New Year occurred or when Easter or Christmas occurred and basically there was much confusion. And we can all assume that it was not easy for the British Empire, or any of the other countries in Europe to adopt the new calendar, or new designation of a year. But, eventually, for necessity, over time, it was done.

There was clearly a need for a common point of time then as there is now. It took a very long time for the West to sort out both the days and the year, but over time there was agreement (actually it was quite recent). It took far less time for the West to impose their concept on the rest the world.

Part III - Other Current Options

If this is 2013 in the Western Christian tradition, what year is it in other traditions? Listed below are some of the currently used and no longer used traditional years based on the more popular cultures.

- Hebrew (based on creation or AM)   5773
- Byzantine (based on creation or AM)   7522

- Fundamentalist Christian
  (Bishop Usher's AM)   6017
- Current/ "Christian" dating –
  based on the conception of Jesus   2013
  - Ethiopian Christians disagree
    Based theirs on the year of the
    "announcement of Jesus"   2005
- Muslim (based on the year
  of the Hijra)   1435
- Iranian (based on
  a royal calendar reform YZ)   1392
- Buddhist Era or (BE) Based on the
  death of Buddha
    (two schools on that date of death)
    – so either   2557
    or   2496
- Hindu (of the current era
  – with many cycles of eras previous)   5114
- Chinese (a Western import in
  setting this date – first emperor   4711
- Baha'i (based on their founding,
  or the Baha'i era)   170

We also can state what year it would be if some of the ancient traditions had continued.
For example:

- The Assyrians started counting years
  based on the dedication of the first temple
  at Ashur   6763
- Ancient Egyptian (from the
  establishment of their calendar)   6255
- Olympian (Ancient Greek)
  dating from the first Olympics   2789
- Roman tradition
  (from the founding of the city)   2766

We also have efforts to create a new era in relatively recent times, such as:

- Based on the resetting of time by the French Revolution — 221
- Founding of the People's Republic of China — 64

Part IV - What Is Wrong With All of These Indications of "Year"?

As we can see from the listing of currently used and ancient (unused) designations of years, almost all are based on a religious concept of either the creation of the world or the critical event in their religious or social history beliefs. Science has disproven the religious determination of creation, or the AM counting, as used by the Jews and Eastern Orthodox and Fundamentalist Christians of the West. The "significant event" approach is clearly too idiosyncratic to the particular religion or cultures. While every group has that right to try and establish their group concept as the best measurement criteria, using anyone's date causes a foundation for complaint by the others: Why should we use Jesus's conception rather than Buddha's death (and so on)?

Also, perhaps, if the French Revolution had been more "successful" and maintained its focus their reset of the year may have lasted more than just a few years. If so, maybe even today "the radical' section of Europe would have a different year than the "conservative" sections (as happened many times in the past). We could have even seen a struggle over the designation of the year throughout the world as the ideals of the French revolution took hold in one country or another, with the acceptance of the French date as an official or just symbolic break from colonialism and religious dominance of the past (or something akin to the centuries-long battle over the Julian or Georgian calendars).

Or perhaps the new time counting system may have even been reset based on the American Revolution, and we would be living in the year 237 ADI (after the American Declaration of Independence). And perhaps if China does come to dominate the world, the new designation of a year labeled APR may appear (after the People's Republic).

Obviously, looking for a new means of setting the "year" is not new with me or my thinking. The simple change from AD to CE, the effort during the French and Chinese revolutions, shows that the issues I raise have been of concern for hundreds of years, as the world adjusts to "first contacts" between cultures, cultural dominance by one culture over others, and efforts to develop more universal acceptance of cultural differences (and adjustments to culture based on new scientific discovery).

We have also seen these efforts to adjust the counting of years away from the Christian system in literature and mass culture. In *Brave New World*, Aldous Huxley projected a future world dominated by mass production of everything including human life, using the new time designation of AF or "after Ford," for the developer of the modern mass-production-line technique (Henry Ford). We also see in all the Star Trek series and movies an effort to make time calculation non-religious based with its use of "star date." (More than one early episode worked into the dialogue that the events were taking place in what "you would call the late 23rd century.")

Part V - Some Options for a Brave New Year System

So we come down to the question of if there is a "universal" significant event that can be seen as a means of tracking the years that does not offend one culture or religion or over promote any one culture or religious worldview? The easiest answer is, of course, "no," since the cultures and religions of the world are so diverse and apparently set in their ways. There just seems to be too much disagreement on so many issues.

We can't even find a universal acceptance among peoples of the "age of the Earth," as provided by science. Some people or subsets of groups reject the findings of science as anti-religious and reject the age of the Earth as now known. (The universe is some 17 billion years old and the Earth itself is some 4.5 billion years.) It is likely that with the billions of people living without access to modern education, far fewer than half of the world's population knows or accepts the new science findings on the age of the Earth.

Besides, this Earth-based year count, like the old Turkish or Post World War I German currency, is just too large to use effectively. Imagine if we used the 4.5 billion date as the basis for time, saying:

- "I was born in the year four billion, five hundred million, six hundred and fifty two thousand and fifty"?

Not easy to do.

Then, is there a more universal non-religious profound earth-changing event that impacted almost all cultures? There are some candidates.

One obvious idea could be to use what is now called 1492 CE, when about one-quarter of the world was connected to the other three-quarters (much to the negative impact of the "new" world's peoples).

It was definitely impacting, but maybe not so for much of Asia for some hundred years or more. While religion had a major impact on how things played out, the event was not a "religious" thing. This "first contact" did occur but only initially involved the West and the Americas. It was very significant and greatly changed three continents right away (Europe, the Americas and Africa) and Asia and Australia over time. So it comes close, but it's not really "universal" right away. Besides "the age of discovery" is the point where the real rise of Western imperialism begins, and perhaps it is best not to glorify that process any more.

Perhaps we should consider 1776, not just for the American Revolution, but because of the invention of the steam engine and the publication of *The Wealth of Nations*; all three of these events greatly changed the world and continue to do so. But again, the initial impact was not universal, with the changes first occurring in the Western world and then spreading out.

Perhaps the answer lies in the stars. After all, the "ancients" knew the "heavens" quite well and understood the passage of time not just in years but in epochs. Almost all the "ancients" developed the understanding of "astrology" and created similar horoscopes with the idea of celestial twelve houses (with different names). We also see how the ancients knew about the winter and summer solstices and the true length of a year. We see the remnants of this great tracking of time in Stonehenge and thousands of other locations across the world.

In fact, the Hindu conception of the great cycles of time lasting some twenty-four-thousand years is highly correlative to what we call today the (scientifically proven) "Great Year." We know that the appearance of the sky and the location of the rising of the summer solstice sun changes roughly every 2000 years and appears to move across the heavens in a retrograde fashion from one astrological "house" to another.

Therefore, our current understanding of the "Great Year" and the Hindu understanding of "eras" are both the same, roughly 24,000 years. Based on what we know through science today, the Hindu work on tracking time is perhaps the most sophisticated of all the ancients (with the possible exception of the Maya and some other Mesoamerican peoples).

The ancient Hindus, based on their understanding of time, could and did track the age of the world in millions and billions of years. They were not bound by the "Holy Bible trap," which led to the debate in the Christian world of whether the Earth was created some seven-thousand-five-hundred years ago, or six-thousand years ago.

The Hindus, as well as the Chinese, never lost the astrological knowledge of the ancients that was purged from Western thinking by Western Christian dogma. Both these ancient cultures, along with the ancient cultures of the Americas, and Mesopotamia, Egypt (and societies that existed that we know almost nothing about), all understood the skies and the passage of time based on "the movement of the stars."

Perhaps it would be the most universal and anti-Western chauvinistic approach to return to tracking based on the "Great Year." And since there is clearly a "near era" coming based on all the major cultural astrological settings as well a modern science (the wobble of the earth changing how we see the stars is clearly a fact), perhaps we can go back to tracking years based on these "universal" scientifically based events.

In doing so we would be more or less able to keep the current year, since the "great year" eras last about 2000 years. And a new one is coming any time now. Therefore, we'd simply refer to the current year 2013 PA (Piscean Age) or maybe year one of the Aquarian Age. We would also start counting what we call before the Common Era or BCE as part of the various ages. For example, if we give, say, 2012 years to each age, Caesar would have been assassinated not in 44 BCE, but in the year 1968 AA (Arian Age). Incredible, how they year 1968 seems to be a year of assassination, under more than one system of counting time. And of course, we can all start singing about the dawning of the Age of Aquarius. Well at least in the West and in the Northern Hemisphere. The Chinese and Indians have a different name for the new age, as for all the signs of the Zodiac. And of course herein lays a major problem with this concept. Whose astrological names do we use?

In addition, the skies of the Southern Hemisphere differ from the Northern, and the astrological designations do not fit well in the Southern skies. And of course, use of an astrological-based time setting is an affront to many Western religions and would cause a great deal of problems in that arena.

Also, there would be all kinds of trouble in going back more than twenty-four-thousand years, since we'd be in a repeat of the age, and setting the time of the dinosaurs would be very difficult. However, perhaps we can limit this time tracking to the advent of "humans."

So, perhaps returning to the system of the ancients is filled with unsolvable problems. Therefore we need to find a modern solution, by looking for a modern moment that is so profound, so significant, we can actually say it issued in a new age; a moment that can be agreed to as universal and impacting almost everyone. What we need to find is a moment that is not based on a religion, or on one person, or the impact of one person on history or one culture and a moment that seems to impact everyone (or almost everyone.)

Perhaps one event does exist that was truly worldwide in its occurrence, felt by almost all peoples, and truly changed the nature of the world; World War I. (Although it was obviously not the first world war, or war occurring on several continents at one time. Unfortunately there have been many of those prior to the WWI and the conflict that occurred between 1914 and 1918.) Perhaps we should start counting time again from what we call 1914 CE, the year the war began, or maybe 1918, the year the war ended.

First of all, World War I was not a religious event but an international sectarian occurrence. And the event truly changed the nature of the world and finally ended (for the most part) the rule by a strong monarchy, something that had dominated the history of humanity for at least five thousand years. (Just prior to World War I, 85% of the world was "ruled" by 13 monarchs and two presidents, with the other 15% under authoritarian strong men, minor monarchs or mock democracies or republics.) The stopping of the war mostly ended not just the conception of "nobility" and its rights, but greatly undermined the historical concept of "empire" and "colonialism." The war brought on a new era of the "common man/person" where the driving force of society was no longer considered to be the ruler, but the people; this is truly significant.

The impact of the war made the concept of "self-determination" something desired universally, and it also laid the foundation for the idea of "a world safe for democracy." In addition, the rights women won in the last century or so, and the rights of minorities throughout the world were initially "given" based on their contributions to the "Great War."

Most of the leadership of the twentieth century that reshaped the world away from millennia of tyranny and towards personal and political liberties or towards a worse form of tyranny and dictatorship as an alternative to monarchy, either

fought in the war, or served in governments involved in the war, or, perhaps equally important, resisted the war.
In addition, the war was the casual factor for the far greater use of industrialization throughout the world and sped the improvement in devices ranging from automobiles and airplanes to changes in food production and use of such new items as rubber. All these inventions and improvements coming out of the war soon became "essentials" of a new world order based on consumerism.

The war and the aftermath were not localized to Europe; battles were fought on three continents and in the Pacific islands. Fighters came from every continent and almost every "nation" at the time. Also, China's famous "May Forth Movement", Japan's new Empire, the ending of the Asian Turkish Empire all came from the War.

Also, the Russian Revolution and the establishment of the foundation for the world communist movement, the rise and fall of democracy in Germany, the eventual establishment of the state of Israel, the creation of an American presence in world politics, and on and on, can all be traced to the impact of World War I, never mind the eventual collapse of the "winning" English and French empires that dominated so much of Asia and Africa prior to the beginning of the war.

It is clear that the "Great War" changed the world more universally then any event in history (with the "Age of Discovery" starting in 1492 coming a close second). The chaos and terror and the great advancement in cultural tools and in the overall way of life of the 20th Century can all be seen as the direct impact of the war or to misuse the famous quote of Clausewitz in the impacts created by the "continuation of the war by other means." In addition, much of the conflicts of the 20th century and of the world today are directly a result of the fighting and the incredible chaotic settlement of the war known as the Treaty of Versailles. Clearly nothing in history was so universally felt and so impacting as World War I.

Therefore, since the world order changed so much, we can clearly argue that World War I can clearly be seen as the starting point of a new world, and worthy of an new restart of time counting; a starting point free of all religious and cultural overviews or prejudices. Therefore, as the world slowly works its way through the consequence of the war and the ending of colonialism and concepts of cultural chauvinism, and in recognition that there are so many religions each with their own natural views on their own importance, and claim to correctness, I propose that we end this particular Christian religious dominance of the world culture, and we shift (over time) to a new restart of the counting of time.

We can revive the tradition of having two names for years, as the Chinese, Buddhist, Muslim, Persian, Jewish and many others still celebrate their own culture's year count. So there is no reason why the Christians cannot maintain their count of the years from their significant event right along with the other cultures. We can let them have "in the year of our lord" back, without offence because we would say it as year "x" after the great war, in the "y" year of the Christian era (or Muslim era, etc.) However, the Christian count would just become another one of many respected cultural events in the world, not the forced dominant "common era" imposed on the other cultures. So the year would be ???? (finding the right term for the new marking of time/2013 or ????/1435 or ????/2557 and all are served and none offended.

Then let us therefore have another of the many historical resets of time. This time we can have the reset on truly a significant event that impacted all cultures over time. Not a localized event of impact as we have in the past, but truly a global impact. An impact not based in religion, funneled down to use with cultural myths, but an event based in hard political facts.

Let us recognize that we now live in a new era with a new designation. Now here is where we need to determine how to mark the time those question marks used above: Should the year be 99 PWWI (or Post World War I), or perhaps 99 FGW (From the Great War)? Or maybe it should be based on counting from the end of the war and we're in year 95 PWWI or FGW. As with all these inconvenient shifts in time, there is lots of room for argument here.

And as with all the resets, it can take a long time for it to occur and disputes worked out (or continue on over time.).

Second Essay about Time

Setting the Stage

We live in a time and in a world where the vestiges of colonialism, religion and even more importantly the monarchal or imperial mindset still dominates our political thinking too much. This dominance, or imperial chauvinism, comes in many overt and covert forms. This essay attempts to show how even the structure of our marking of history, and time, how we define the coming and going of "ages" is still dominated by the West's view of the world.

Or perhaps better stated, the Western fascination with the Roman Empire and the governance of that "state" continues to ripple through not just our view of history, but our views of what was positive in history. Much of the history of the Western culture is linked to a desire to somehow recreating the Roman World, including recreating the Roman Imperial form of government. The goal of the essay is to show the need to rethink history from a perspective of the struggle for the old imperial concepts and the new concept of "freedom." If we define the new concept of freedom as the basis for the modern world, we have to ask the question of when did in fact the "ancient world" end and when did in fact the modern world start?

When Did This Modern World Start?

We tend to understand history from a Western chauvinist point of view. Even the fact that we call this year 2010 is from a Western Christian timeline based on the misplaced time for the birth of Christ. (Since most historians now put the date of the birth at 6 or 7 BCE, perhaps we are already in 2017 CE.) Of course, the Chinese, Indians, Muslims and Jews (just to name a few) have a different take on what the current year is based on their own traditions and religious views. The basic worldwide agreement on the current designation of the year has more to do with the success of Western imperialism and colonialism than much else.

Following along in that vein, the concept presented to us as the "stages of history" is also mostly a creation or "social construct" of Western thinking, and reflects that Eurocentric point of view of history. We have been handed the idea of when the "ancient" and "classical" world ended and when the modern world began by the same type of Western chauvinist thinking that makes us agree that this is the year 2010. In fact, there can be a strong argument made that we are just now entering what can truly be called the modern world, a world free of "Empire," with the construct of the state based on "democracy"; where the focus is on the needs of the many, not the wants of the few.

This Western chauvinism dominates almost all our thinking on history, at least in the "West." One of the more striking examples of this Western chauvinist view of world history is the period we refer to as the "Dark Ages" (roughly 600 CE and 1200 CE), when Europe was in a state of intellectual stagnation, controlled by Christian mythology, and beset with one wave of invasion or local wars after another.

This time period where Europe was mainly a "dung hill" was in no way a "dark period" in the rest of Eurasia and North Africa (or, from what we can tell, in the Americas). This time was one of great political and intellectual expansion of the Muslim world. China and India during this time also continued to have burgeoning intellectual and cultural development. The T'ang and Song Dynasties of China achieve great heights of economic and cultural success during the very time of the "dark ages" in Europe. In this time period, India was involved in mighty struggles between the traditionalist Hindu culture and the newly arrived Muslim invaders, with both groups creating dynamic cultural advances. Also during this time Buddhism saw a great rise and fall mainly in China.

So for this time period, the "old world" (again a Western construct) was only "dark" in Europe; but since Europe soon came to dominate the other sections of the world, and colonized all of the Americas, our understanding of the timeframe comes from that Eurocentric point of view.
I am not saying anything really new here from a "modern" thinking point of view; the victors discount the conquered, and for a period, Europe and the United States conquered the world. So they wrote history from their perspective. The children of India were made to learn the list of English kings; and world history was taught as if the struggle of the tiny Wessex kingdom of Alfred "the Great" was vastly more important than the great empires of India and China, never mind the extensive and wealthy cultures of Africa. American history was presented in many ways as if the world began in Plymouth, and came to success in 1776.

The concept of the Dark Ages, or that of what year we may be living in, is not the only ways Eurocentric views dominate our view of history. We are given, thanks to European thinkers and "organizers," a timeline of history that tends to try and neatly present our past in chunks of easily defined segments. While historians of the last few decades have worked hard to break down some of this neat organization and the primarily Western chauvinist view, we still mainly conceive the history of the world as moving from the "ancient" world to the "classical" world to the dark ages and the medieval world, into the "Renaissance" and the "modern" world. We also now tend to add the "industrial age" as a new element beginning roughly in 1776 (with the invention of the steam engine, the publishing of *The Wealth of Nations* and the American Revolution).

We are told there are precise events that tend to mark the ages: the fall of the Roman Empire ended the Classical age and began the "dark ages." We are told the Middle -Ages ended with Columbus's sailings of 1492 and the opening of the Americas to European expansion and exploitation. The historian Paul Johnson (in *Birth of the Modern*) sets the beginning of the modern world in 1815 with the defeat of the British at New Orleans (rather than, interestingly enough, the defeat of Napoleon at Waterloo in the same year).

How neat and clean it has all been to the Western mind, all this clear structure, and how problematic to the holders of the current model that it concept of historical structure is being assailed by historians and cultural nationalist from all over the world.

In part this Westernized timeline does not work well any more due to the demands of the rest of the world to be recognized as part of history (the Muslim world was not "dark" in the dark ages, and so on). And, it is not working well any more since we are realizing, through good research, that the Western chauvinist historians got it mostly wrong on so many points.

For example, Gibbon, in his culturally impactful work called *The Decline and Fall of the Roman Empire* gave the world his definition of the end of the Roman Empire as 476 (CE), when the "last emperor" was replaced by a Germanic king (although he did include reluctantly the Byzantine Empire in his work) It is now clear from the study of the writers of the time, and of the next millennium, that the concept of the Roman Empire continued in the existence of the Emperor in Constantinople even in the allegiances of the German "successor states," and that the Roman Empire still lived in the minds of both the

Europeans and Asians until at least the final fall of Constantinople in the year 1453 (or the Emperor of Trebizond till 1461).

Much of the politics of the West over the next 1500 years has been an effort to recreate that empire. First came the Holy Roman Empire (starting in 800 and ending only in 1804,) then the Spanish monarchs and the French "Sun King" then Napoleon and others pretenders, great and small who tried to claim the mantle of unifying Europe again.

When the Eastern Empire finally fell to the Turks, the rulers and Kiev and then later Moscow claimed imperial rights and inherency, ruling with much the same powers as the Byzantine emperors at the height of their powers. It was until 1917 that the Czars of Russia claiming to rule the "Third Rome."

Later the Germans, when finally unifying (in 1871 CE), claimed their newly crowned Emperor to be Kaiser (or Caesar). The Germans used this "new" title to revive the claims of the Holy Roman Empire as the true heirs of the transference of imperial right in the West (from Rome to Charles the Great to Otto the Great and so on down the line to the new German state).

The significance of the concept of Rome and of Empire was not only important in the West, and with the Germans. The Turks, too, claimed to be nothing less than the true successors to Rome, with a true purified version of the religion of God (as opposed to what they saw as the corrupted message of Christianity). The first major Turkish state established in Anatolia (around 1100) was named the Sultanate of Rum (Rome), and the name was continued by the Ottomans as their conquests reunited all of the Eastern Roman Empire at its greatest extent (including North Africa) and beyond (into Iraq, deep into Arabia and into Sudan).

Truly the Ottoman sultans came closest to Roman style power and claimed much to the chagrin and shame of the Western powers of the time, the right of being recognized the true successor state in the East. Their effort to completely unite Europe under their "Roman Empire" and their "one true religion" only finally failed with their defeat at the gates of Vienna in 1683. Funny, how this close run thing has been left out of most Western history books.

So despite Gibbon and Western-oriented historians, it can be clearly argued that the "Roman Empire" (or at least the claims to the Roman Empire) died, not centuries ago, but with the mass revulsion of the people (both of the civilians and soldiers) of the mass deaths in the trenches of World War I, and hatred of the ruling classes that could be blamed for the death of millions of fighters and non-combatants alike.

While the kings, Czar and Kaiser and all their nobles still claimed to be "God's select," the mass of people finally had enough of the concept of this view of government. The result was in one way or another, violent and non-violent, from the Russian steppes through Germany and in central Europe, and into the "republics of the West" a major revolution not just in government but in conception of the right to govern.

It was not Romulus Augustus in 476, or Constantine the IX in 1483 who was the last "Roman" Emperor, but Nicolas the II, Czar (or the Russian version of Caesar) overthrown in 1917, or perhaps Fredrick II Kaiser (Caesar) of Germany abdicated in 1918, or the last Ottoman Sultan dethroned by Kemal Ataturk in 1922.

It seems that the Roman Empire did not end in 476 CE but, at least in the minds and often titles of the ruling classes, it extended out until 1917 or maybe 1921 with the end of those claiming the title of Caesar, Kaiser, Czar or the Sultan of Rum.

This concept of the continuation of the Roman world (or a culture that worked to emulate the Roman world), lasting into the 20th century brings into question the whole effort to neatly package history into that neat timeline so often presented to us. With the point of view that "Roma" or its successor states continued at least till the end of the World War I would also tend to argue that the "modern world" actually begins with the ending of the "War to End All Wars" and with the death of the "concept of Empire."

The killing fields and the death of so many of the ruling classes, along with their servile populations, in such numbers in Flanders and Gallipoli and in the battles in Russia or Italy finally led to a worldwide uprising against the philosophy that had dominated society under Rome or the Holy Roman Empire (or the Roman Church or in princely and nobility state or in the kingships of medieval Europe or traditional empires of Asia or the "modern" worldwide empires. And the killings of millions continued, as the ending of empires during the 20th Century led to extensive numbers of "wars of national liberation" against the imperial nature of the world and the remnants of empire mentality as created in in the West by Rome.

This concept of Empire that dominated society for millennia had one underlying principle; simply put, it was that the mass of humanity was there to service the few, the nobility or Emperors or the Church higher officials, the ruling elements of the "State." The modern world truly begins with the worldwide acceptance of the idea that the rulers are there to serve the needs of the many. The true concept of the modern world, what really divides the "ancient" from the "modern," is the shift in perspective of the people and the state that society should be designed to benefit the "masses", not the "noble" alone. The modern world is based on the concept of people being "endowed ... with certain inalienable rights," as opposed to "God Save the King" or "Long Live the Czar."

This concept of the mass of people being the important part of society is the dividing line between the "old" and "new" world, the age of "Empire" and the age of the modern "civil society." And based on how slowly this idea of the rights of "man" (or, better stated, "humanity") took to reach the wide world, we can argue that we are still in the very early stages of this period of modernism.

From this point of view the Twentieth Century should not be seen as just a period of mindless mass warfare of mega-state against mega-state, or as a time of popular uprisings against mega- states (both colonial and dictatorships), but as the (final?) bloody transition between the ancient and modern world. None of the revolutions we have seen were pro-monarchy or pro-nobles, they were all, at least in terms of the old Soviet Union propaganda, designed to support the "freedom loving peoples of the world."

While the Fascist and Stalinist Communist state used the same concept of rule as the empire world, they claimed to be anti-noble. But of course their states where were "you could not tell the men from the pigs and the pigs from the men" (as George Orwell stated in *Animal Farm*). These states professed that they ruled to benefit the "Reich folk" or the "workers of the world."

The fall of Communism, just some twenty years ago, may finally be the tipping point that has finally brought the majority of the world away from an "imperial" view of rule towards this concept of modern thought. While most of the successor states of that rose from the Communist fall, and the independent countries created by the end of colonialism are by no means perfect, they almost all at least speak in terms of modern political terms (democracy, freedoms, justice and protection under the law). While many of these states do not quite have freedom, in principle the rulers rule for the benefit of the many.

Of course resistance to the "ancient empire" model is not new, and we can find actual resistance to the rule, as well as writings against the concept dating back to almost the beginning of writing.

Some six thousand years ago, the people of Uruk prayed to the gods to find a way to relieve them of the tyranny of Gilgamesh. In the Bible in I Samuel Chapter 8 the prophet wars against the rule of monarchs ("He will take your sons ... your daughters, your fields ... your sheep").All forms of events and writings remain from the "Ancient and Classical world" that shows resistance happened. Of course one of the most famous and critical of these events is the assassination of Caesar, ("an ambitious man"). Despite the efforts "republicans" (or actually oligarchs), the West rulers slowly evolved into the same format as the rulers of the East; the god-kings that had so disgusted the Greeks.

The transition between Roman Republic to Roman Empire and the evolution of the empire to total dictatorship is far too great a subject to explore here. However, we must remember that there was extensive covert and overt resistance against this new style of rule while the Roman Empire evolved away from the Roman Republic. Most noted in these efforts were the three great Jewish wars of resistance beginning in 66 CE and only ending in 136 CE.

In the later stages of the united Roman empire and then in the period of the fall of the Western Empire and the slow decline of the Eastern Empire, the form of resistance took on a religious tone. At first the resistance was shown as maintaining the "old gods" against the demand of the State that all people become Christian, (as late as 400 someone was offered by the Senate of

Rome the imperial title if he would only allow the worship of the old gods.) and then later in the great debates over the nature of God and the "Son" that led to numerous splits in the Christian Church; the profile of the political dissenter of earlier days soon evolved into the religious "heretic."

Christianity had other effects on the Empire, for example:

- Gibbon argued that Christianity created a belief that a better life existed after death, which fostered an indifference to the present among Roman citizens, thus sapping their desire to sacrifice for the Empire. He also believed its comparative pacifism tended to hamper the traditional Roman martial spirit. (see) http://en.wikipedia.org/wiki/The_History_of_the_Decline_and_Fall_of_the_Roman_Empire#Controversy:_chapters_XV.2C_XVI

In the resistance throughout the "dark ages" and the revolts of the Reformation period (including the many peasant rebellions) we actually see the "modern origins" of the demands that the State serve the people rather than the people serving the ruler starting in the writings of the late 16th century. Over time (more than several hundred years) these thoughts evolved beyond the English demands for noble's protections from the king to "equal protection for all" and were finally embedded publically in the US Declaration of Independence and the Declarations of the Rights of Man proclaimed in the initial stages of the French Revolution (where a new "year one" was started to show the beginning of the new and transformative idea).

Still later these ideas were manifested in the Carlist wars in Spain and in the rise of Liberal thought in England and in the Marxist and Anarchist movements in the 19th century. But as a whole, this view of the "modern state" didn't develop as a driving force worldwide until the collapse of empires at the beginning of the Twentieth Century.

Following this logic of the modern world actually just beginning a relative short time ago we need to look at world history with a new definition, with those "stages" of Classical, Middle etc. not from the Western perspective, but from a more global and political perspective. We must look at the stages of history not as we have but as:

- the first rise of the "state",
- with the slow rise of the age of Empire germinating in the "West" with Babylonian, Egyptian and Assyrian concepts, in which the state becomes more powerful and the rulers more "god like."
- through the Persian expansion of the god-king throughout most of Western and Central Asia (before and after Alexander)
- the long struggle in which eventually the concept of God/King of the East prevailed in the West (starting with Alexander the Great and continuing into the rise of the Roman Emperors). Included in this stage is the crushing of resistance to the Empire concepts in the West (in Gaul, Judea and against the Spartacus Revolt, to name a few examples of resistance.)
- The ongoing dream of the "imperialist" to recreate the absolute power of the later Roman Empire throughout history to the near present time.
- And lastly, the long struggle to change the world from an Imperial to a Republican or more democratic view of the State.

While we have been taught to celebrate the victories of the mini-states of Greece against the god-king of Persia, we should see the victories of the Greeks as a stopgap event (or a pyrrhic victory) against the rise of the "State." We are also taught to relish the history of the Roman Empire yet what we should see is that the creation of the Empire crushed and destroyed the concepts of freedom defended in Thermopylae, creating a love of tyranny by rulers lasting unchecked until the Glorious Revolution of England and the rise of America and Revolutionary France.

The victories the Greeks were overturned by the creation of the Roman Empire and the imposing on that empire the concept at first of the god/king and later the king unchallengeable since they were the anointed of the one and only god. (The "one-god- one Emperor" concept was floated by emperors for about one hundred and twenty years with other religions, before they found Christianity willing to make that bargain of endorsing tyranny on earth for a share of the power and a tyrannical hold on the afterlife.)

Even with the new competition from the "liberal state" and "democracy" the concept of Empire continued to rule the Western mind, and through colonialism and domination of intellectual fields, mostly prevailed in almost all the lands of the world. They prevailed that is until the collapse beginning mainly with World War I.

In fact, if we look at the decade just prior to the commencement of World War I, say the world in 1907 (a year or so after the Russo-Japanese War), we see the almost complete triumph of "Empire," with virtually the whole world's population governed by roughly fifteen men, of whom a baker's dozen claimed rule by right of monarchy (and the will of God or the Mandate of Heaven). These rulers were (in no particular order)

1) The Emperor of China
2) The Shah of Iran
3) The Sultan of the Ottoman Empire

4) The King of England (with also the title of Emperor of India) - The sun never set on the English Empire at this point in time. (OK really the prime ministers ruled, but in name the king)
5) The Kaiser of Germany
6) The Czar of Russia
7) The Emperor of Japan (with Korea and new territories recently gained from Russia)
8) The ruler of the Austro-Hungarian Empire
9) The King of Portugal (with extensive holding in Africa)
10) The King of Spain (at this point the smallest of the imperial powers, though at one point by far the largest - with still some holdings in Africa, but thanks to a war with the United States much of their vestige of Empire gone)
11) The King of Holland (having all of Indonesia)
12) The King of Belgium (having the huge area of Africa call the Belgium Congo)
13) The King of Italy (recently united and just about to gain some African territories starting in 1911)

The two claiming power through the right of election and the "people's will" were:

14) The President of the Republic of France, and
15) The President of the United States

While the free Spanish-, Portuguese- and English-speaking countries of the Americas all claimed to be republics, most were military dictatorships with few real rights for the people and an intense oligarchy that ruled much like an imperial state along Roman lines. Brazil had only stopped being an "empire," in 1891 (and only abolished slavery in1888).

This time period just before World War I saw concept of Empire considered more than legitimate (with its class and racist philosophies as its intellectual underpinnings). Social Darwinism became new justification. The trust to finish off the division of the world yet unclaimed was called the "scramble for Africa." was nearly completed. The old empire of the East in China was being challenged by the newly invigorated and centralized empire of Japan. (Who had recently shocked the "white world" by defeating Russia). Japan was laying the foundation of claiming "Asia for the Asians" - (their own version of the Monroe Doctrine?) by expanding in the Pacific and Korea.

The United States, supposedly non-imperial in nature, continued its march toward being a republican imperial power (like France); having taken half of Mexico it continued its expansion with the acquisition of territories (including the purchase of Alaska from Russia) through what and creating "revolutions" beyond the mainland of North America (Hawaii, Guam, the Philippines, Puerto Rico, and the creation of a Cuban Protectorate).

There were a few places in the world not directly governed by these imperial powers (Scandinavia, some Balkan countries, Afghanistan, Ethiopia, Thailand and Liberia as the most notable). But these countries themselves maintained states mimicking the empire mentality with kings of their own (except Liberia), states designed to service them and their circles. And with the exception of the two presidents, the other rulers of humanity clearly felt that society was there to benefit them or to utilize the "royal we" and make reference at the same time to the extreme tyranny of the Borg, from *Star Trek, the Next Generation* fame, society was there to "service us."

Then starting with the revolts in Iran/Persia (1908), the great peasant uprising in Mexico (commencing in 1910) and the proclaiming of the Republic of China (1911) all before the World War, and the ensuing failures in World War I, one by one the "emperors" fell or were stripped of their ancient powers by revolts.

Those Empires which survived World War I (England, France, Japan Holland, Belgium, Portugal and the United States – and the Spanish monarchy), were faced with another seventy-year period of resistance by their colonial territories. World War II destroyed the Japanese Empire and made shells of the other empires (except for the US), leading to the period of rapid decolonization far too often actualized in war rather than a peaceful transition.

With this line of thinking presented in this paper we can represent the intellectual and political struggles between the Communist, Fascist/Nazi, Socialist, Militarist and Liberal Republican States that dominated the Twentieth Century as a process to find an adequate replacement for the imperial, or Roman Empire concept of the masses serving the state rather than the state serving the masses. We have witnessed states trying to create a new way of existing, of governing in a society, of evolving away from thousands of years of Empire: With the main alternatives offering different views of how to either "control" or "serve" the people.

- With the Communists and Fascists we saw the imperial mindset reinstated with different rhetoric (and far harsher rule than ever experienced under Empire but sounding populist as they did so).
- The Militarists tended not even to mask their pretensions with social justice rhetoric. They ruled to maintain order (and control by the elite.)
- With the liberal and social democratic states, we saw an acceptance of responsibility for servicing the people but with great internal struggles on how much service needed to be provided and by what means.

In both the liberal and socialist states we've seen the struggles played out, not so much in street battles and political purges, but in debates over tax policies; with the major difference between the democratic socialist and the liberal capitalist states being how much the rich would be taxed to benefit the mass.

But only now, just a little more than a century after empires began to fall, with the extensive defeats of Fascism, Militarism, Communism and Colonialism, the idea of the state serving the people is taking strong root throughout the world.

There are challenges still with religious fundamentalism trying to force an imperial-type rule in some countries and the rise of new forms of "strong man" rule as economic instability is present in so many places. In addition, we now face a new form of "colonialism" and ruling class in the form of the new corporate oligarchy, which can be seen as the new potential rulers of a worldwide empire.

But a century of limited success and only some twenty years of dominance of a "new world order" is such a short time in world history. It is unclear how long this modern worldview will dominate, even superficially. It's also unclear how these new style governments can respond to the crisis of global warming, the energy crisis, overpopulation and the general sense of rising expectations.

We may, in fact, not be at the real beginning of a new era but just in a brief interlude prior to the return of Empire (much like Greece after the Persian Wars or the 1920s in Europe). We had other times where we thought the madness was over.

Like other Enlightenment t thinkers, Gibbon held in contempt the Middle Ages as a priest-ridden, superstitious, Dark Age. It was not until his own age of reason and rational thought, it was believed, that human history could resume its progress.

See http://en.wikipedia.org/wiki/The_History_of_the_Decline_and_Fall_of_the_Roman_Empire#Controversy:_chapters_XV.2C_XVI

With limited clarity and no claim to clairvoyance, we cannot, like the older Western historians, put exact moments for the end of one period and the beginning of another; we are now in fact in a long transitional period that is murky and uneven in its progress towards a modern world. However, we can see that the mindset of the Roman Empire is, at least for the moment, finally fading and truly a worldwide (including "every place in the world" as part of term) effort is underway to create a modern world.

As with all historical changes this move to modernism is happening not in some neat process, but in a hit and miss and forward and backwards process as has always been the real route of history. We know that in history, changes in mindset take so long to accomplish that those living through the changes often cannot see the transition in process.

We know that there are still today so many who wish for the return to the times of Empire and rule of the many by the few. Yet, in every section of the world where there was once empire, we see states claiming to work for the people (not always well, but at least claiming). We see everywhere rulers seeking to be responsible to the people rather than demanding order and obedience.

- In just some one hundred years, we have seen, almost everywhere, elected governments replace divine right rule (the right of the Emperor) and military dictatorships.

So perhaps it is best to end this paper by paraphrasing one of the best Western Chauvinist historians, Winton Churchill, by saying ... this time period we live in may not be the end (of Empire), but it is, perhaps, the end of the beginning .... (of the stages that will bring about the modern world) (Copyright laws prevent compete original quote).

Setting the Stage

This essay attacks the basis of much of our folk culture and American myths. We want to focus on the Pilgrims and the early settlers fleeing to America for religious and economic freedom, the shining city on the hill: Today we want to present these settlers as setting the tone for modern America. However, through this myth we have wiped clean from our collective memories the reality that most of these colonies over the first seventy-five years of settlements were economic disasters.

Only when a different model, one not coming from Europe, a model not based on freedom and opportunity, but based on mass slavery, was introduced to North America from the Caribbean, did the economics of the new colonies change rapidly (for the better). This model first came into South Carolina and from there spread throughout much of the country. This essay argues that while we see our history mainly as the development of the North, in reality, until so recently, the real history and political development of America was dominated by South Carolina and those who followed her model.

Is South Carolina the Most Important State in US History?

Part I

How to measure the importance of one state over another is difficult for so many reasons. However, there is a strong case to argue that much of the history of the lands that became the United States, and subsequently the history of the United States altogether, have been influenced by South Carolina perhaps more than by any other state. Since this relatively small and relatively less developed state is not currently an economic or, apparently, social driving force, few people readers of history would point to this state as such an important catalyst in the past and current economic and social makeup of the nation.

However, in this brief review, I hope to show that in fact

- the ideals and economics (and social construct) behind the development of South Carolina created the source of some of what in retrospect appears to be the worst of the history of the US (what Lincoln referred to as the "House Divided"); and
- this influence started in mid- to late-Colonial times, and continued through the creation of states in the expansion West, and to the Civil War; and
- this influence continued throughout US history past the Civil War into present times.

Today, however, South Carolina is perhaps attempting to create influence in a new and possibly positive fashion that could once again change this country greatly:

- Electing the first female governor of (Asian) Indian descent, and
- Appointing a Black conservative congressmen to the US Senate

Therefore, by doing so, making the Conservative Movement more attractive to African-American leadership and populous alike: and

- continuing the great influence this one state has on the nation.

To understand South Carolina's seminal influence we need to understand the unique origins of the state of South Carolina as distinct from all the other "original 13 Colonies." In fact, they were overtly unique in two aspects, and had commonality with only one other colony in another aspect, that one other being New Jersey.

- New Jersey and South Carolina both were created as personal gifts to loyal supporters of the Stuart line during the period of Civil War and the period of "Restoration" to enrich their personal wealth.
- One of the South Carolina's unique aspects is that, among all the colonies, they were mostly peopled by settlers (voluntary and forced) not directly from the British Islands or Holland (or a few other European countries).
- The other unique aspect is that the colony was majority slave (and therefore majority Black).

In addition, there were three other aspects that made South Carolina different from the other colonies:

- It generally had no concerns about religion or any real conflict with the State of England
- It was extensively pro-nobility and hierarchy, with its founders having very little interest in the interests of anyone other than themselves.
- And, unlike any of the other colonies, they were economically very successful right from the start.

We today have little understanding of the foundations of the eventual thirteen Colonies. Their founding and development were not a neat and orderly process as often presented in our social studies or history classes. At times it appeared there would be only a few official colonies of England, and at other times it looked as if there could be fifteen or more (if Canada was included in the picture).

The process of determining what was a colony and what was not is beyond the scope of this paper, but just to point out a few aspects:

- Originally Carolina was to be one colony, and New Jersey two.
- Vermont was never recognized as a separate entity until after the Revolution, even though the settlers there had established a separate government.
- Almost all of the mid-Atlantic area was one colony and, in fact, not English at all but Dutch.
- The Crown also looked upon the areas of Canada added after the French and Indian wars as more North American colonial areas, more or less the same as the colonies to the south.

So, each of the "thirteen" had a rocky road to establishment and success. But again, South Carolina's route was different than all of them.

Most of the colonies were created as "refuges" of one form or another. The social and religious wars leading to the creation of the Commonwealth of Cromwell and the eventual collapse of Republican England go well beyond the scope of this paper. However, in one way or the other these wars (and the other religious wars throughout Western and Central Europe) had a great influence on the creation of almost all of what eventually became the "thirteen colonies."

Principally in that almost all were created, or populated, in one form or another by peoples seeking haven for whichever of several religious or social groups who were out of favor in one place or the other. (Massachusetts by Pilgrims, and later other religious dissenters, and then Connecticut and Rhode Island by those oppressed by the Massachusetts new religious establishment, Pennsylvania for Quakers and Maryland for Catholics, Georgia for convicts seeking a new start, etc.)

Another reason of course for colonial development was economics; with the hopes England in this area mainly focused on of Virginia. However the Dutch were great competitors of the British in settling North America south of Canada (along with the French and even the Swedes and Danes) in the realm of economic development as all these countries sought vast new farm lands available, the mass forests and trade with the native peoples for furs. For some forty years, what is now New York, New Jersey and Delaware, along with a goodly part of current-day Pennsylvania, was all part of Dutch North America and just one colony under the Dutch (only to be all lost to the British after one of the three Anglo-Dutch Wars). The English later divided the area into initially five colonies and later four.

While economic in nature, the Dutch were, at least on paper, highly tolerant of religion (except for Catholics).

This went so far as requiring (after a court case on the issue) the city of New Amsterdam to be the first to place legally allow Jews to settle in North America. That toleration continued in these areas even after British rule began.

Along with desire for freedom of worship (at least for themselves) and economic opportunities, a third factor driving immigration of new settlers was a motivation to be free of the traditional bonds of the "old world" making most of the settlers strongly "anti-nobility." This is not to say that most of the settlers were pro-Republican/Cromwell (while many were), or anti-King, which many were not. Most settlers were anti-noble for three main reasons:

- Forced Religious Conformity:

With the religious conformity of Europe, for centuries it was assumed that all people (commoners and nobles alike) were Catholic. However, with the conditions created in the lead-up to the English civil war, and then the Republic, religious diversity developed. Nobles pressed to ensure that everyone in their lands followed the religion of the overlord. Therefore, if the noble was a Catholic or an Anglican or a Quaker or a reformed church group of one kind or another, the noble would typically insist that all of his people follow his faith. This pressure led to a new layer of conflict between nobles and "their people" that had not been seen before. Many of those settling in the New World sought to get away from the imposition of a noble's demand for accepting religions that conflicted with their personal beliefs.

- Avoidance of nobles' claim to land and taxes:

The new world offered the opportunity to almost anyone (male and white that is) to acquire vast amounts of land the size of which were virtually incomprehensible in Europe of the time, in their own name and free of obligation to any noble (for tax and military obligations or other fees or levels or tithing During the colonial period, no Earl of Maryland or Duke of New England could have been created without massive resistance by the settlers.

- Opportunity for Social Advancement.

Along with the economic changes came the ability to create a culture in which social status was not just based on birth (into a noble or royal family) but could be created by personal skill and capacity. This opportunity for advancement was not available to most individuals in the socially rigid nobility-dominated Old World, but was dramatically available in the New.

Therefore, there was a strong anti-nobility concept among most of the colonial settlers (whether English, Dutch, French, German or Swedish). This sentiment ran deep in almost all of the colonies, with the exceptions of Virginia, New Jersey and, eventually, South Carolina.

Now, while the initial leading settlers of Virginia were more inclined to support the concepts of nobility and even longed to obtain titles from the king (as George Washington had wished for long into his adulthood), the majority of Virginians were in line with the new concepts of a New World, where accomplishment was obtained by one's capacities (and of course, God's will), rather than by birth. While the leadership of Virginia attempted to create a "new England" in their boundaries (including religious conformity), short of adding nobility, the land areas were so great and the government so limited that outside of the core areas, the settlers were able to do much as they pleased.

This "freeholder mentality" of the "frontier" areas was extended south in-to what was called the Carolinas. The original settlers of the Carolinas were so anti-State they mainly refused to even establish towns. The area of North Carolina, filled with small freeholds and highly independent minded people, could not even establish a seat of government for the Revolutionary government until well into the war period.

The attempt to import nobility and pro-noble ideals into the colonies in the newly formed New Jersey failed with the complete corruption and incompetence of the friends of the king given the lands as gift.

Eventually, to restore order, and to create a functioning government, the gift was rescinded and the area was made a Crown Colony with a royal governor. The land was mainly peopled by those coming from other colonies and those seeking respite from the economic limitations created by the nobles in England. Therefore the people of this new Crown colonial areas tended to be as anti-noble as most of the other colonies.

Part II

Now we come to the founding of South Carolina, and we begin to see how this colony differed from the others in outlook in religion, in economics and even in the origins of its populations. From the history of the development of the area, we see South Carolina's settlers as

- solidly Anglican and with no religious diversity issues (and with a limited geographic area to control could enforce this conformity if at all needed);
- Not only pro-king, but pro-nobility and all that entails; these were people who were descendants of nobles or clearly noble "want to be";
- opposed to social change, not seeing the need for social advancement of any class other than themselves.
- In addition, the settlers of South Carolina brought a new element into the North American colonies:
- the plantation culture completely dedicated to the concept of an elite ruling basically a slave population (with a small "overseer class" completely dedicated to the "noble" rulers.)

There were virtually no freeholder independent-minded settlers allowed in the area of what became South Carolina (cut out of Carolina through a gift from the king). Those few who had been there prior to the separation of the Carolinas were either forced north or became absorbed into the new social establishment as the overseer cast.

The key to understanding why this area developed so differently than the others in Eastern North America is looking at the origins of the settlers. The first major (and most successful) settlers of South Carolina came specifically because the plantation economy had been well established and the mass enslavement of the population had been in place for some one hundred and seventy years. Furthermore, in South Carolina the new settlers were "nobles," some in name and some only in wealth and status (though their wealth often bought marriages into nobility).

- For the settlers of South Carolina came from Barbados and other Caribbean Islands, where the Sugar Plantations and the horrific form of chattel slavery that dominated the sugar economies of the New World had been in place, and highly successful, since almost the time of Columbus.

The settlers of South Carolina were therefore not religious or economic or political refugees seeking asylum of some kind; they were children (often the second and third sons of plantation owners who would not inherit the land of their fathers) of highly successful and powerful families coming from an area that was simply was running out of land.

They were not looking for a means of creating a "new world"; these people were looking for a means of expanding their "old world" into new areas. They came, dragging their slaves with them, wanting to duplicate the success of their fathers in creating a "plantation culture" (a "more Roman" concept of society then even English) that happened to exploit the cash crop economy of the time: sugar.

Part III

To understand this development of these sugar empires, we need to go back even farther into history to the discovery and exploitation of the New World (again, a full discussion of this is well beyond the scope of this paper). We need to understand that after the Spanish had sacked all the wealth of empires of the Native Peoples, the wealth of the New World was in the new food crops found there (and in the vastness of the land available to grow the crops),

- With the three most important being potatoes, maize (corn) and, most important of all, sugar.

We need to also understand that for the first hundred or so years, all the New World belonged to the Castilians (later to be transformed into Spain) and Portuguese, based on papal Decree. Only with the Reformation and the rejection of the Pope's laws, could other countries even begin to seek lands in the vast new areas.

And only when Spanish power was broken in the ninety-year Dutch War of Independence (and other European political and religious wars) along with the loss of the Spanish fleet (in the effort to suppress English support for their fellow religious reformers; the Dutch), could any effort be made to "colonize" (or steal from Spain and Portugal) any part of the New World.

We also need to understand how little the Spanish really cared about what is call North America. To them this was "ca - nada" or the "land of nothing." To them the real wealth of the new world lay in the lands where sugar could be grown (and potatoes and maize was grown to feed the slaves, at first Native peoples, who quickly died off, and then Africans, imported as replacements for Native populations who worked the sugar plantations).

These areas were also the focus of the new Reformation states (and the big Catholic rival of Spain, France) who began to attack and seize the lands where sugar was grown. At first through "pirates" and then through formal wars or conquests, small but highly valuable lands became part of the territories of the newly rising powers of Western Europe (England, France and Holland, and even Denmark got into the picture a little). England gained Jamaica, Barbados and a number of smaller islands; the Dutch, the ABC islands (Aruba, Bon Air and Curacao); and the French, what is now Haiti, along with some other islands. They also each grabbed a small chunk of South America as well.

- Through these islands, sugar flowed to the "Old World," transforming both cooking and the social order. Those who went to the "West Indies" and established plantations (and survived the fevers and slave revolts), became incredibly rich.

These colonial upstarts took on airs of lords and masters, to the point that they were seen as an embarrassing mockery of themselves by to the traditional nobles of their period.

And all this time, North America was considered almost economically worthless, except as a source of furs, since the key cash crop of the day, sugar, could not really be grown in most of the area (with the exception of Florida, which the Spanish did maintain as their territory into the 19th Century).

The northern lands of America were primarily settled by those who were seeking religious and economic and political asylum, often with much support from those whom they would rebel against, for after all if the dissenters were far, far away from the home of the establishment, they were less likely to cause trouble, or be a local embarrassment.

The economic history of the early North American colonies shows how right the general view of the establishment was. For the most part the colonies struggled, and the freeholders had to supplement their efforts at farming with fur trading, providing Europe with fish and lumber and sending slaves and food stuffs to the Caribbean plantations. The only potential cash crop that seemed to grow well in the area was tobacco and, for many years numerous European countries outlawed its use, though it nonetheless was very popular among the wealthy classes, used as "snuff." In many ways the early wealth of Virginia was created through the selling of an illegal substance that was snorted up the nose (much like Columbia is gaining wealth today).

Therefore, up until the late 17th and early 18th centuries, North America was looked upon by the European powers as an economic dung hill, but militarily important (protecting the Northern flanks of the Caribbean trade routes).

The lands were claimed for national pride (to poke at the very soft underbelly of the Spanish Empire) but little was really done to exploit or develop the area, other than providing for resettling undesirable elements of the society. No real means of making the Colonies profitable could be seen.

The developers of South Carolina changed all of that. They not only brought in the plantation culture, fully developed, but introduced cash crops that were highly valuable and "needed" the plantation culture to be successful: rice and indigo (able to be grown in the marsh lands of South Carolina). The rice was used to feed the slaves (with surpluses being sold to the Caribbean markets), and indigo to provide dyes for the demand for blue colors among the elite of Europe.

South Carolina therefore was unlike all of the other colonies in yet another way: they were an economic success basically from the start. And they linked their success to the plantation culture from which they came, which they understood and knew to be successful based on the creation of the sugar states in the Caribbean and elsewhere. For the first time, mass chattel slave culture came into North America and was highly successful.

Slavery at this point (using roughly pre-1700 as the baseline) was legal in almost all of the colonies, and in fact most of the slaves in North America in the beginning of the 18th century were concentrated in the "cities" (New York, Boston, Philadelphia and Charleston) where they worked as household slaves and as stevedores in the ports. Many were also rented out to local smaller farmers throughout a colony as "hired hands" or "share croppers" for part of the farming year. (Many farmers could not afford to maintain a slave all year but gained access to them for critical times (planting and harvesting.)

For a long while there were more White "slaves" then Black ones. Up until the development of the South Carolina Model, most slaves (both Black and white) were indentures who worked for periods of time and then became free people (based on the Bible story of Jacob and Rebecca, the time of indenture usually lasted seven years).

- Once freed, both Black and white) they had all the rights of all free men (if they were men) and even could become land and slave owners themselves.

As noted in most of the colonies, this somewhat held true for Black slaves as well as whites, with some variations on lengths of slavery and rights after freedom. (This is the origins of the free Blacks populations of the North and South among whose historic accomplishments long before the civil war and general emancipation included the first person to be killed in revolutionary activities against the British (Crispus Attucks in the Boston Massacre) and volunteering for what became "the most reliable" regiments for Washington's army (despite Washington initial rejection of free Black regiments for the revolutionary army).

- At the time of the Revolution there were some 40,000 Free Blacks in the Colonies. Of these some 5,000 fought for the Revolution and perhaps another 20,000 fought for the British many in exchange for freedom from bondage.

Virginia only began to put limits based on color on current and former slaves in the late 17th century (including making Black slaves lifelong property). More limits ensued in the 18th century after they began to fully incorporate the South Carolina model in their state. With a few exceptions, Virginia was the only one of the original Colonies with plantation-style farms and with large number of slaves, mainly for tobacco farming. Maryland and Delaware also had some of these styles of farms, but in limited numbers.

Prior to the success of South Carolina, most of the slaves in all the colonies were not treated with the cruelty and low regard as the chattel slaves of the sugar areas. Once Virginia changed, the other states followed and they all started to impose harsh limitations on Black slaves (including making them slaves for life.)

The life expectancy of a slave coming from Africa into the sugar industry was only about five years; most of them died quickly and quickly had to be replaced.

Thus the need for a constant flow of slaves in the industry to keep the process moving (and the great profit of the slave traders, including those from New England, flowing).

Therefore that's why, over the first three hundred and fifty years of the New World, 95% of Africans were funneled into the sugar-growing areas of Brazil and the Caribbean. The sugar plantation culture saw no need to look after the general welfare of the slave; or even to allow the development of families. The slave was simply a replaceable "thing" that would soon wear out and be replaced again. This was part of the mind-set of the settlers of South Carolina that was not part of the mind-set of even the largest of the tobacco plantations.

To the large owners of slaves in the tobacco areas, slaves were valuable and often hard to replace. Whereas in the Caribbean and then in South Carolina, slaves were not of much value because they died quickly and could be quickly replaced. The South Carolina port of Charles Town (soon Charleston) became the point of entry for most of the 5% of slaves who ended up in the new North American slave market, needed to feed the plantation model.

So here is one of the major changes that the founders of South Carolina brought to North America: a massive change in mind-set towards slaves, and especially towards Blacks in general. These founders of South Carolina barely considered the slave human (a social justification for the brutality of the sugar slave system), barely considered them of value. The Black slaves were not slightly different than others, as white indentures or urban Black stevedores as seen in most of the other colonies.

To the Caribbean migrants the Black slave was severely different and with no rights under any conditions, and barely a soul. In the Old World, in medieval times most nobles viewed their peasants in almost the same fashion as these New World plantation lords. As noted, they ruled these slaves with all the pretension and power of the ancient Roman or the European noble, or Eastern European boyars.

Despite social revolts and religious revolutions, the nobles living around the development of North America still viewed their peasants as having very limited rights or capacities. In Russia, the "serf" was a person almost akin to the Black slave of the plantations of the Caribbean. In the West the peasant or serf were slightly better viewed. In England, the views were less severe, based mainly on labor shortages. As stated, in the founding of most of the North American colonies, settlers resisted and hated these "noble" views of the world.

However, in the Caribbean world, the limited restrictions on the nobles and limited rights ascribed to the peasant were completely ignored when it came to the Black slave. Here, we find the noble view as if on steroids, stripped of almost all limitations. This "noble" view established itself in North America, through South Carolina, and eventually spread throughout what we refer to as the Southern States, along with the successful plantation model of the Caribbean, into the lands that become Mississippi, Alabama, Louisiana, East Texas, and Florida.

The model also soon supplanted the other plantation models of Virginia and displaced many freeholders in North Carolina. It influenced the views of the settlers of Tennessee, Kentucky, Missouri and Arkansas, especially their views of Blacks, even though the lands of those regions did not fit the model well.

Despite the historical trend in the colonies to hate the power and pretensions of nobles, soon for many that hate and fear of nobles was replaced with awe of the new planter class; a new American nobility only without titles.

Therefore, the initial anti-noble impulses of the founders of the original colonies were successfully challenged by the concepts of the founders of South Carolina, in a third of, if not half, the nation over time. In addition, the view of the Blacks as:

- being sub human
- of little value, and
- not worthy of investment of almost any kind

spread not just to what became the South, but throughout most of the nation.

Again, the creation of anti-Black racism in the US and the long and ongoing struggle against this worldview is beyond the scope of this paper. However, clearly this mass hatred of Blacks was first to introduce into the mainstream of what became the United States with the founders of South Carolina, who came up from the Caribbean, where these values and economic models had developed in the creation of the sugar empires of the New World.

Despite the early success of the South Carolina plantation model, there was no assurance that it would become as widely replicated as it did. Rice and indigo could not be grown in most areas, and, while successful in South Carolina, there was not such a huge demand for these products that it could form the basis for the economic development of new areas, also modeled on South Carolina.

Initially, the westward expansion of the new nation in the late colonial and early independent periods came from the land-hungry, freedom-loving, free landholders, much like those that had dominated North Carolina and New England. Tennessee and Kentucky and the failed state of Franklin were initially created by this type frontier people (the Daniel Boone image). It appeared at first that these areas would become regions of small farms with few if any slaves, and strongly anti-noble in nature. However, major economic revolutions occurred that changed the future of these and many other territories, if not the whole nation.

Part IV

Much of the social and economic revolutions that did occur and that led to the success of the plantation model is again beyond the scope of this paper. However, certain key factors had to independently develop to allow for the spread of the model into other colonies and later into added territories of the new nation. While there were many key events, the three most important were:

- The eventual legalization of tobacco and the eventual spread of smoking the weed instead of just using it for snuff. This created a far greater demand for tobacco, worldwide, and the spreading of tobacco plantations (with great financial success) in the colonies, and later the US, to meet this demand.
- The creation of cotton as the new cash crop with the cost factor of "de-seeding" the plant solved by the creation of the "cotton gin" (1793). The demand for cotton became so great, eventually the term "King Cotton" was used to describe the economic impact it had on the development of wide areas of the new nation (spurring the desires of so many to become plantation owners).
- The creation of the industrial age, which both set off a world-wide massive demand for cotton, for the new textile mills of England and later New England and generated the means for the cotton to be effectively

transported from what had been remote lands to distant markets via steam river boats, and railroads).

With these changes, new lands could be opened and used for the new cash crops, and the new crops could be transported to markets.

Therefore, the lands of the Southern and Central new nation were prime locations for expansion of the South Carolina model. And these lands were cleared (of both woods and the native peoples who had lived there) and new plantations and eventually new states were developed to meet the cotton demand.

Mississippi and Alabama were specifically developed to expand the plantation system, Louisiana was transformed for the model, and eventually Texas was "liberated" from Mexico for a new source of cotton land. (Slavery had to be re-introduced in the new nation of Texas, since Mexico had outlawed the institution some ten years before the battle of the Alamo.)

One of the areas of social needs of the time that did not get too impacted by any inventions of the time was fertilization.

Both cotton and tobacco tended to waste the land quickly, and people were unaware of how to revitalize it once it was worn out by the crops.

Therefore, part of the cotton mania created in the US by the worldwide demand was the need by the plantation model owners for greater expansion, to gain control of more lands to be exploited and depleted (a version of slash and burn farming techniques). This led to one political crisis after another in the US, including the Louisiana Purchase, the expulsion of the Native Peoples from the southern areas (the Trail of Tears), the acquisition of Florida, the Texas Republic and war with Mexico, as well as intense domestic arguments over the allowance or non-allowance of slavery in these newly added lands.

The intellectual leadership that provoked many of the crises came from South Carolina, with the prime example being John C. Calhoun. It was he who not only almost started the Civil War in the 1830s with his argument for the right of nullification, but it was he who also clearly declared slavery to be a moral and social good.

As noted in the Wikipedia article on the politician, http://en.wikipedia.org/wiki/John_C._Calhoun

> Calhoun was shaped by his father, Patrick Calhoun, a prosperous upstate planter who supported Independence during the American Revolutionary War but opposed ratification of the Federal Constitution.
>
> The father was a staunch slaveholder who taught his son that one's standing in society depended not merely on one's commitment to the ideal of popular self-government but also on the ownership of a substantial number of slaves. Flourishing in a world in which slaveholding was a badge of civilization, Calhoun saw little reason to question its morality as an adult. …
>
> Calhoun believed that the spread of slavery into the back country of his own state improved public morals by ridding the countryside of the shiftless poor whites who had once held the region back] He further believed that slavery instilled in the white who remained a code of honor that blunted the disruptive potential of private gain and fostered the civic-mindedness that lay near the core of the republican creed. From such a standpoint, the expansion of slavery into the backcountry decreased the likelihood for social conflict and postponed the declension when money would become the only measure of self-worth, as had happened in New

England. Calhoun was thus firmly convinced that slavery was the key to the success of the American dream.

In a famous speech on the Senate floor on February 6, 1837, Calhoun asserted that slavery was a "positive good." He rooted this claim on two grounds: white supremacy and paternalism.

- Here was the conception of the "noble" view of the world fully-exposed.

But Calhoun was just carrying on the tradition of other South Carolina leaders, intent on promoting their ideals onto the rest of the land.

It was the South Carolina delegates to the Revolutionary Congress that forced the elimination of the mildest of anti-slavery references in the Declaration of Independence. (Edward Rutledge took the lead in that effort, and who also did all he could to keep free Blacks from joining the Continental Army)

The conflict over slavery was between those who wished to allow the free holders model of most of the original colonies and the Plantation model of South Carolina was the driving force in early American history; the Plantation model won out in most cases.

The supporters of the model forced "compromise" after "compromise" (1820, 1850) which allowed for the expanding of the South Carolina model at the expense of the freeholder anti-noble model. Here was "the house divided against itself; half slave half free" to which Lincoln referred.

Part V

Another unique aspect of the South Carolina colony and state was a population that was in fact majority slave, as with the Caribbean islands dominated by plantations. Along with the intense racism of the island and South Carolina cultures came intense fear of slave uprisings, or even worse, slave liberation of some kind, or even slave enrichment on any level. This fear explains many actions throughout both Caribbean and US history.

- For example, when the newly created French Republic declared the end of slavery in both France proper and all French colonies, the French plantation owners of Haiti turned themselves over to England, their arch rivals, in order to preserve the existing order. (The slaves rose in revolt in the name of France, beat the English, only to have to fight against the slave support Napoleon later.)

It also explains why South Carolina, the colony most in favor of noble and elitist society, would side with the Revolution, and in fact be the first to declare independence from the king. For two forces played into? the actions of South Carolina;: the pressure by England to create a standard Crown law everywhere, and the ruling of the Crown Courts that slavery was not legal in England proper (*Sullivan vs. the Crown* 1772).

Therefore, in the eyes of South Carolina, if a standard Crown law was imposed, slavery would become illegal throughout all of the British Empire. Therefore, after Sullivan, South Carolina became the leading Southern voice in favor of independence. (Even thought at the time the Sullivan ruling was specific to England proper and had no impact on the colonies, the fear of the potential outlawing of slavery was enough to drive South Carolina to revolution.)

Later, after extensive efforts to have no limits on slavery in the US, when the new Republican party won for the first time, with Lincoln, with a platform to limit the expansion of slavery in the West (no direct threat to existing status of current slaves), South Carolina headed up the secessionist movement, became the first state to actually secede, and provoked the Civil War, when negotiations and compromises were being offered, by firing on the Federal Fort Sumter.

As with *Sullivan*, the Republicans offered no direct threat to existing slavery, the fear of any limits and potential political impacts later led South Carolina once again in to revolution.

When the war was lost, once again South Carolina (along with Mississippi, as state founded on the South Carolina model) provided leadership to the plantation orientated states by introducing the *Black Codes,* which created a virtual state of slavery for the newly emancipated Blacks. While forced to be repealed by the Reconstruction governments, they came back within a few years under the guise of what was called "Jim Crow" laws which created the American Apartheid system that, along with the *Black Codes,* dominated Southern life for over one hundred years.

Once again, when the first efforts to address the racial inequities of Southern life came to the fore, starting in the 1940s, it was South Carolina that provided the "moral," intellectual and political leadership against all efforts to end segregation.

Primarily this effort was personified by the long serving senator and presidential candidate of the States Rights Party (also known as the "Dixicrats"), Strom Thurman. In the critical election of 1948, the party carried South Carolina along with Mississippi, Alabama and Louisiana, the states most founded on the South Carolina model, nearly costing the Democratic Party the election.

- The transformation of the South from a completely race-based oligarchy, a "noble" system, to the current society is again beyond the scope of this paper.

However, it should be noted that South Carolina was one, if not the most resistant state to the Federal mandates to integrate society.

Yet again, this state provided what became an intellectual basis for resistance, through what was called "segregationist folk theology," a blending of Biblical and social justifications that echo John Calhoun.

- The paper of the capital "State of Columbia", urges all Southern states to resist together, for if any state gave in, it made it harder for others to resist. (See Massive Resistance, Southern Opposition to the Second Reconstruction.)

The historical tradition that had always kept South Carolina leading the efforts to maintain white supremacy and a "noble" view of society continued on late into the 20th century, having changed little in outlook than its founders.

From this brief review, it is clear that South Carolina is the origins of much of the race and class issues that have caused such pain and social conflict throughout the United States. It is clear that the economic success of the plantation model, and the massive support for the old world elitist noble concepts of society spread out from South Carolina, to be directly mimicked throughout the whole "deep South" and was envied and accepted by many people in all the South.

In addition the deep hatred and great fear of the Black slave inherent in the Plantation culture soon became ingrained in American life in the form of White racism throughout the land. This inherent racism and long-time acceptance of slavery and Black peonage has dominated political and social issues for most of the history of this nation.

- Therefore, South Carolina's role as the colony in which this culture was created and dispersed and supported, makes South Carolina the most important state in US history, the one that has influenced the politics and culture of the nation the most.

And, as this nation has evolved out of the plantation concept and become more diverse, through constant waves of immigration (mainly to areas other than the Deep South);

and as the mixture of the old colonial views of the freeholders and modern national views of equality forms a new American culture, the holders of "conservative values" (the evolved successors of the noble class and the "Know Nothings" and "Dixicrats" and the aging white racist voters) are losing power (at least in national elections).

Experts all point to the changing demographics as the potential death-knell of the remnants of those so influenced by the South Carolina of the past, which currently seems to dominate the Republican Party.

However, once again South Carolina is providing the political and intellectual framework that may yet allow for the continuation of what they see as conservativeness, while working to actually move away from the racist foundation of the past. Currently the leadership of South Carolina has moved to attempt to make "conservatism" no longer for whites only. They are attempting to make their values appeal to minorities and to women.

- If we look at the government of South Carolina, we see a very conservative governor, who is of East Indian descent. We also see that she, with almost no opposition from the white elite of the state, appointed a very conservative African American to the U.S. Senate.

This is not to say that South Carolina continues to be a virtual single party state (as it has been since its founding) nor are the parties in the state really integrated; in general the party of the whites is still Republican and the party of the Blacks is still Democratic.

However, these changes in which an African American can be appointed to the Senate from South Carolina and become the leading contender to win the 2014 special election for the seat shows a dramatic change of events in the South; one in which race and race hatred takes a back seat to the concept of "conservative values." We could get an inkling of this type of change coming through the actions of Strom Thurman when he actually hired as a staff member, James Meredith, the first Black man to attend the University of Mississippi (and whose enrollment set off wild riots of protest).

We can see and hear the differences in the "new South" where white governors speak openly of racial equality and the "mistakes of the past." We hear them argue that the Voting Rights Act is no longer needed since all the restrictions against voting have been removed.

And we know that mostly it is a façade. Most of these states have gerrymandered the Blacks into underrepresentation, and no African American has won a statewide office in any former Confederate state. South Carolina is 1/3 Black with only one Black Democratic member of Congress (the other eight in safely designed districts, are all white male conservatives).

Perhaps it can only be South Carolina, the traditional Southern states leader, who can lead the rest of the South to really put aside race hatred and once again become the most important state in the Union in this time. If Tim Scott, the appointed Senator, does win statewide election in 2014, it will truly be a landmark occurrence, once again coming from South Carolina.

Setting the Stage

Racism and hatred of the "other" still play a critical role in how we view our society. Currently the focus on these "others" is immigration and reform of existing immigration laws. What is often left out of the discussions now, beyond the statement that "we are a nation of immigrants," is the overwhelming good that immigration to the US has had on not just the people who did come here but a positive impact on the places from which they immigrated. This essay looks at the African American experience in the US as that of just one more group of immigrants, and focuses on the impact on them and their "homeland."

The premise of the paper is that we should really look at the issue not starting in 1619 with the first African slaves arriving in Virginia, but starting in 1914, with World War I and the cut off of cheap labor from Europe, and the American industrialists turning to a new source of semi-literate peon labor which who could become the next source of cheap labor so critical to profits. We need to look at African Americans' "outcomes" in comparison to other waves of immigrants and compare over the timeframes used for those groups. The election of Obama as president (which I added to the original essay at a later date) fits nicely into the premise which I first presented in 2001.

What Is the Second Most Important Date in the History of African Americans?

There can be no doubt that the most important date in the history of African Americans was the passage of the Thirteenth Amendment to the US Constitution banning chattel slavery. While the emancipation proclamation is often more cited as the date of "liberation" Lincoln's edict did not in fact free all slaves but only those in territories still in succession. Slavery itself was not fully outlawed until the passage of the 13th amendment, (with citizenship rights later provided with the 14th and 15th amendments.)

However, what should we consider the second most important date, or event? The introduction of slavery into Virginia (before the Mayflower), or one of the positive or negative Supreme Court rulings, that allowed Jim Crow or moved toward ending the American Apartheid? The "I have a Dream Speech" or Jackie Robinson's entry into (white) professional baseball? (Or after this paper was first written - the election of President Obama?) There are just so many possible events or dates that stand out in the long-term struggle for African Americans to achieve success in the United States.

However, if we look at issues from a slightly alternative perspective, I would like to propose a different idea for the second most important date in African American history that is not typically considered to have any connection to the African American community.

- That date is June 28, 1914, and the event is the assassination of Arch Duke Ferdinand of Austria, the event that began World War I.

I offer this date not for the long-term impact of the African Americans who eventually served in the US military (in mostly segregated units) and created a core group of empowered persons that came home expecting a different world. No, I offer this date because with the advent of World War I the much-needed source of cheap labor (Europe) that had fueled the American economy since the foundation of the nation, was now cut off. And as a result of this termination of cheap labor from Europe, the industrial heartland of America turned to a similar group of peoples (semi- or fully peon populations with little or no education, living in dire economic and political repression in their homelands) for its source of cheap labor, the peonage population of the African Americans living under Jim Crow in the southern United States. Between 1914 and 1945 (with some big gaps with the world-wide Depression), some four million African Americans eventually participated in the "Great Migration"

And these four million African Americans join in the great heritage of the mass migrations of other oppressed peoples fleeing from the servitude and hopelessness of Europe into the great American cauldron of the industrial heartland. And as it turns out, these African Americans, despite racism and the past history of slavery, have, for the most part, prospered and progressed at the same relative pace, using the same means for progression, as the other major immigrant groups who also descended upon America. Therefore with the end of cheap labor from Europe, the African Americans were given the chance to break free economically as well as culturally and politically from the Jim Crow era and move significantly along the path to political equality.

In addition, what each of these immigrant groups, despite low wages and mostly deplorable living conditions, were able to do, besides prospering themselves, was to develop a rare commodity: surplus wealth. As with other immigrant groups who came to America, this surplus wealth, in part, went to improve the living and political conditions of their "fellow countrymen (people who never made it to "the promised land of America."

So we not only see that the modern civil rights movement in the US was supported in large part by the small contributions of the "migrants," but we see also that the establishment of the Republic of Ireland was mostly funded by descendants of Irish immigrants to the US, and the creation of the State of Israel was demanded by and mostly funded by Jewish Americans. In addition, efforts to bring about reforms in Russia, Poland, Germany, Italy, and many other countries were greatly supported by, if not majority funded, by the "surplus" wealth of the immigrants and their descendants to the US.

But this similarity and its long-term benefit to the efforts to end tyranny around the world is only one of so many similarities between the immigrants to the US from other countries and the African American immigrants from the almost "other" country of the "Southern states."

But before going on we need to define a bit better the groups we are talking about. For example, the large wave of Scandinavians immigrants of which helped to populate Minnesota and Wisconsin does not really fit well into the major immigration patterns in US history. Primarily this group does not fit well in that the Scandinavians who came were mainly "middle class" and rather well-educated for the time, and they tended to stay in one highly concentrated area. They came primarily to continue their lifestyle (farming) in a place that offered far more land than they ever considered possible. And while there were some ethnic conflicts between the Norwegians and the Swedes back in Europe, it rarely rose to a level where the Norwegians were at risk of life.

However, for the other key immigrant groups of the late 18th and throughout the 19th century and into the early 20th century that came to populate and repopulate the American industrial "heartland,"

- the Scots, and poor English, and then later the massive waves of Irish, and then Italians, and then great waves of Slavs, including Russians, Poles, Bohemians, and, in the West, the Chinese, and the last of the pre-World War I massive wave of Russian and Polish Jews.

that all came to the US to become the cheap source of labor for the American industrial "giant," they had a much different experience then the compact groups.

These peoples were very different than the Swedes and Norwegians. These people were almost all desperately poor (at least for America), they were fleeing economic, and, often, political repression, and though they clustered in urban settings and neighborhoods, they spread out throughout the whole of the Northern US (with the Chinese, primarily on the West coast). And except for some people who came over to be miners (and had been miners in the "old country"), mostly the people came to do jobs they had never done before, and perhaps had never conceived of before.

- Typically these were poor peasants with almost no knowledge of modern technology who were being thrown into relatively modern cities and went to work in massive factories with "those huge machines."

Also, for the most part these new immigrants were extremely religious, and practicing a religion that was not the "accepted" one of the new nation. While the Americans were primarily some variety of Protestantism, the new immigrants were mainly Roman or Eastern Catholic, or Jewish. To the "nativist Americans" these religions were either the long-term oppressors of the majority of the US population – the Catholics; or the most hated and repress of the religions of Europe – the Jews; or an almost unknown aviation of the Catholics – the Eastern Orthodox.

To the "older Americans" the immigrating peoples had had little impact to their traditional cultures from what we call the "enlightenment" or modernization. In the main these people appeared to be very superstitious uneducated persons (who all appeared to have endless amounts of children).

In addition, almost all the groups were frightened of "outsiders" since the "outsiders" were the oppressors:

- The Irish were greatly repressed by the English, and there was great deprivation at the time of the major wave of immigrants (the potato famine).
- The Italian's economy had collapsed and the people had to deal with the old tyranny of the Catholic Church and local dukes, and also a newly united-state with a new king, as well as the long-term terror of the local gangs.
- The Slav's economy also had collapsed and the people were mainly ruled by absolutist kings who were often German and Protestant (Prussia, Austro-Hungarian Empires), and the people were often "cannon fodder" for the frequent wars in Eastern Europe.
- The Russians has just been "liberated" from some 400 years of virtual slavery (as serfs) but had little economic access to land or education and were still treated as mostly non-humans by their ruling elite.
- The Jews faced what seemed like an endless stream of attacks from almost all people, and the Jews of Russia were faced with the new effort of the Czarist government to make the Empire of Russia "Jew Free" by a policy of "one-third conversion, one third deportation and one-third starvation."

As we can see the African American community fits well into this pattern:

- After some 340 years of legal slavery in the US (with the most intense period being after the invention of the cotton gin in the 1790s), Blacks were awarded their legal freedom, much at the same time as the Russian serfs. And much like the serfs, the initial "liberal" efforts to train and educate the Black population (Reconstruction)

were mostly abandoned based on pressure of the old ruling elite (the White landowners in the South, and the Barons in Russian) and on near civil war in the areas of the US south.
- As with the serfs of Russia, the African Americans of the south were mainly left to fend for themselves and rapidly fell into a state of near slavery or legal peonage.
- And for the most part, while there were some long-term "free Black" communities in the north and pockets of successful African Americans in the south, there was roughly a 50-year period of loss of rights and social and economic isolation.

And they were frightened of "whitey" since "whitey" was often ready to kill African Americans without any fear of redress of the law. It is estimated that a minimum of 14,000 African Americans were killed in "lynchings" or other acts of racial violence (the original meaning of the term "race riots") in the forty years between the end of "Reconstruction" and the beginning of the Great Migration.

Then came the "guns of August," in 1914, and the empires of Europe found a new use for their "surplus" populations that they had been all too happy to ship off to the Americas.

- But now they were needed as soldiers and workers in the new war machines required for this new, modern war.

But American factories still needed labor, and cheap labor. Since the continuous flow of competitive cheap labor kept wages down and Unionism only a pipe dream, the need was critical to the industrialist who feared "labors'" demands. By the time of World War I almost all the major countries of Europe has successful unions and even major socialist parties (based on the concepts of the Second International). Not so the

US; the constant flow of labor enabled the factory owners to rid themselves of union organizers and socialist agitators with ease: For every worker fired there were often two or three waiting to take the job. The classic line offered by the industrialist of the time was, "I can hire one half of the working class to kill the other half." This foundation of anti-unionism was only possible if the flow of cheap labor continued.

In Europe, with their limited movement of populations, the strong sense of nationalism (even in relatively newly formed countries) and extensive classism, and old "guild" concepts, both Unionism and Socialism were successful, since there were no replacement workers waiting in the wings, and European industrialists had to come to terms with their "workers." In fact, at the beginning of World War I the majority party in the German Parliament was the Socialists (who quickly abandoned their pledges of international worker solidarity in opposition to the war, to one in favor of German Nationalism and Germany's sacred right to fight).

But in America, the industrialist needed to keep the flow of labor coming in to keep the competition going to keep down wages and unionism. The best source of peon labor that was readily available and easily transportable was the African Americans caught in the tyranny of Jim Crow; and the word went out and the Great Migration began.

And what awaited the new African-American immigrant in the cities of the North was the same as what awaited all other immigrants; overt hatred from the "native persons" (the descendants of earlier immigrants):

- Discrimination in jobs and housing, and being used by the industrialists against other groups of labor.

The Irish were the first to face the overt hatred of the Americans, with the inflow of Irish even leading to a political party that looked to "control the American borders, and ban new immigration." The American Party, the political arm of what is known as the "Know-Nothings," were active politically throughout the 1850s and won governorships and mayoralties based on pledges to end immigration throughout the country and ran third in the 1856 Presidential elections.

The overt hatred towards Blacks was no worse than that towards Chinese in the western US, or Irish and Jews on the east coast of the US. In fact the case can be made that the Chinese were treated even with more contempt than Blacks as the anti-Chinese groups managed to expel much of the Asian populations from many states and to ban their further immigrations (and later, during World War II, had some 150,000 Japanese placed in concentration camps based solely their race).

All the major immigrant groups faced the rage of the "nativist" groups and were subjects of overt anti-immigrant humor, as well as almost a complete barricade or social blockage from the "normal means" to progress to wealth. As late as the early 1960s there were "quotas" for the number of Jews that would be allowed into any given college (especially the elite schools), and tokenism prevailed (having a "Jewish seat" on the US Supreme court, but almost never more than one Jew at a time would serve).

Therefore, almost all the immigrant groups took virtually the same seven means to acquiring wealth and power in a hostile capitalist setting (these seven are discussed below).

But before discussing success, we need to remember that these groups on the whole, during the first wave of immigration, were not very successful.

- They worked in the proverbial "sweat shops" and mass industrial complexes, and, during their first generation of immigration, typically failed to progress very far away from this setting.
- Most of the immigrants who came over as cheap labor, worked and died as cheap labor, and often the same could be said for the children they brought with them, and the first children they had in this country.
- The majority of the progress for all the immigrant groups came, if at all, in the form of "class creep," meaning a slow rise from cheap labor to middle class families, over the course of some three to five generations.

It can be clearly argued that the poor white populations in the rural areas and even most urban areas of much of the South are basically 8th- and 9th- generation failed immigrants. They arrived in the US in the late 1700s (if not before) and became farmers and tradespersons in the areas of Tennessee, Kentucky, West Virginia, and out to Missouri and Oklahoma. They did not do well in the agricultural age and little better if not worse in the industrial age, and are still relatively failing in the information age as well. And they were and often still are the butt of bad jokes and stereotyping (Okies, Hillbillies, etc.) but are really failed descendants of failed immigrants.

But the urban immigrants had other means at their disposal for acquiring wealth and power, other than the traditional means of industrialism. And those who did find success did so primarily through the use of one or more of seven options –

- the military, policing, local government and politics, popular entertainment (and sport) and also crime (mainly the sin crimes of gambling, prostitution, and, when the country went "dry," alcohol and later, other drugs). In addition, of course there were the shop keepers who on occasion developed ways and means to turn local shops into major industrial forces (Sears & Roebuck, for example).

We can see the ambitious and talented immigrants working their way into these settings (and we can see them in the clichés of the times, such as the Irish cop, or Custer's troopers at Little Big Horn, or the Italian gangster or Italian crooner). We see the world of entertainment move from the Eddie Cantors and Al Jolson's to the Frank Sinatra's and Tony Bennett to the Michael Jackson's, Will Smith and almost all the rappers of today.

Boxing (the middleweights at least) were dominated by Jews in the 1920s (who replaced the Poles, who had replaced the Irish and Italians as the dominant fighters) and now, it is the Blacks and Hispanics (the latest immigrant group) that dominate the fight game. Basketball use to be called the "Jewish sport" in the 1920s and the description of the "sly and shifty Jew" in sports papers mimicked the overtly racist description of African American ball players that was the hallmark of the early 1950s and even into the early 1970s. We saw baseball dominated in its early days by Irish players only to be replaced by Italian players, then to be replaced by Black, and now, Hispanic players.

Irish gangs, which "controlled" much of the poor sections of major cities (and were the foundation of the Kennedy family fortune) were replaced by Italian gangs (and in many places, Jewish gangs), which have now given way to Black and Hispanic and Asian gangs, all controlling the non- government controlled "sins." (The old numbers game is no more because the states created the Lotto systems.)   Cities went from having Irish mayors to Italian and Slavic mayors to Jewish and Black mayors.

- In 1910, 90% of the prostitutes in New York City were Jewish, now the "trade" is dominated by Blacks, Hispanic and Asians.

But what I have only brushed on partly is that all groups took three to five generations to reach at least tolerable social acceptance in the mainstream culture.

It was almost one hundred and thirty years, or roughly five generations, between the first rushes of the Irish to America to the first (and to this point only) election of an Irish Catholic president. Now on St Patrick's Day, everyone tries to "act Irish," whatever that means.

We also see the social acceptance of the foods of the immigrants as "American food": Bagels are now sold at McDonalds (with ham and cheese on them, Oy). Pizza has become more or less the national American food. Jazz is recognized as the most-true of all American art forms. And so on and so on. But all of this took time and during that time it was rough for both the immigrants and the nativists who so strongly resisted their "un-American" ways.

Clearly we can see that, for the most part, acceptance into the mainstream culture takes three to five generations. While some, such as Chinese and Japanese and the Jews seem to have been accepted somewhat faster, that is mostly appearances, and not fact; the Asians and Jews were hated minorities for many generations prior to their recent successes. And in addition there continues to be many poor Asians and Jews in the United States.

It is mainly the newer immigration policies of the US that enables larger numbers of highly educated Chinese and Japanese (and Indian) to come and appear to be highly successful and accepted right away. These subsets of immigrants are more like the Scandinavian farmers then the mass waves of unskilled peoples that dominate the history of US immigration.

In addition a study of immigration clearly shows, that very few immigrants actually achieve great wealth, though (in almost all cases) within five generations the majority of those who survive tend to reach American middle class status, and some far higher; however, within every group at least 1/3 fail [to make it].

As noted we can see this failure in Appalachia and the Ozark regions. But we can also see it in South Boston, where there are still generations-old Irish poverty (or at least lower working class), and in the Lower East Side where numbers of poor Jews have been for close to five generations. And in cities like Buffalo and Cleveland and Akron or even Chicago, we still often find closely knit Slavic and Irish communities in conflict with each other as well as with the Blacks, for what little resources remain in the old rust belt cities. These communities have been intact for generations and primarily have little change in economic status during the entire history of the neighborhood.

So, not all immigrants succeed, and not all the children of the immigrants succeed, and during the three to five generations of social integration, the nativist point heavily towards the most unsuccessful, the lowest one-third of the immigrants, and try to generalize failure of this portion of the immigrant population to all the members of that group. Today we hear extensively about Black school failure and African American males in jails, but hear relatively little of the ever expanding numbers of African American college graduates and persons who are successful in a wide degree of economic arenas.

We primarily hear about the failures, and in fact this is normal in the American experience. We used to hear about all the stupid Poles, and Italian Mafia, and Irish drunks, and every group's "ladies of the night," and again, this is normal and standard. It sells papers or TV ads to feature the failings of the latest competitors for jobs and housing, etc. It wins votes for politicians to campaign on fear of the latest groups to appear different with their different religion and strange clothing and customs that don't seem at all modern.

- But again we have seen this occur in the US in the most horrible of fashions for every group that came over as poor cheap labor.

The elites had to feel like elites, and our journals and newspaper archives are filled with writings that were more than socially acceptable at the time that would not be believed by modern readers. But over time, and through social acceptance by use of the military, police, government, and crime, as well as commerce, but most importantly, through the arts and sports, each group has won its place in the US culture and has greatly added to (and therefore changed) the culture, but it takes time.

Experiencing the massive waves of Irish or Jews into this country at the time it was happening must have been amazing. The people seemed so different in religion and outlook and clothing and beliefs and habits, etc. They seemed so dirty and ugly and they couldn't speak English or communicate properly. They seemed lazy and so secretive. They all had terrorist groups within their communities aimed at destroying America and American values (the Molly Maguire's, the Jewish Communists, the Italian and Russian Anarchists, the German Fascist, the Black Panthers and in some ways the Black Muslims, etc.)

But over time, over generations, the language was learned, the dress changed, the names changed, often the religion would even change, and the "terrorist groups" became more like the Elks and the Rotary than the Communist party cells.

The children grew up and hit the American streets and wanted to be "American." They changed the streets to make them their own, adding their culture to the mix and even coming to dominate the "street culture of the time.

Also children grew up and many went to college and became more established and more successful and moved away from the old neighborhood. So today you find neighborhoods in the suburbs that appear to be homogeneous which are in fact a hodgepodge of ethnic and cultural backgrounds that after these three to five generations have become so American they often relate little to their own cultural history.

Using this time line to view the African American experience in this process of "immigration to America," starting with the advent of World War I, we see that the African-Americans are right on track, despite the "race issue."

We are just moving into the third generation after the end of the Great Migration, and we see the black population doing so much better in the "mainstream" then ever projected (and again, there is still a great deal of failure, but this is true with all immigrant groups).

But just consider the change in role of Blacks as spokespersons for products on TV or starring roles in movies (where now it the goofy white sidekick for the super smart Black action hero). Who could have projected that Allstate insurance would have an African American spokesperson, or that Black women would be seen as role models for beauty and as spokespersons for beauty products? (Or we would have an African –

American president.) Go back twenty-five years and say that would happen, and imagine what type of reaction you would have received.

Also the latest data from the US Department of Education shows that, on average, a black person stays in school slightly longer than the average white person (some 12.8 years, as opposed to 12.4 years for whites). This is a far cry from just some sixty years ago when the average African American attended (segregated) schools for no more than four years.

So in the midst of the nativist anger and rhetoric, and the still-blatant attacks on the one/third who are failing (and attempting to generalize that one/third to all Blacks), and in the midst of the dramatic changes happening in the culture due to the next wave of immigrants coming in in such great numbers (Hispanic, Chinese, Africans and Arabs), it is hard to step back and take an objective long-term view of the traditional positive outcomes for most members of the third-through fifth-generation of immigrant groups.

It is hard, but so needed in order to give a solid argument against the new Know-Nothings' attacks on the new people who are coming to continue the tradition in the United States of reaping endless benefits from immigrants.

By providing these immigrants the chance to become "modern" and acquire that scarce resource called "surplus wealth" we will allow for new internal movements within all the countries of origins of these new waves of immigrants to help end the tyranny that engulfs their homelands.

But it all takes time, three to five generations to be exact. Unfortunately we all tend to live in the here and now and cannot project out three more generations, so all we can see now is the conflicts and the crises, and the natural struggles between the nativist and the newcomers, and see nothing more than that conflict. We fail to see the standard process of cultural integration from a long-term perspective, and we fail to see the eventual hope, and only look at the current problem. And, perhaps worst of all, we fail to learn from the previous processes and therefore tend to allow the same mistakes in the integration process to occur over and over again.

Section Two –

Relatively Modern Times

Glenn Young

Setting the Stage

This is an essay written in 2003. Little has changed to alter the paper. If anything the position of fundamentalism has grown stronger and their points of view considered more legitimate.

While most of Europe retreats from religion, especially Christianity, the United States has become ever-increasingly religious. We are by far the most religious of all advanced economic nation. We are the nation where socially conservative religious groups are the most politically powerful and socially influential (with the possible exception of Israel). Much has been written and argued about as to why such a thing has happened.

While this upsurge of fundamentalism fits my conceptions of the Hegelian conflict of modernism and religious fundamentalism, this essay has a different spin on the matter.

This essay looks at our brand of religious fundamentalism as a very specific variation of recognized mental illness, that, in its more recognized form typically impacts a scant few people a year, but in its American strain is epidemic in the US. I am not saying per se that belief in religion, or Christianity, is a mental illness, as some others do; in this essay I attempt to link this American creation to something called the Jerusalem Syndrome.

American Christian Fundamentalism: Is America Being Taken Over by People Suffering From a Form of Mental Illness?

Part I – Conflicts in Perception

As a public speaker, I know the need to vary my presentation to the audience, if only to add a joke or some kind of allegory to which they can relate. Speaking as often as I have I found myself making these insertions almost organically, without really thinking about what I was going to say, more or less trusting my instincts. So, when I found myself presenting to an audience of government officials from Southern states, giving a presentation on systemic change, I, without much thought (actually without any thought), said something to the effect of ….

We know that systemic change takes a very long time, and it faces internal resistance on almost all levels. For example, the world did not accept Jesus directly from the cross. It took more than three hundred years between the time of the crucifixion and the establishment of Christianity as the state religion of the Roman Empire. And during that time you needed a Paul, and the writers of the gospels, and there were also the repressions and the martyrs, and then the schisms and the extensive councils to resolve them, and then finally the support of the Emperor Constantine the Great.

I thought it was a brilliant price of example pulled from my other "world" of "enthusiastic amateur" historian. I felt it gave people an example that was close to their hearts and spoke of the extensive efforts often needed to bring about acceptance of a new idea (or systemic change). And after all, what I said was pretty much the truth, even leaving out many of the more obnoxious things the Christians actually did on the way to, and once in, power. That element was not needed, and I was glad my little mouth did not go on a tangent into those realms (which I have been known to do more than once or twice).

Most people who spoke to me afterwards didn't comment on the Christian moment of the speech, only on the general subject, and most of the comments were very positive. However, two "Pentecostal Christians" came up to me after and told me that it was one of the most "anti-Christian" speeches they had ever heard and they intended to take it up with my superiors. I was actually in deep shock over this; I had no idea that I had said anything offensive. I was just giving historical fact to support a concept.

Their feeling of insult never manifested into formal complaints (after I begged a bit and tried to explain I had no intention of insulting them or their religion). I never really learned what it was that I said that was so offensive. They were not fully ready to express it then, and once I got it all calmed down, I didn't want to return to the subject.

But what this event made me do is to think about how to talk about religion with people who are religious, not just socially religious, but deeply so. And how does one make arguments about the meaning of this, or that, or the fact that this or that occurred, with people who are not basing their concepts in fact, but in faith and belief? I had been puzzled by this problem of communication for years prior to this event and continue to be so now.

With the current world situation, the post-911 world and the world in which fundamentalism is on the rise everywhere and in every religion, the idea of communication with people who are followers of any "faith" seems even more important than my little run-in with the Pentecostals. Yet, I find that there is almost no common frame of reference between myself and people who are "deeply religious" to the point that they are "true believers" in a holy book (and there are many holy books from many religions, which to choose, not just the Bible). And the believers take the representations, writings, manifestations, in these books to be the "truth" no matter what other facts can be shown to dispute them.

To paraphrase Bill Maher, the comedian, statement in his HBO "*I'm Swiss*" he argues that there is basically no way to have a reasonable conversation about much when that person believes that the world was created 6000 years ago and was completed in six days: Maher said he felt there was simply possible common ground to have a serious conversation. (Copyright laws prevent the actual quote.)

Yet what does this mean, that there is nowhere to go with these people? Deeply religious "true believer" people are a part of the body politic in the United States. We need to have serious conversations about the world and the future and politics and such with them. These conversations are increasingly important when so many of these people who believe in this Bishop Usher view of world history are in relatively strong positions of social and political power. They started with the school boards in the 1960s and now have progressed to the Congress, and many could say they have a major influence on the Presidency, never mind almost all professional sports teams ("I want to thank God for helping me score that touch down", and so on.)

I find it hard to understand how in this day and age, people can believe in the "stories" of the religions. I can understand how people, especially in the past, often need a god and feel strongly that this existence was not the only life. Since life then was "nasty brutish and short" there had to be some other form of existence, or even reincarnation. I understand that belief in the past, when we had so few answers for what went on all around us, and those we loved died so quickly and frequently. And I understand how many hold on to that belief today. What I don't understand today is the literalist, the ones who are fundamentalist to the point that they believe in every word of the Bible or the Koran or whichever holy book one fancies. I understand the need for the macro god, but not this micro god. How can people be still trying to understand the meaning of the verses of the Bible, such as of Genesis 6:2 or 6:4:

- Gen 6:2 That the sons of God saw the daughters of men that they [were] fair; and they took them wives of all which they chose.
- Gen :4 There were giants in the earth in those days; and also after that, when the sons of God came in unto the daughters of men, and they bare [children] to them, the same [became] mighty men which [were] of old, men of renown.

Wasn't God supposed to have only one son? Who are all these sons of god getting it on with the fair daughters of men ... and who are these men of renown, who are nameless and we never hear from again? /// OK, never mind. I know the Christians have come up with some answer for these questions long ago, but, their answers are simply silly, but were through cohesion accepted.

The first time a rocket went through the clouds and we didn't hear a giant "ouch," should have ended beliefs in the stories of God. Never mind the centuries of disproving the stories of the Bible through a host of sciences. How can people hold on to the stories in the face of such new knowledge developed by archeologist, zoologist astronomers and so many other fields of science and research?

I want to know how to talk to them. But then again, perhaps there is really no way to discuss the new facts of the world with fundamentalist who have such strong beliefs in predestination and also in the actual, literal stories of the Bible. Perhaps this essay should be a mocking effort (mocking a trashy crazy book called How to talk to a Liberal) called How to (or not to) talk to a Fundamentalist.

Perhaps we really can't talk to them. Perhaps my friend from Afghanistan is right when he talks about the religious fundamentalist in his country (the Taliban and others). He has said for years, "KILL THEM ALL!!!!!" "You don't understand them," he tells me. "The only way to stop them is to kill them all. Send them all to the paradise they seek. Make them happy, because if you don't, they will make you miserable."

My Western liberal juices get going when I hear this type of rant. But, I often wonder if we could have stopped the Nazis in 1923, if we had "killed them all" after the Beer Hall Putsch, instead of letting Hitler use his few months in jail to write Mein Kampf. Would we have been better off?

Surely our fundamentalists are a long way from the Nazis or the Taliban; surely there is still time to talk. Maybe there is a way, or then again, maybe not. Perhaps the best way to really describe the fundamentalists of today is as a form of "fifth columnist," an internal supporter of our fundamentalist enemies in the war on terrorism. For they are in many ways so like the Islamic extremists in hopes and desires (something the Christians would greatly dispute). And then again, perhaps the best way to look upon them, these true believers, is as really just insane people in our mists. In either case, talking to them is almost impossible.

Part II – The Written Word

Perhaps the conversation should be between the non-believer, and those who are believers, but are open to diversity and not absolutists and bypassing the fundamentalist completely. We, the non-religious, the semi-religious and the non-fundamentalist believers, need to work together. We need to do this to salvage America from this rising tide of fundamentalism that is threatening our very freedoms from enemies without and enemies within.

Together, we "others" can no longer allow the insanity of the fundamentalists to play such a strong role in our politics and daily lives. With every election in the US, we see their power growing. Even the most liberal of politicians end speeches with "God Bless the United States." The fundamentalist version of the world seems to be more and more represented by the mainstream media of society,

 We are on the verge, so far only the verge, of another plunge into ignorance and religious tyranny and with this "fall" we will lose the right to think (or to think differently). This type of darkness towards which we are heading is that kind that happens when any religion becomes the absolute determining factor in any society. History has taught us, that in this type of society, dissent is never tolerated, new ideas are never tolerated, freedom of choice, freedom of movement, freedom of all kinds are not tolerated. This right to be different has been the cornerstone of America (with notable exceptions) since its inception. America came about largely by those seeking these freedoms. What irony.

I am not saying this change, this triumph of fundamentalism, is a given, or that it inevitably will happen. ("Nothing is written," to quote TE Lawrence or at least the movie about him or to put it in terms of rejecting some forms of Christianity nothing is predestined.) There are many options and turns of events that will stem this flow. Perhaps the most likely thing that will save us, save our county, is the new wave of immigration. Perhaps these politically active fundamentalists are actually just another version of the Know-Nothings of the 1840s and 50s (an anti-immigrant, anti-Catholic political movement), and in time will fade away, overwhelmed by the new immigrant' growing political power.

But we already see that as these people of "faith" gain more control of the civil systems, our freedoms are already at great risk. For, they not only want to be left alone with their beliefs, but they want only people with their beliefs to be in positions of power. They want to increase the role of religion in law and education. They only want fundamentalist school teachers and fundamentalist politicians, fundamentalist judges, fundamentalist law, etc.

- And they, our American Christian fundamentalists, don't see that they are offering the same type of society as the Islamic fundamentalists (who want fundamentalist teachers, fundamentalist politicians, etc.) because they see the Islamic as "wrong" while they are "right with God and Jesus."

In Iraq and Afghanistan, we in America are in a war in which we are talking about bringing freedom to the world. While we are marketing freedom of thought and actions abroad, these very same freedoms are under attack at home. The "enemy of freedom" (our fundamentalists) at home seems to be very similar in thought, patterns and beliefs as our major "enemy of freedom" abroad, just different stories.

We have seen what happens when fundamentalists gain control of the politics or political agendas of a nation. Whether it's Spain with the Inquisition, or China with the Taiping

Rebellion (the leader thought he was God's Chinese son), the Cromwell era of England, states run by religious groups have been repressive and dogmatic, and, in the end, have failed. This cycle of oppression is obviously also true for those nations under control of a "living god" such as Mao, Stalin, Pol Pot. It is not solely the concept of religion, or religious fundamentalism that is at root here; it is the problem of what happens when people who are in power have an absolute belief in themselves or their religion, or their mandate that does not allow any room for question or for compromise. How can you

Part III - Which Side Are You On?

If we can learn anything from history it is that societies are not stagnant. The ebb and flow can be dramatic, and what was a haven for freedom can become death camps. I use to say that "being Jewish meant that you always kept one suitcase packed."

- No matter how good things looked at any point, the history of the Jews has shown that culture changes and scapegoats are needed (Spain 1492, Russia 1888, Germany 1932, just to name a few).

The rising tide against diversity and freedom, which has come in the guise of religion or as a massive social movement, always seems to look somewhat good to so many in the beginning. "One nation, one people one religion", the call of the Spanish monarchs of the late 15th cent, later echoed by Hitler, sounded good to a divided and threatened people both in the 15th century and 20th century. The fundamentalist demands for greater focus on family and a "culture of life" of no drugs and less sex all seem within reason and actually good for the greater American society.

They all seem to sound good at the beginning. Even the Taliban sounded good in the beginning. They called for the end of the 20-year civil war, the end of corruption, a return to the traditional values of Islam and Afghanistan, and peace. Hitler was elected to power (OK with never more than about 40% of the vote). In the 1970s, the Khmer Rouge was greeted as liberators from the American "puppet government" of Lon Nol by the Cambodian people.

In his book *Terror and Liberalism*, Paul Bergman lays out a clear argument that Islamist fundamentalism is of the same root and branch as the massive anti-liberal movements of the 20th century (Nazism, Fascism, Communism, and the Spanish movement of Franco), in that they all saw/see:

- liberal democracy as a failure, and corrupting people
- a glorious future by the elimination of liberal freedoms (dictatorships of the righteous)
- their vision of the future is based on some distorted vision of the past (the Roman Empire, the German Folk, the Spain of Isabella, the community (Ummah) of Mohamed
- the need for a scapegoat (a group of people) to condemn, to blame all problems upon (the Jews, the capitalist, the Communists, the Zionists, American cultural imperialists, etc.).

Bergman also sees that with in the Muslim world, the anti-liberal forces took two models; the Islamist who looked to the time of Mohamed as their past point of glory, and the Baathist (the party of Saddam Hussein, and the Assad's of Syria) who modeled their anti-liberalism on the Russian Communist Party.

Bergman is using the term "liberal" in the classical historical definition; not that of the American late 20th Century bogey man of the right. The liberal movement as it developed in the 18th Century had three basic thrusts:

- individual rights (equal justice before the law, and so on)
- property rights (the right to own and grow wealth regardless of "class," providing the basis for the development of capitalism) and
- a role for government in the welfare of the people, including education, public health and civil rights.

This last point was mainly presented in terms of separation of church and state. The liberals thought that people should not have to participate in a particular religion to gain education (so non-church schools, public schools, were established) or have to participate in a church service to gain some food, so public welfare programs were established, or follow church dictates for marriage (and divorce), so civil marriages laws were developed.

Bergman calls upon American liberals to support the War on Terror all over the world, including Iraq, as a continuation of the struggles of World War II and the Cold War. (He agrees that there is much room to argue about the tactics in which the war is handled, but not in the idea of the war itself.) He argues that European colonialism and imperialism repressed the anti-liberal movements in the Arab world (during the period leading up to and including World War II), and only now, as the grip of colonial (and neo-colonial) rule fades, is the anti-liberal movements, crushed in Europe, now coming to full scale maturity in the Muslim world.

Clearly there is room to argue against Berman's projections (including that, unlike Europe, there had not truly been a democratic or pro "liberal society" movement in the Muslim prior to the anti-colonial wars). However, overall he presents an interesting evaluation of the times.

More to the point, based on Berman' model, doesn't the fundamentalist movement of the United States meet these same criteria?

- They see the liberal democracy as a failure, and feel it is corrupting people.
- They see a glorious America if we get "right with God."
- They see the past featuring a "God-fearing" America. Claiming America was founded on Christian values," (which it was not, it was conceived on the writings of the "liberal thinkers" of their time (Locke, Paine, the writings of the "Glorious Revolution" of England time period" etc.) Most of the founding fathers were, at best, Deist.
- Their scapegoat is the "liberals." (At least for now.)

Yes, the American fundamentalists are the same as those anti-liberals in the past. The message may sound good and even rational, but the underlying message is one of elimination of freedom, elimination of reason, elimination of knowledge and control through faith and faith alone.

The politics and the direction of the American fundamentalist religious activist are the same as our "terrorist enemies." So to be consistent, as part of the war on terror, we need to fight the anti-liberal force here, as part of the war against the concepts of fundamentalism. In the 1930s during the rise of Hitler, there was a "Bund" movement in the United States in support of Hitler, and of a fascist government for America. Can we see the fundamentalist movement of today as just a manifestation of the "Bundist" movement of the 1930s?

It is the common everyday fundamentalist person ("well, ya know, I'm a Christian") who vote people who they see as fellow "true believers" into positions of power. There is nothing wrong with voting for politicians who represent your desires.

However, it is the goal and desire of this everyday fundamentalist to eliminate the separation of church and state (one of the four pillars of the anti-liberal movements). They want to, more or less, establish a "church/state" rule, with their version of Christianity setting the laws and behaviors for all (rule by the Ten Commandments?).

These everyday Christians and the politicians they elect do not believe in the separation of church and state. (And if they succeed, God [OK, got me] help those who disagree with them.) And again, they think it is for our own good, the good of America. They fundamentally believe that all who do not believe like them are damned

In 1936, when the Spanish army revolted against the socialist-dominated government, they advanced upon Madrid in four columns. When a member of the press asked General Franco, the leader of the revolt, which one of the columns would take Madrid first, he answered, "the fifth column." He was referring to the expected rising of the population of Madrid in support of the fascist revolt. The term grew to imply any internal supporters of a national enemy.

While the Christian fundamentalists would never say they support the Islamic fundamentalists, if they are both after the elimination of freedom of thought and instituting a new church/state, and they both take steps to develop those goals, then they are both supporters of one another goals. The efforts of the Christian fundamentalist greatly support the aims of the Islamic fundamentalist, even if not intended. Therefore, the

American fundamentalists are really fifth columns whether they intend to be or not.

Part IV – DSM and the Bible

Theologians of today all seem to me insane. They seem to me to be rejecting all the knowledge of the world gained in the last three or four centuries. People searching for meaning and an order to life where they explain it through God, is one thing. That level of belief, I can discuss and comprehend. (John Lennon said something to the effect of God being a measuring tool for determining our level of pain (copyright laws prevent the direct quote from the song *God*) But holding on to the absolutism of any "holy book" in this world of knowledge about the sky, and the nature and cause of life and death, and the depths of the universe, the Hubble Telescope, and, of course, history, is just frankly absurd, if not worse. Those who think they hear the word of God are to me absolutely insane.

So of course for me, the most insane are the fundamentalists. I am not offended by them. I am downright scared by them. They think that I am damned, the worshiper of the devil or worse, and are absolutely offended by my non-religious beliefs. I am equally as offended by them and their insistence that they are superior and among the saved, and their belief that they have to save me.

As we have seen, these fundamentalist perspectives are akin to other anti-liberal movements, but they also show clears signs of what could be considered insanity.

- On a recent NPR broadcast about the 80th anniversary of the Scopes trial, a woman from the town in which the trial was held stated that "Darwin was just a theory, but Creationism was a fact because I feel the presence of the

Lord in my heart, I hear the voice of the Lord, therefore the Bible has to be a fact."

They hear voices, telling them what to do and when to do it? The American Psychiatric Association's (APA) *Diagnostic and Statistical Manual of Mental Disorders (DSM)*, the manual on psychological disorders, would classify this as a symptom of schizophrenia. Those who think they hear the word of God are to me absolutely insane.

Any effort to have a serious discussion of fact about religion with the slightest reference to sources other than the Bible can create a sense, on the part of these people, of being attacked and ensuing defensiveness. Again, this defensiveness is a symptom of many psychological disorders, including schizophrenia. They also have an extensive belief that they are "saved" and therefore superior to others, despite material signs that would say differently (narcissism?).

In fact, one of the most frightening things about this type of person is that they feel that pushing and forcing their religious views on another is for that other person's own good (extreme narcissism?). They only want to save the souls of the unbelieving, or non- believing. They see themselves as noble and vastly superior and possessing the power to save you (personality disorder?).
They feel that they are absolutely right and that all others who differ with them are living at risk of loss of their immortal soul, condemned for eternity to hellfire and other torments. They ignore any fact that does not fit their view of the world, and if need be they "rewrite" history to support their beliefs. These are clear signs of bipolar disorder.

Their retort to any confrontation of them is, "I will pray for you." They never clearly state what they will pray for, your downfall or your salvation, but we are supposed to be somehow intellectually satisfied or in some way happy and rest assured that they will be praying for us ... But it actually is a way for them to end all debate, and assault on their beliefs, by proclaiming their superior knowledge of the universe and their ability to access the almighty. They are trying to use faith to counteract reason and rationalism. Therefore they are a "good" and "superior" person. Again these are signs of severe narcissism.

And after all what they really are waiting for and wanting so much to happen is the return of Christ.

- That, of course, according to their sacred writings, will result in a massive war with incredible destruction and deaths of untold billions.

But this is what they are hoping for .... Won't it be glorious?

Again, should not hoping for the death of billions and the total destruction of the world be considered a sign of insanity? And what should working towards that goal be considered?

This belief of the destruction of the earth with the return of Christ comes from the Book of Revelations. This book has become a major cornerstone of American fundamentalism. The focus on this book is somewhat unique to American fundamentalists. In fact many Christians throughout history have rejected Revelations.

As late as the 9th Century it was yanked out of the Bible entirely, only to be put back in again some two hundred years later. The Greek Orthodox have so little faith in this book, even today, they don't include it in their readings of the Bible; but not so among our American crazy Christians. They want the "Second Coming" ... and they are looking forward to it; they want the end of the world.

Is the belief in the Second Coming (or "parousia"), after so many failures, not also a sign of insanity? Isn't the classic description of insanity doing the same thing over and over again and expecting a different result?

So let's see, these Christians, actually Christians through the ages have been expecting this "Second Coming," dare I say it, forever. After a brief review of history of their writings, this second coming was supposed to happen, just to name a few ...

1) within days of Christ's death
2) within a few months of Christ's death
3) within the decade of Christ's death
4) within the first hundred years of Christ's death
5) with the ending of the Roman Empire
6) with the first millennium
7) with the taking of the Holy land by the Crusaders
8) with the cleansing of England, then France, then Spain of the Jews
9) with the setting up of perfect communities of God in places like Munster during the Early Reformation
10) within the first 1500 years of the birth of Christ
11) to save Constantinople from the Turks
12) and more than I can count ... even to now when the

Second Coming was supposed to happen within the 2000th anniversary of the birth of Christ (which, by the way, has now been determined to be in 6 BC, so the Second Coming should have been in 1994).

Aren't these fundamentalists doing the same thing over and over again and still expecting the same results? They continue to wait, even though in Matthew and Mark, Jesus is quoted as saying "before this generation has passed away all these things will have taken place." Meaning, that Jesus laid out a timeline for his return. He said that he'd be back in the lifetime of his followers.

- C.S. Lewis (the author of the *Chronicles of Narnia* and a noted writer on Christianity in the modern age, called this "the most embarrassing verse in the Bible."

It didn't happen. Christ did not come back then and it hasn't happened, but still they wait. They come up with changes after changes in the interpretation of the Bible to justify this wait. And when the next announcement of the time line does not work, they just come up with a new interpretation. Is this faith or insanity?

- In the early 1960s a comedy group called "Beyond the Fringe" did a routine on this insanity with their skit call *Will this wind be so mighty?* Peter Cook and Dudley Moore (of the group) saw this belief as insane then.

But as the Christian fundamentalists have taken more and more control of our culture, belief in this insanity is not only socially acceptable, but belief in this Second Coming is almost a prerequisite for an American politician to win any election.

- There is actually a clear psychological disorder associated with Christianity.

When I went to Jerusalem, I stayed with a relative of a friend.

My host was not only a very good historian, he also was a psychiatrist attached to major hospital in the city. He told me about a mental disorder referred to as the "Jerusalem Syndrome. According to the Wikipedia website http://en.wikipedia.org/wiki/Talk:Jerusalem_syndrome

- The Jerusalem syndrome is the name given to a group of mental phenomena involving the presence of either religiously themed obsessive ideas, delusions or other psychosis-like experiences that are triggered by, or lead to, a visit to the city of Jerusalem.
- The best known, although not the most prevalent manifestation of the Jerusalem syndrome, is the phenomenon whereby a person who seems previously balanced and devoid of any signs of psychopathology, becomes psychotic after arriving in Jerusalem. The psychosis is characterized by an intense religious theme and typically resolves to full recovery after a few weeks, or after being removed from the area.

What my host told me is that the people who develop this disorder are almost exclusively Americans, from the center of the country and from a stable home that was greatly involved in religion as part of their family activities. The profile was of a person who was from a relatively straightforward Christian church: A male, white, mid-20s to the late 30s, who has a relatively "closed world" environment. In many cases this was their first trip overseas, and first real venture outside of the comfort zones of their "limited" lives.

They heard about Jerusalem all their lives, and how important Zion and the life of Jesus were to them. Then, they come to their "holy city," and have the shock of their lives. Jerusalem, especially the old city, is very small and relatively unimpressive. The Christian holy sites seem almost a joke as the six or so Christian sects try to out shout each other during the prayer times.

(The Christian sites seem so small as opposed to the very impressive Dome of the Rock Mosque, or the Jewish Wailing Wall.) The actual Christian population is only about 2% of the city. And the real political and religious battles are between the Muslims and Jews.

Arab and Jewish vendors rent out crosses (with wheels) so you can carry the cross on the Via De La Rosa and visit all the Stations of the Cross. The Christian holy sites in the other cities (Bethlehem, and so on) are under Palestinian control and most of the Arab/Muslim populations in these areas are friendly but quite distant, almost disdainful of these weird Christians, who violate the basic laws of their (and Jewish) religion by making images of their god. They want the Christians to visit for economic reasons, but want no part of their religious beliefs.

The true-believing fundamentalist seems to be able to look upon this non-Christian environment with either sadness, or to interpret the events as showing them what a mission they have ahead of them bringing the holy city back to God. Or the fundamentalist simply wrap themselves in "rapture" and ignore everything around them but what they want to see. But, not these particular young people from the American heartland.

The major manifestation of the syndrome is that the person cannot handle the contradictions of the image they have had all their lives of Jerusalem and Jesus, and they basically "freak out." The Syndrome manifests itself with the young man thinking they are actually Jesus, come to fight with the money changers in the temple, or they are John the Baptist coming to make ready the highway in the wilderness. These young Americans strip themselves naked and look for something with which to beat them self; or to make into a crown of thorns for their heads. They run through the streets, naked (or in a loin cloth), yelling for people to "repent."

- They may run through the streets trying to baptize Muslims or Orthodox Jews (NOT a good idea in Jerusalem).

They urgently have to correct this contradiction between their beliefs and their "world view" with a manufactured reality that is presented to them in Jerusalem. They are therefore, as part of the mental illness transformed from just an ordinary American young man, to the very "Second Coming" he had hoped for all his life, or at least as the one who prepares the way for that "glorious event" that will do away with all the contradictions just presented to him.

I think that the American fundamentalists, as a whole, are actually suffering from their own form of Jerusalem Syndrome. They cannot handle the apparent contradictions between what they are expecting from life as "good Christians" and the reality of American society. They only need to visit any American "Jerusalem" (or big city) to encounter what they see as the corruption of society. They have been raised to think that this country is a "Christian country, based in Christian values."

Instead they see a pluralist society, with a wide diversity of lifestyles that include many in contradiction to what they see as the Bible saying (gays for one, single parent families for another) and they have basically "freaked out."

The fundamentalist attacks on abortion clinics, gay lifestyle (manifesting in "rescuing" gays) and the countless other "values" issues are their modern form of "running through the streets naked." They are trying to get the world to repent. It is upon them that the responsibility to be like Jesus or John has fallen.

- But the disorder cannot subside, since they never "leave the area."

They can't move away from "Jerusalem." They stay within this comfort zone (their American world) and their insanity becomes reinforced by that limited environment. Therefore, unlike the victims of the actual Jerusalem Syndrome, the insanity does not subside, it intensifies. And it is now these people, with this ever-growing insanity, that are, more and more, setting the political agenda for the United States.

Part V – The "Word" as Propaganda

In terms of relative world history (say some 10,000 years of civilization, if civilization is based only on the concept of urban (civil) life,) we find that, in the West, we are just a few hundred years from of the domination of faith over all aspects of the culture that lasted close to 1500 years. From the time of the edict that made Christianity not only the state religion, but the only tolerated religion in the Roman World (AD 325) to roughly the 18th Century, with the coming of the Age of Reason, the Western mind was essentially held captive by church dogma. (See Charles Freeman's The *Closing of the Western Mind* for a documented history of the efforts of the Church in this period to basically outlaw independent thought.)

Yes, there were brief flurries of free thinking in the supposed "Renaissance" and extensive efforts under the Reformation to think differently, but all of these were basically within the constraints of rethinking the church and the Church beliefs, and limited to intellectuals and universities. The freedom to think independently and free of religious oversight or free from religious constrain, until very recent times has been one of the rarest of all human experiences.

The mass movements calling for freedom of thought and belief were met with extensive violence (the Peasant Uprising right after Luther began his reforms) and often led to extensive wars (30 Years War in which 1/3 of the German population was killed.) In fact, the new churches or new governments of the Reformation were often more oppressive of dissent than the Medieval Roman Church. (See Robert Cohn's *The Pursuit of the Millennium: Revolutionary Millenarians and Mystical Anarchists of the Middle-Ages*, for how these movements can be seen as the origin of Fascism.)

But, how far are we really from the age of Copernicus, who, knowing the punishment for his knowledge of the real structure of the solar system, waited till he died to have his works published, to avoid the stake. (The Pope ordered his bones dug up and burnt anyways.)

Those who challenge the religion of the moment are never promoted well, and those who support the religious fervor are paraded in front of us constantly, some even masquerading as reporters. How is it that the broadcast media of this country is filled with religious propaganda that is all based on "faith"? Is it really just the marketplace driving it?

Can we really present new theories about religion in general and Christianity in particular that are critical and have them not mostly repressed or ignored? Thomas Paine has been largely written out of history because he wrote the book in 1796 called the *Age of Reason* in which he pointed out the contradictions within the Old, and within the New Testaments (showing how the Bible could not have been written by God or any individual writing at the time of the events depicted).

Prior to this book being released, Paine was considered one of the real founding fathers of America and was right up there with Washington and Jefferson in being given credit for winning the Revolution. His writings at the time of the American Revolution ("these are the times that try men's souls") rallied the people to the revolution and to the army, far more than "we hold these truths to be self-evident." While Jefferson wrote for intellectual statesmen in other countries Paine wrote to the "people".

Later Paine's "Rights of Man" was incorporated into the new constitution of France, and is considered one of the greatest writings on freedom ever penned. His book on religion actually gave the title to the epoch (the Age of Reason) and yet is almost unread and nearly forgotten today. The *Age of Reason* crossed the line; it clearly stated that man wrote the Bible and that it was not even well edited (Even God needs a good editor?). When this book was published Paine became hated and attacked by so many who use to love him, especially among the "common people of the United States. His old friends in the American Revolution, from 1776, who actually agreed with his religious writings, were now politicians, and couldn't afford to show him support. Paine, the man who held the Revolution together and gave a name to the new age went too far when he dissected the Bible and died alone and broken.

How different are we today? Is there really a politician anywhere who can openly criticize the Bible or even Christianity? Two wonderful books called the *Religion of the Occident* (from 1964) and, as already mentioned, *The Closing of the Western Mind* (2002) are fine examples of well researched and well-presented works that focus on the disastrous impact of the Christian religion on the Western world and then eventually on the entire world. Yet these works get little play, while the fantasy that is the *Da Vinci Code* is "investigated" endlessly. (The four Frenchmen who create the "Priory of Sion" hoax have long ago confessed, but the fantasy lives on and is built upon with lie after lie, sorry, "faith after faith.") We never see the authors of fact-based books on Fox or even Larry King. What we get is just endless dribble about endless dribble. Endless hours of "Mysteries of the Bible" or "Hour of Power," never mind whole networks dedicated to religious propaganda.

I recently meet some very nice people at a party. We began talking about our various experiences in Jerusalem. They told me, as Catholics, how exciting it was to see places like the Via De La Rosa and other important places from the Bible. It made them feel good to see these places and how inspired they were by the events.

They asked me how I felt about seeing these things. I tried a polite answer. But they sensed that something was different. They pressed me, and I told them that I was somewhat of a historian and began to talk about some of the history of the Church. I told them that, to me, the sites in Jerusalem were far less impressive than those in Istanbul. They pressed more, and I leaped forward.

I started telling them that I had just recently learned how the Church had put an end to the Olympic Games (AD 393) that had been going on for 1240 years or so, because the games were dedicated to Zeus. Not only did they end the Olympic Games, but they banned all athletic games of that sort on penalty of death.

I went on to tell them how the Church had killed more than 100 times the numbers of those with "pagan" beliefs or "faulty Christian" beliefs in the first 20 years of their power than in the entire 300 years that Christians lived in the Roman world under old-pre-Christian Roman law. In fact the Romans rarely persecuted Christians over the three hundred years, with only one real "national" campaign (Diocletian's of around 300 AD), and no more than 2000 or so were killed for their religion.

I told them that these are not beliefs but clear facts based on historical research and supported by multiple sources. These

comments were seen by these two people I met as insulting them and their religion. And these nice people were just run-of-the-mill Catholics, liberals in fact, supporters of Kerry, in fact. But they have their beliefs and their love of their Church. They prefer their comfort in their myths of religion than to have other information.
There is an old saying:

- Treason cannot flourish, for if it flourishes, none dare call it treason. (Ovid)

In fact, these American fundamentalists are actually treasonous to the American way of life. They fit into the very profile of the anti-liberal movement that has infected the world for the last century and has led to mass exterminations of peoples all over the world. Their movement and their efforts are building a major anti-freedom movement here in the US. They are more than a "fifth-column." But they still "sound good."

I think the Catholics I meet and the other run-of-the-mill believers find it more comfortable with folks like themselves than with me (a facts-based historian, an outright atheist, and a former Jew, so one who never ever believed in Jesus in any fashion). They have more of a common frame of reference with the fundamentalists than with me. They (the run-of-the-mill religious people), remind me of those who went along with the Nazis because, after all, they were Germans themselves, and they had more in common with the Nazis than with the Jews.

The run-of-the- mill believers are allowing the fundamentalists to flourish because the alternative would mean that they need to reject the basics of their own Christianity. That reject project is often unwanted as well as considered un-needed, and in the end anti-social. We know that the majority (the vast majority) of Americans are, like those everyday religious people I meet, trapped by their comfortable beliefs. Therefore the non-fundamentalist Christians try to address their need to maintain their beliefs and at the same time challenge the fundamentalist. Such a position is in the long-run unsustainable.

The moderate Christian position is so difficult because religion in the U.S. resembles more religion in Muslim countries then almost anywhere else. Of Western countries, the US is by far the most religious of any other; some 95% of Americans declare a belief in God, and some 50% belong to and attend some form of religious center. (In France only about 5% of the French attend church on a regular basis; in Italy and Spain it's about 20% attendance.) In the U.S. religious belief, like in Muslim countries, religion is the norm. While Muslim countries tend to be mono-religious (with a great deal of exceptions) in the US we have multiple forms and variations of religions, most of these however can be grouped as Christian of some variety or another. Therefore, whether, Baptist (white and Black), Catholic, Protestant, Mormon, or seemingly endless independent or non-denominational churches, they can all be linked as Christian.

With religion so part of the norm, and Christianity so dominate, the more moderate of these Christians are really unable to oppose their fundamentalist fellow believers on the broad basis of religion itself. The more liberal Christians and even moderate ones too, can and do say that the fundamentalist are using texts too literally or can reject the effort of the fundamentalist to impose religious views in the public sector. However, they cannot completely reject the notions of the fundamentalist without basically rejected the premise of American style of Christian belief. And without rejecting the fundamentalist outright, there is a form of acceptance and toleration, a form of being a fifth columnist for the fundamentalist cause.

What does this say about our culture? Perhaps it is saying that we are in great trouble, not as the fundamentalist would have us believe, because we have not enough Jesus, not enough religion, but in fact because we have far too much religion. If we can learn anything from history, times when religion has had strong control of society have been some of the worse times in human history (with possibly the sole exception being Buddhist influence in China and India).

These periods of tyranny are true for religions with hidden gods (Jehovah or Allah), living/dead gods (Jesus, Osiris) or living gods (the Pharaohs, Stalin or Mao). And the times when religion has had minimal influence has been the times of most growth and freedom. The China of Lord Kung (Confucius), the Americas in the Revolutionary period, the period of Islamic rule right after their major conquests, the golden age of Greece, were all times of great human progress where religion was limited in its importance.

The whole concept of modern capitalism and the role of the modern state (English liberalism) were based on limiting the role of the church, and the influence of faith, by replacing it with rational thought. However, when religion, or pseudo-religion, was mainly in power, rationalism and progress came to almost a standstill. Repression and fear and terror largely reigned.

One of my favorite sayings from American politics is from old mayor Daley of Chicago. During the 1968 Democratic Convention riots, he said that:

- "The Police are not here to create disorder, but the police are here to maintain disorder."

So while I should be trying to end this paper with a series of statements on what can be done to solve the problems of the rising Fundamentalism, I cannot. Nothing I will say will really be more than speculation.

The one thing I would raise though is that there are howls for a constructive effort to revive the term "liberal."
We need a push to teach the meaning of liberalism and its three main premises: equal justice, property rights and a role for government in civic affairs (separation of church and state.) If we can link the fundamentalist movement to the anti-liberal movements of the world, the Fascist and Communist enemies of our recent past, we can possible stop the momentum ….. of getting the more moderate Christians to really step forward and not become fifth columnist perhaps, perhaps, perhaps. But, as a person who is not Christian, not heard, and not part of the norm, I can only say this as a means of creating disorder.

Part VI – Answers to no Question

I recently got an answer to the question of why my speech to the Southerners was so "anti-Christian." I received a call from my sister who lives in Australia. She is another one of my siblings who have become stronger "believers" as she has gotten older. At least she is only an Anglican.

We fell into a discussion of how she believed that rationalism had failed, and basically destroyed the culture (yes, one of the first bases of the common framework of the anti-liberal movement)

She said that the rationalist movement has led to the ability of people to question everything, but the movement has given no answers to anything. Therefore, people have been led down a road that ends in an emotional, intellectual and spiritual dead end. She said the rationalists' effort as having allowed for the breakdown of family and social structures, by focusing on the rights of the individual at almost any cost, and had resulted in people isolated and alone with their own thoughts. The rationalists have led to people questioning religion, questioning personal relationship and roles, and questioning the family structure to the point that all they really are left with is questions. They lose the family connections, the community connections and the religious connections that have been the mainstay of culture since its inception. Without these connections society degenerates into individualism.

This conversation led me to telling her of my run-in with the Pentecostals, and my bewilderment over their view that my comments were so anti-Christian. She said it was obvious why they were seen so. (I was quite amazed that she saw it as obvious since no one else I to whom I had told the story recognized an obvious cause.)

She said that what I had done was to lower the whole rise of Christianity to just another political event. What I had done was to put it on par with any other human event. I had rejected the concept that it was predestined and ordained that the word of God would be accepted. They saw the coming of Christianity as the fulfilling of prophecy, as inevitable, a fulfillment of a promise from God. I presented it as a consequence of circumstance and power politics. I had denied the divine, and therefore was anti-Christian.

Her insight was pretty precise. I do reject the concept of predestination (as do many Christians --- what is free will?). I do see the development of the world as random political acts that are driven by the forces of humankind and natural forces (earthquakes, and so on). And I do not see these forces as driven by a "universal design" or God.

In the long run, this understanding of the way of the world (not belief, but understanding based in fact and history) is what maintains my hope that we will get through this fundamentalist movement epoch. In fact, following the logic of Hegel, the rise of fundamentalism is the new "antithesis" to the current domination of the thesis of rationalist-modernism. The result of a long-term struggle may be the development of a new type of rationalist society that incorporates the needs of the fundamentalists for maintenance of family, community and religious connections demanded by the fundamentalists throughout the world.

The "signs" of this new age, the time of struggle between the thesis and the new antithesis are all present. Just a quick study of these "Hegelian shifts" shows that the early period of shift are always marked by great acts of terrorism.

But the "shifts" have also always led to great periods of horrible wars. The new merged society is not a given. Freedom could lose and we can fall into that abyss of the absolute church/state. One of the determining factors for this negative outcome is when our culture or freedoms are undermined by the enemy within, by the fifth columnist of the anti-freedom forces. It has happened so often in the past.

The repression of freedom of thought by the Catholic Church in what is now called the Middle East and Egypt is considered one of the critical factors why, in the early 7th century, the Islamic conquest was successful. The populations of those areas saw the Islamic forces as liberators from the forced religious uniformity imposed by the state and church. Can such a thing happen again?

Setting the Stage

It has been proposed since political writing began that for States to control their own and other people, there is a need to maintain a level of fear and dread. Since we in this country have little collective memory or understanding of the past, it is hard for us as a people to assess how difficult or dangerous is the world's politics and how much of a threat to us actually exists.

This essay, written in 2005, attempts to demystify the State-presented level of world disorder there was, at that time as well as today, when compared to other times in history. I intend to show we are actually living in perhaps the most peaceful of all times, and the constant message that we should fear the world is more right-wing politically based than reality-based. Little has changed since I wrote this to disprove the premise.

The Real Peace Dividend

In these days of terror, war in Iraq and the destruction and the Gulf Coast of the U.S. it is hard to realize that the world is in one of the most peaceful stages seen in the last century. And perhaps this is the most peaceful it has ever been. There are almost no wars currently happening anywhere. How this differs from fifty to seventy-five years ago, twenty years, and even fifteen years ago.

Perhaps the much talked about "peace dividend" hoped for in the early 1990s (projected based on the end to the "Cold War") may actually be coming about. The dividend may not be in the form of tax cuts for Americans (as projected then) but in a planet where new markets open up for American goods as the earth moves toward a world free from war.

The definition of "war" includes four major types of conflicts:

1) formal conflict between two or more nations
2) a nationalist uprising against an occupying power (an insurgency or a partisan war)
3) a civil war, or an internal war between two or more factions within a nation
4) a separatist movement, an internal war aimed at creating a new independent state from a portion of an existing nation.

The recent concept of a "war on terror" is a false premise. Terror is simply a tactic used by one side or the other in one of these four efforts. Bin Laden sees his terror efforts as a means associated with the second type of war listed. (He sees his main effort as getting the foreign power out of "Muslim lands".)

The IRA terror campaign was associated with either the second or the fourth type of war, depending upon one's perspective. There are often problems in fitting a conflict clearly into the second, third and fourth categories.

- As is often said, "One person's insurgent is another person's bandit." Or, "one person's freedom fighter is another's terrorist."
- And also, it is often a point of argument whether a land is really part of a given nation or occupied by another (Kosovo, Palestine.)

However, in 2005, there are no formal wars currently active in the world.

There is technically a formal state of war in Korea, since the 1950-53 fighting was ended only with a truce that has been in place for some fifty-two years. There is also a technical state of war existing between Ethiopia and Eritrea (over one village), which has not had any combat in over two years. But that is it.

There are type two wars (insurgencies/partisan) in Iraq and in Afghanistan. There is also an active "Maoist" insurgency in Nepal. The ongoing 20-plus-year old insurgencies in Columbia and Peru are far less active and have mainly degenerated into conflicts over control of drug trafficking, rather than overt efforts to topple the government.

The fighting in Congo, Sri Lanka, Kashmir, Chechnya and Tibet are examples of wars that could fit into either category 3 or 4, since they may be seen as either civil wars or wars of independence. However, there is currently little fighting in any of these places.

In addition, the Sudan has settled their long standing thirty-four year old war by dividing into two countries. Kosovo is also quiet, as is the whole Balkans area. The most active fighting is in Southern Philippines, where Muslim separatists continue a limited armed insurrection for independence;

- There is the Palestine/Israel situation, however there the fighting is mostly restricted to suicide bombers and State retaliation.

There is also Western Sahara where there continues to be a nationalist war for independence from Morocco (with the fighting very limited).

There is also a clear civil war in the Ivory Coast, and a semi-state of civil war in Nigeria.

But the casualties in these conflicts are in the hundreds or thousands they are not in the tens of thousands or millions.

That's it. Right now, that is all the wars going on in the world: All the other major conflicts on earth that have captured our attention for the past decade or fifteen years, are quiet, and even resolved. This is an amazing time.

Why is there this new stage in world history? The answer seems relatively straightforward. The two major causes of post-World War II wars, (colonialism, and the residue of colonialism, i.e., unnatural borders, and so on, and the US/USSR rivalry, and the overlap of the two major points) are gone:

- All the US/USSR surrogate wars (Angola, Ethiopia, Mozambique, Nicaragua, El Salvador, etc.) are over.
- Almost all the "national liberation" wars are over.
- The Sudan war is over.
- The Balkans, if not stable, are under control.
- Pakistan and India are playing national cricket games against each other.

Even the massive internal repressions that were termed "the dirty wars" (Argentina, Chile, etc.) associated with anti-communism, are over. Major war in South Africa was averted by the introduction of democracy. Southeast Asia is at peace, even if most of the governments remain repressive.

- Most remarkable of all perhaps is the fact that the USSR fell without a major war.

The new goal of almost all governments and peoples around the world is to better position themselves to compete in the new global economy, rather than for the next military campaign.

This is perhaps the real "peace dividend" coming from the end of the Cold War and of colonialism. The "new world order" is in fact in place, and the promise of world peace is coming closer to fulfillment.

The Islamic extremists do not really offer an alternative to the rush to replace war with consumerism. They are only a major inconvenience. 9/11 and the other terrorist acts should not be a new justification for supporting repressive governments and new "dirty wars" (although this is what constitutes current US policy). The momentary war in Iraq will not slow the march of the rest of the world toward peace.

This peaceful world is the real peace dividend that was promised. In the long run, it is far better than a tax cut.

Glenn Young

Setting the Stage

The main themes of this collection of essays found in this book includes: Western Chauvinism, religious views dominating our conception of history, and lack of knowing about the past limiting our views of realistic options for complex issues. All these come together in this apparently far-fetched solution for the ongoing "Middle East" (a Western chauvinist term) crisis.

- The goal of this essay is to show how the "nouveau riche" mentality of the West is not only insulting to the rest of the world, it prevents us from looking for solutions based on events that took place prior to when the West was dominant.

Like the way the Great Powers of the 19th century used to solved problems my solution can work by ensuring that everyone gets "a piece of the action," This essay looks to find a win/win/win/win solution; it evens includes something for the American Right. While this essay was written long before the financial crisis of 2008, that event, and so many that have followed, shows the viability and the need for the broad solution offered.

Current politics and myopic thinking make all approaches to the Israel issue seem very much unsolvable. But I recall a political crisis of the near post-World War II world, where we also seemed faced with an unsolvable issue: the expansion of Soviet Union power around the world. Few in the US wanted a new war with the Soviets, and almost none wanted unrestrained Soviet expansion.

As we went from one local or regional crisis to the next, there was a broad-based solution that was relatively obvious to high ranking people, but none dare speak of it publicly at the time for fear of looking weak. Soon an anonymous article appeared in the *Journal of Foreign Affairs*, submitted by a person only identified as "X," and within a few months, what could not before be mentioned became US policy under the rubric of "containment."

This broad-based solution most likely saved us from World War III. This is not to compare myself to George Kennan; nor is my solution the only solutions; what is similar to "X" is that I put out ideas for solutions that no politician or religious leader could say publicly. However, once out, and discussed, perhaps it really could lay down the foundation of a broad and non-myopic solution, based on historical facts, to what seems unsolvable.

Israel for Sicily

The United States is a "nouveau riche" country. In fact, the main Western countries (UK, France, and Germany, for example) are all "nouveau riche" societies when compared to the great histories and former wealth of such countries as Persia, India, China and Egypt. As is the tradition with all "nouveau riche," after the first generation of wealth, the Western countries try to do all they can to wipe out the history of their "humble origins." The histories of the "rags to riches" have been rewritten by many families and nations to the point that Stalin would be proud of the whole process.

This process of "reshaping the past" may have benefit for the "nouveau riche" nations (and families), but it gives the leaders and the populations of these a vastly distorted world view, especially in the eyes of the nations who are somewhat akin to the "fallen nobility of the 18th and 19th century" of Europe (those with all the pretensions of nobility, an actual family history going back centuries, but no real resources to support the lifestyle).

It is perhaps this "nouveau riche" mentality that explains why Americans mostly hate the study serious history. Yes, we may want to know some Greek or Roman history (our pseudo ancestors). But we shy away from the history of any other nation, especially nations that we consider less important than us (which just about means all the other nations). It may be that this information will contradict our self-conception and challenge our "nouveau riche" rewrite of history.

We, as a culture, support this limited knowledge of the past. Our schools teach little history, and have made it so "politically correct" that what knowledge is passed along is "pabulum." I've heard American historians state it was more important that American know the "legends" of the United States, than the actual history. We know so little about our own real history and the history of the world that it is insulting to other peoples.

An Egyptian friend once said to me, after spending some time in West Virginia, Ohio and Tennessee, that the "stupidest fellaheen (Egyptian peasant farmer) knows more about the history of the world than those people 'out there.' I could not argue with him.

It's not just the average American who is "ignorant" of history, but our leaders as well. I know someone high up in the "military industrial complex" who believed that Jesus and Mohammad were contemporaries. I have yet to meet an elected official, or a high ranking military officer who has heard of Hasan ibn al-Sabbah, the historical inspiration of Osama Bin Laden.

This utter lack of a foundation of history leads to bad choices by our leaders. The Iraq war is only the most recent example. The Viet Nam War and the support of dictatorships around the world can all be linked to the distorted view of history that our leaders have, and the views of those who elect them.

In addition, it leads us to fail to understand potential options to solve current world. We are trapped in our thinking by the very limits of our knowledge. We think mostly of the world as a stagnant situation, when the history of the world is one of the constant movements of peoples and borders. Lands have been occupied by one people only to have another come in within a few centuries (if not sooner) and the population and the cultures changed, almost completely.

(Perhaps we don't want to remember the 200 years of wars with the Indians in what became the U.S. that came with the establishment of the nation, endless broken treaties and eventual "ethnic cleansing in the 1830s.)

Lands have been conquered and held for hundreds of years only to be lost again based on new wars or new waves of immigration. (Perhaps we don't want to remember that we only conquered half of Mexico some 160 years ago, which is almost nothing in world history, and now the Hispanics are coming back.)

So our "nouveau riche" view of a stagnant world keeps us trapped in the idea that things have to remain as they are, when some of the best solutions may be to make a major change in the current locations of peoples and ownership of land. Some of the problems we face are really quite ancient, and perhaps we need a modified version of ancient solutions to address these issues: the ancient solution of moving people.

Israel maybe most noted for this "people movement." For centuries, the land was fought over by the Hebrews, Canaanites and Philistines. Eventually the Hebrews (now Israelites and Jews), were expelled by the Assyrians and Babylonians respectively. The Israelis never returned (the infamous "Ten Lost Tribes" and the Jews returned with a newly refocused religion (many historians believe the Bible was first written while the Jews were in exile in Babylon). But the battle over the land currently called Israel did not end with the Jewish return under Persian protection, and then under Greek control. Over the last 2000 years or so the land was owned and occupied by many civilizations and peoples.

- The older Jewish state of the Hasmonean descendants of Judas Maccabee gave way to Roman rule around 40 BC. (or BCE)
- By 140 AD (or CE) or so, Jews were expelled and (after three major wars of independence lost by the Jews), completely banned from the lands.

The lands were occupied by Greeks and Romans as well as some Semitic peoples. This was the status of the land for close to the next five hundred years, with the culture shifting to Greek and Christian from Roman and Classical (with a few incursions of Persians, one lasting for about forty years).

Then, next came the Arabs and Islam; these new rulers did not expel the Greeks, but created a new educated and elegant Arab/Greek culture, with Islam slowly replacing Christianity (and the Arabs allowed the Jews back in).

Then, after some 400 years of this transition, came the Crusaders, who slaughtered all they could, including the entire population of Jerusalem. They tried to repopulate the land with Germanic Franks and descendants of the Vikings. But the majority remained Arabs. This Christian rule lasted to some degree for about one hundred and fifty years until the Turks (under the leadership of a Kurd, known in the West as Saladin) took the land.

Since about 1200 AD or so, one Turkic people or another occupied the area with the population being primarily Arab, but with large amounts of Turks and some Christians and Jews. The Ottoman Empire held the land from about 1600 until 1918, when the English gained control.

- British rule lasted less than thirty years.

While the Turks allowed Jewish immigration into the land during its rule, there were less than 50,000 Jews when the British took over, and only about 600,000 at the time of Israeli independence (the increase coming mostly from the remains of European Jewry). Now, in just the past sixty years the population rose to over 7,000,000 in Israel (mostly Jews but some Muslim) as well as 5 million Palestinians Muslims in the two sections of the area called the Palestinian Authority. The huge growth in population of Israel is largely the result of massive relocation of Russian, Persian and Arab Jews. So, now the land is once again mainly occupied by Europeans, with a large Semitic minority, as it was under the Romans, and under the Crusader states.

But, as dramatic as this story is (since it also mixes in the issues of religion,) this is not the territory in the European/Mediterranean world that has changed hands and populations the most. That honor actually rest with Sicily. As stated in the Wikipedia Encyclopedia http://en.wikipedia.org/wiki/Sicily#Geography

The original peoples of the island were Italic peoples (or possible Iberians). The island's location made it the center of conflict of the ancient world (much like the location of ancient Israel.) At first there was the struggle between the Phoenicians and their colony of Carthage and the Greeks (who occupied all of Southern Italy and eventually half of Sicily. The two sides fought over the island and its center to trade for over 350 years. The land was populated and repopulated time and again. The Carthaginians brought in tens of thousands of Gauls, Celts from what is now France. The Greeks brought in Greeks from what is now the coast of Turkey, as these Greeks fell under the control of the Persians.

The Greeks ended up fighting each other as well. The greatest military disaster of Athens was their effort to conquer the Sicilian city of Syracuse. They lost their entire fleet and army, upwards of 40,000 men.

But perhaps the most remembered war over Sicily is the Punic War, or the war between the rising Roman state and the aging Carthage. By 242 BC, the Romans had won the first round of the war, and occupied the island. They began to repopulate it with Roman and Italian stock.

However, as stated in the encyclopedia:

The initial success of the Carthaginians (Hannibal in Italy) during the Second Punic War encouraged many of the Sicilian cities to revolt against Roman rule. Rome sent troops to put down the rebellions (it was during the siege of Syracuse that Archimedes was killed). Carthage briefly took control of parts of Sicily, but in the end was driven off. Many Carthaginian sympathizers were killed—in 210 BC the Roman consul M. Valerian told the Roman Senate that "no Carthaginian remains in Sicily."

The famous statement about Roman conquest was: "You make it a desert and call it peace." Carthaginian was a prime example of this concept of "total war."

For the next six centuries Sicily was a province of the Roman Empire. It was something of a rural backwater, important chiefly for its grain fields, which were a mainstay of the food supply of the city of Rome. The empire did not make much effort to Romanize the region, which remained largely Greek.

With the decline of Rome, Sicily again became a major strategic battlefield. For the next 350 years Sicily was ruled by a series of different peoples, including the Vandals (for three decades). For the next six decades the Ostrogoths and the Byzantines (Greeks saying they were Romans) fought over the island, leaving much of it in ruins and depopulated. The Byzantines won out, and ruled the island (again repopulating it with Greeks from the Balkans). The Byzantines ruled more or less unmolested until the island was invaded by the Muslims from North Africa.

Starting in 827 the war of conquest continued until 902 and the land was occupied by Moors (Berbers) from North Africa. Like in Spain under Muslim rule, the island became the center of progress and religious tolerance. The Kalbid dynasty made Sicily one of the, if not the, richest kingdom in all of Europe. But the descendants of the Vikings, the Normans, invaded the Mediterranean in 1060 and started a thirty-year systematic conquest of Sicily. They basically became a ruling class of Berber (Arab), Greek and German population, and maintained the tolerance of the former Muslim rulers.

However, with the coming of the Crusades, and a new ruling house of Germans, toleration ended, and persecution of Muslims (and the small Jewish population) became standard. In 1224, the last of the Muslims were expelled.

Soon after France conquered the island, but only held it briefly. In 1282, Aragon invaded and brought a "Spanish" presence. Either as part of the independent kingdom of Aragon, or as part of the unified Spanish Kingdom (Aragon, Castile and a few other smaller parts), Sicily remained in Spanish hands (and with Spanish-speaking rulers) for some four hundred and fifty years.

The population's ruling classes became Spanish-speaking and many Aragonites moved into the island, bringing another new population change. Also, in 1656 a major plague hit Sicily hard. Spain ended up importing Italians from the mainland to help repopulate. It was only then that the island got its first major populations who actually spoke Italian.

In the early 18th century, the island was under the rule of Savoy, then Austria and then a French monarch who, starting in 1734, ruled the island and southern Italy under the name of the Kingdom of the Two Sicilies. (From Wikipedia)

- Sicily was the scene of major revolutionary movements in 1820 and 1848 against [the monarchy's] denial of constitutional government. The 1848 revolution resulted in a sixteen-month period of independence from the Bourbons before its armed forces took back control of the island in 1849.
- Sicily only became part of the newly formed kingdom of Italy in 1860. However, it was not a "happy union" and in 1866 there was a major revolt. Descent and revolts continued, leading to the collapse of the economy and the massive movement of Sicilians off of the island. As noted in the Wikipedia site;
- Palermo revolted against Italy. The city was soon bombed by the Italian navy ..... Italian soldiers summarily executed the civilian insurgents, and took possession once again of the island.
- A long extensive guerrilla campaign against the unionists (1861-1871) took place throughout southern Italy, and in Sicily, inducing the Italian government to a ferocious military repression. Ruled under martial law for many years, Sicily (and southern Italy) was ravaged by the Italian army that summarily executed hundreds of thousands of people, made tens of thousands prisoners, destroyed villages, and deported people. The

> Sicilian economy collapsed, leading to an
> unprecedented wave of emigration.

Depopulation of the island took place as millions moved to New York and other areas. The island itself fell mostly under the control of local "lords" or organized crime networks commonly known as the "Mafia." Sicily's status within Italy as being something different from the mainland was recognized when Sicily was made an autonomous region starting in 1946. Despite reforms offered, the relationship between the island and the mainland government continues to be uncomfortable at best.

With a serious review of the basic history of Sicily, we see that the perspective of Sicily as a quaint happy Italian island is mostly false. It is not happy, and it is actually barely Italian. In its people's histories are Celts, Phoenicians, Greeks, including Greeks from Asia and the Balkans, Romans/Italics, Germans of several groups, Arabs and Berbers, Scandinavians, Spanish, French, Austrians and the modern Italians. Each one of the groups ruled the land from a few generations to hundreds of years, bringing about many changes in culture and religion with each shift in rulers and populations.

Israel and Sicily have had extensive changes, as we have seen. However, other nations and lands have similar stories, if not as dramatic. For example, if we look at the history of the "Hungarian Plain;" the area today known as the Ukraine; the Balkans; as well as all throughout the Americas, and as we learned the history of Africa better, we see a similar pattern in much of the southern part of that continent of the frequent changing of peoples and cultures in any given area: Peoples, states, cultures when looked over the long haul appear to be almost constantly moving.

So, why did I do this long review of the land and populations changes in Israel and Sicily? Because, if we look at history from a long view, we see that "things" are not stagnant. With this understanding we can start to think of a potential solution to the crisis in the "Middle East" from an "ancient view point," that of looking at the fluidity of the populations' movement. What can we learn from this long-term perspective?

1) Land occupation by any nation can be tentative at best.
2) Land is often exchanged as part of a war and peace process.
3) Peoples around the world have relocated many times.
4) Often people relocate to avoid destruction and war, other times they do so for economic reasons (including population increases).
5) The occupation of lands by new people can bring about destruction or it can bring about a great expansion of wealth and culture.

From a "stagnant" point of view, we see the crisis in the Middle East as two peoples (Israel and Palestinians) fighting for the same land, each making claims to the land based on history, religion and by right of conquest. Both sides have holy places under their control and not under their control that are bound tight to their, and others, religious foundations. In addition, both groups see their land as a place of salvation and security, having both experience extensive discrimination, (with the Palestinians only having this experience as people living in exile during the last 60 years or so, while the Jews have faced destruction many times, in many locations and for centuries).

In the stagnant world view, there seems little that can be done but to try and divide the land in some fashion (which most Arabs, and a minority of Israelis, do not want). It has taken some 40 years of war and terrorism to get the parties to roughly agree on a "two state solution," but in fact this seems not to really satisfy the Arabs, as witnessed by the election victories of the Hamas party, which is still dedicated to the elimination of Israel.

The policies of the West, and Israel, caught up in the stagnant view, are possibly leading to another war of extermination of the Jewish people. The signs are everywhere. The radicals, such Hamas, gain power throughout the region (with Iran supporting their efforts towards a new war). The existing governments of the Arab world are hated by the citizens, in large part for their failure to defeat Israel, and are seen by their own people as the tools of the old and new Christian/Jewish imperialism (who appear to the "mob" to control the policies of France, England and the US).

The "Arab street" has a strong argument. Most of the current nations in the Middle East have "unnatural borders" of the existing countries of the region are the remnants of European imperialism. These boarders are mainly based on the failed treaty ending World War I, and its aftermath. Iraq is nothing more than a creation of British and French needs and has not historical basis. Israel, Jordan and Arabia are also manifestations of this period. The lack of "Kurd state" is also linked to the post World War I politics.

The Arab peoples are also far better aware of world history then the people of the West. They tend to see Israel as the reincarnation of the Crusaders states. It took the Muslim world more than 200 years to rid them of that old imperialist venture. Israel has only been there for sixty years. The Arabs see time as on their side. Most Westerners, when they think of the Crusades, think on terms of the valiant Christian knights trying to protect Christian pilgrims.

The Arabs also see demographics as on their side. The population of the area is growing in leaps. Clearly the younger population is expressing a new "peoples' will." Sooner or later, in some fashion or other, the local older populations' governments representing the "imperialist" will fall and the "will of the people" will come to power. That new "people's will" is extensively pro-Islamist and, extensively, willing to go to war with Israel no matter what the cost.

In addition, the outward migration of Muslims into Western Europe and the United States make them and their political and religious views important in these democracies. Israel no longer has the monopoly on the internal Western advocates on the Middle Eastern regional politics. How these demographic changes in the West will affect the political support of Israel by Western powers will play out over the next fifty years.

- (If the Western powers are still the world dominate powers some fifty years from now.)

The shifts away from Israel are already beginning, and the trend towards at least a "more balanced approach" is clearly in place. President Bush calling for a Palestinian state was a major sign of that shift.

What is apparent, however, from a "stagnant" world point of view, the future is not good for the region. It seems apparent that in the long run the "two-state solution" will not last. It seems clear that eventually Israel will fall, or be destroyed. It is also clear that the war possibly will lead to a worldwide nuclear war. Perhaps the "Biblical Prophecies of Armageddon" will come true. Perhaps, the "fire next time" will be the fires of Iranian or terrorist nuclear weapons with replies by Israel and the US. Or perhaps the sequence will be a pre-emptive strike by the US or Israel. It does not matter, if the outcome is a nuclear war.

However, if we look at the situation from a non-nouveau riche," non-stagnant worldview, we see that there are options. In addition, there is now the wealth in the world, in the Arab lands and among the relevant world powers, to make options possible. There are also precedents in the potential warring parties that could give them the basis for accepting options.

Before the option can be expressed, we need to look at the given needs of the two warring factions:

From the Arab point of view, Israel is an imposition of Western Imperialism that has led to:

- the disposition and impoverishment of millions of Palestinians, and
- the loss of control of holy sites central to the religion of Islam.

The Arabs also see it as a religious obligation to regain control of lands lost to the "Ummah" or Islamic community.

Israel, or the Jewish people, sees based in history that:

- there is a need for a "Jewish state"; the real need is for the Jewish state to exist within "safe and secure borders";
- the land was promised to them both by God and the British Empire and the world through the UN.

They also see the land as the "promised land" and the only rational place for a Jewish State. In the early period of the "Zionist movement," Jewish leadership rejected several options for the location of Israel in places other than the Near East, including Uganda, parts of Argentina and even parts of Utah.

There are several ways for the two points to be phrased, but the real issue seems to come down to having Israel, as a safe and secure place, as a nation with a Jewish majority and culture. Demographics, the desire of the Arab masses and many other issues show that this bottom line appears not maintainable over the long haul in its current location.

However, the massive anti-Semitism of the last 150 years, starting in 19th Century Russia on through the Holocaust and into the modern Islamist movements, has more or less proven the need for a Jewish-dominated state. That point almost all will concede. So from the stagnant worldview, there seems to be little solution. However, from the fluid worldview there is another solution.

- Move the Jewish State (out of harm's way).

To many in the West, this sounds like an absurd solution. Yet, as nouveau riche, they forget their own histories. Each of the States of the West (except for perhaps Norway and Sweden) consists of peoples who started in one place and migrated to another. Often there were multiple movements and relocations. Remember, those who created the Kingdom of Spain can trace their origins to nomadic horsemen from the country now called Ukraine. Most of the Balkans nations are populated by peoples with origins as far away as Siberia.

So, just for the moment let's put aside all concepts of absurdity, and ask a critical question: How in this modern age would you go about moving a nation? Especially how do you go about moving a nation without causing a war?

- The answer seems to be buying the nation, and, then using that money to buy some other place to relocate.
- Currently, with all the oil wealth in the Arab world, there is actually the wealth available to buy Israel. All

that would be needed is to determine a price (and what can stay and what can go).
- The Arabs would regain the lands they so sorely want, and they would do so without war.

In fact, the Arabs had actually sold the lands in question; during the crusading period, Fredrick the Emperor of Germany, during the sixth Crusade, basically bought all of the "West Bank" and Jerusalem (except for the Dome of the Rock) from the Sultan of Egypt, in exchange for cash and military aid (February 1229). This in fact was the least costly, least bloody and most successful of all the crusades.

- Its outcome was rejected by the Western leaders (including the Pope) for failure to fight with the "infidels." This rejection led to more (lost) wars and the final collapse of the Crusader states.
- Perhaps the Arabs leaders would be able to not make the same mistakes as the Pope.

So, if the land of Israel can be "bought" by the Arabs, where could Israel go?

- One of the best and clearest options is Sicily.

Besides the fact that the island has a long history of changing of populations and cultures, it is roughly the same size (Israel 20,770 km² Sicily 25,708 km²) and climate as Israel and there is a similar agriculture base. In addition, as noted the island and its people have not really been happy as part of Italy. The people who remain there are in deep poverty.

Therefore, the land is occupied, and in the modern world, peoples cannot be forced to leave to make way for another population.

Therefore, the part of the deal would have to include incentives for the people of Sicily to either move or to accept new rulers, citizenship and the new influx of the new culture. First of all there would be the incentive of money. The property of the people would be purchased, if someone agrees to sell. Second, the citizens of Sicily are citizens of both Italy and the European Union. Currently many nations in the EU are facing labor shortages (most often turning to Turkey for workers), and many people from Sicily could easily resettle in other parts of the EU (with their new cash, and perhaps training and education incentives).

In addition, there would be no absolute requirement for people to move if they accept the new State and the influx of 7 million new people who would be mostly Jewish. Many Sicilians could remain on the island and take on the role that the Palestinians play in the Israeli economy (low-wage workers in the "service economy").

But Italy also needs a reason to sell the Island. First of all, the nation is in dire need of economic help. The income from selling Sicily would assist greatly in getting some needed resources to help modernize the rest of the country's infrastructure. It would also rid them of a section of the nation that is an economic drain on the rest of the nation, and a source of much of the nation's crime.

In addition, the other Western states would benefit with the sale of Israel in that it would release some of the "Petro-dollars" that are currently locked in the Arab world. The sales of Israel and Sicily would help offset the "trade deficit" between the West and the Arab world.

Israel would gain a place where they could have a nation in safe and secure borders, and be able to stop putting so much of their resources into military. Once relocated, the cost of the national enterprise would be greatly reduced, and the more original concepts of the land of Israel could be restored.

The issue of religion and the promise of God and all these other issues will of course stand in the way of any type of settlement for Israel. However, there are several solutions for at least part of the traditional issues that have been barriers to peace.

For example, the key part of the any real solution would most likely need to include the "internationalization" of Jerusalem, especially the holy sites. The city would become the possession of the United Nations, and that organization would relocate to that site. Other specific sites such as the Dome of the Rock, the Wailing Wall, the Masada, and various Christian sites, would become "property" of the United Nations with the delegation of the upkeep and security for these sites delegated to specific countries or groups of countries (with religious sensitivities always at the fore of the process.

In addition, as part of the settlement, the United Nations would have to guarantee the human rights of all peoples who wish to either stay in the area, or to locate there. In other words, just like the Sicilians could not be "forced to relocate," neither would Israelis be forced to leave by the new Palestinian government. Any Jew who wished to remain in the old land of Israel should be free to do so, protected by the UN, and perhaps even given the new status of UN citizens. Many of the Orthodox Jews may wish to do so, and they would need to be protected, by the new government, and by the United Nations.

So, here is the deal … in the sequence that seems to make sense. It actually needs to move backwards. The first step would be Italy agreeing to participate, by agreeing to sell Sicily (and the people of Sicily would have to agree to be part of the deal). Both of these would have to be "in principle" agreements, since the price will not be established for a long time into the process.

Then Israel would need to agree, in principle, to relocate, and to be "bought" (again, in principle), and to massive relocation. Then the Arab governments would have to agree to buy Israel, with the caveats about protections of holy sites and Jews that remain, also with the relocation of the UN. Then, the incentives would also have to be in place eventually to enable the UN to relocate and take on the responsibilities of protection of the holy sites and minority populations.

There would have to be agreements on costs and on a time table for the change (perhaps over the course of 10 to 15 years). Both the Jews and Arabic cultures are famous for their ability to barter; this would be one negotiation for the record books. To quote so many sales persons of the past ... "Such a deal ..." Since nothing else has worked ...why not investigate the options?

Who should broker the deal ... perhaps a major power with the least interest or historical connection to the are ... Perhaps China or Japan ... Since China has a long history of fighting with the Muslims, perhaps better Japan: Or, perhaps a nation with a history of dealing with division, South Korea. Perhaps the Pope, but Arabs and Jews could have problems with that.

By broadening the issues and bringing the whole world into the process, and by giving everyone a piece of the action, we can break away from the trap of looking at this issue as a fight over a small piece of land claimed by two peoples, to a means to a grand bargain solving multiple problems driven by the superpowers of the day. While the super powers of the past often disregarded culture and populations and religions to justify their own desire for empire, the approach they took of grand bargains often averted major wars.

We need to learn from them not to not think of the world as a stagnant place, but now we need to include our modern standards of social and political justice and of course the value of money. This new modern approach to a grand bargain will need to include respect for peoples' long-time history and more flexibility in the options offered based on the true history of the movement of peoples and cultures over time and space. And of course, the spreading of the money brought to the process among all involved, not just some monarchs or conquering generals.

Like in most problems in the modern world, the crisis of the Palestinian and Israeli conflict can be resolved with innovation, planning and enough money spread around. This time, the Muslims have the money, and we need to give them a real plan that will make everyone winners.

Setting the Stage

During the early days of the second Iraq war, (2003) there was much debate in the media and among pundits as to if the war would be like Viet Nam (resistance and eventual defeat) or like World War II, where we would be greeted as liberators. Later there was the discussion of the viability of "nation building." I thought both positions were flawed and missed the real historical parallel (if such construct is really possible). I also thought that the model offered for nation building at the time (post-American Revolution or post-WWII Europe), were also historically bad examples. I saw what was happening in Iraq as something similar to what happened in another of those political eras that most Americans would prefer to forget and therefore cannot learn from. That era was the Reconstruction period after the Civil War, where we could have created a far more free and "democratic" South and failed.

Iraqi Democracy less like the American Constitutional Era, More like Southern Reconstruction

When defending the War in Iraq, the Bush Administration often discusses how difficult it is to start a new Democracy, even comparing the Iraqi struggles to create a constitution with the creation of American Democracy in the 18th Century. The rationale of any historical parallels between those two events is highly suspect given the fact that our opponent during that period had not significantly destroyed our infrastructure, we weren't infiltrated with violent religious fanatics, and we hadn't just overthrown a violent dictatorship that had dominated us from our own shores. To put it another way, America in 1787 didn't have the ethnic or regional obstacles that exist in Iraq today.

No Sense of History

Although I disagree with the assertion that Iraq resembles our fledgling Democracy of the 18th Century, American history does provide a critical example that may be relevant to Iraq, especially with the possibility of a civil war in the region.

- Back in the good old 1860s our own country went through a Civil War, and the reconstruction process of the losing party of the Confederacy faced a long, hard battle to recover for many years.

For nearly a century, the South remained devastated by the lingering effects of the Civil War, including an insurgency fueled by racial hatred and violence that crippled the region and that restricted the rights of many of its citizens. One reason for this was the mistrust of "Yankee" Northerners, who were still considered an enemy. Union troops in the South did much to restore order in the aftermath of the Civil War, but were unable to stabilize the situation in the long-term. Will this happen in Iraq? – we can't be sure, but if Southern Reconstruction in our own nation is any indication of what is to come in Middle East, we are in for a long struggle unless we utilize resources we have today that the Union Army could not in the 19th Century.

In Iraq, the insurgency will always be energized against U.S. soldiers, and they will even take it out on their own citizens who they feel capitulated to American influence. The only solution is to do what the Bush Administration has repeatedly rejected – bring in international help. Other nations have offered to train Iraqi troops but have been rejected. The United Nations has offered to send peacekeepers, but has been rejected. Some Americans criticize the rest of the world for not supporting our efforts in Iraq but fail to criticize the Bush Administration for refusing to accept help when it has been offered!

To understand the parallel between this situation in Iraq and Southern Reconstruction, we need to first look briefly at their similar history. After entering the modern age as part of a colonial empire (the British in Iraq and America), both nations were created by linking together diverse areas without much historical relationship (Kurds, Shiites, Sunnis in Iraq; Virginians, Texans and Louisianans in the US before the Civil War).

Both regions came from economic backwardness to create a thriving economy based on a single product (oil for Iraq, cotton for the South). At the same time, the limited democratic institutions that were first developed slipped slowly into authoritarian rule, benefiting the new elite class developed by the control of the single product, while reducing large segments of the society to semi-to-absolute servitude (Saddam's rule in Iraq; the rule of the white slaveholder in the South).

Similar to Iraq, the South overestimated their power and faced a disastrous war with a far more advanced economic power. In both cases, the war resulted in a massive defeat, with a majority of infrastructure destroyed, the nation occupied, and the army unceremoniously disbanded. There was little planning of the "peace" by the victorious power, and there was little planning on how to address the needs of the country afterwards.

In the haphazard peace process, the former ruling class was stripped of almost all power, and basically banned from governmental activities (Baathist in Iraq; former White plantation class in the South).

The occupying government attempted to establish a new government, mainly based on the previously oppressed classes and races (Kurds and Shiites in Iraq; Freedmen and white sharecroppers in the South). Elections were held and new governments took office and attempted to implement a series of reforms, and to establish its own military and police. The occupying power also sent a number of "experts" and "professionals" to assist the new government to manage the "single crop" economy, creating the appearance that the real benefit was for the occupying power (American oil producers such as Halliburton, "carpetbaggers" in the South).

In the years following the Civil War, there was limited success on the part of the new governments in addressing the unemployment of the former members of the military and former government employees. Feeding on the economic hard times, the old ruling class, in alliance with many members of the dispirited out-of-work military and bureaucrats, raised a protracted insurgency against the new governments.

The insurgents, relying on the old army structure for command and control, used extensive terrorist tactics, including bombing and assassinations. The Union initially responded with extensive attacks and overwhelming force against the insurgency (the KKK in the South), but soon retreated into safe zones as the insurgency became more guerrilla in nature. There is a clear parallel between these events and the events currently taking shape in Iraq.

Although the Bush Administration has pointed erroneously to one point in American history, neither side of the political spectrum has pointed to Reconstruction, despite the fact that comparisons are far more applicable. Furthermore, despite the contention by the Bush Administration that we are ignoring the success in Iraq, such as Iraqi elections, new schools, hospitals, the development of a constitution, and women on the legislature, there were also quick successes (except for women's rights) in the Confederate Reconstruction state governments.

With the aid of the Federal Government's Freedman's Bureau, these new Reconstruction governments established activist progressive governments that even led to African-Americans being elected to the U.S. Senate, U.S. House of Representatives* and into the state legislatures (with an actual Black majority in the South Carolina legislature).

But after the early years of Reconstruction those quick successes began to fall apart, as states back under the control of the old power elite that once elected Blacks to represent them, now barely allowed blacks to vote due to Jim Crow laws, and persistent racism and intimidation. One reason for this retreat from freedom was that many of the changes were forced by the victorious Union power whose presence had garnered extensive resentment. In addition the Union forces could not effectively dismantle (militarily or ideologically) the insurgency in the South (much as we are failing to do so in Iraq).

As the years went by in the South without any neutral peacekeepers and with a diminished role by the Federal Government, the new Reconstruction governments were greatly undermined by insurrections and weren't strong enough to defend themselves. It took a very long time to train a new police and state militia from the newly freed slaves and sharecroppers, and the recruits were a target for attack by the insurgents. The governments had to rely on the occupying power to defend both elected officials and the actual electorate.

This reliance on the occupying power only supported the insurgents" premise that these were illegitimate governments, dependent on outside forces, made up of a despised race or members of a despised religion (most of the occupying US army in the South were Black soldiers or poor Irish-Catholic immigrants only recently arriving in the U.S.). Despite early success at brutal suppression of the KKK uprisings, the seeds were sown for future infiltration by the group. As the lynching and the bombings continued, and the new governments were chastised by the Democratic Party presses, public support in the North for the continued military occupation of the South collapsed. Most voters in the North wanted to bring our troops home right away.

- In reflecting the new public mood, President Grant (the same one who led the Union policy of attrition that destroyed the Southern infrastructure) said, "What good is saving us Mississippi if it loses us Ohio?"

In 1876 the last of the troops were pulled out. Within twenty years of the disastrous war and Southern defeat, the original tyrannical power structure was back in place, and the former slaves were back into a place of near peonage. This white supremacist rule lasted almost unchecked for nearly eighty years. There is not the space here to adequately describe the tremendous human cost to this return of the old order in the South. The same issues of racism, poverty, and corruption were still ongoing in the 1950s, causing the Civil Rights movement to explode internally as a people's movement, almost 90 years after Reconstruction began!

- *Twenty-two African-Americans served in Congress from the end of the Civil War to the turn of the 20th Century, but no more African Americans were elected until 1928, and that congressman came from Illinois.
http://www.senate.gov/reference/reference_item/Outstanding_Afr_Am_Congress.htm

We certainly cannot hold on for ninety years in Iraq, nor can we hold on for five years. If this parallel between the

Reconstruction period and Iraq is valid, the momentary success of elections and new schools should not be seen as promising steps, but as somewhat expected results from the US occupation. However, like the first years of Reconstruction, if the insurgency in Iraq continues, the extensive lack of services continues, and there is extensive resentment of the US occupation forces, our presence may do more harm than good, even among those who welcomed the overthrow of Saddam Hussein.

The insurgents have modern day "scallywags" (those Iraqis working with the US) and "carpetbaggers" (Halliburton) to point to, adding fuel to their complaints and their pleas for support. All these factors seem to point to a potential repeat in Iraq of the establishment of "redeemer" governments of the American South after Reconstruction. And with the latest polls showing only about 35% support for American action in Iraq, we just know that many Republicans of today may soon be asking themselves:

- "What good is it to save Baghdad if it means losing Ohio?"

Renowned early Twentieth Century writer and political commentator H.L. Menken was once noted as saying, "for every difficult problem in the world there is a quick and easy solution that is absolutely wrong." Many prominent critics of the Iraq War are calling for us to "just bring our troops home," but no matter how emotionally soothing that may sound, it will fail to rectify the situation, and will likely make it worse.

Doing so will open wide the door to the return of a "redeemer" government in Iraq and create a terrorist haven that is a threat to the region. American popular opinion will eventually necessitate a withdrawal, but that withdrawal must be anticipated, and planned for accordingly. The Bush

Administration, now famous for failing to create an exit strategy, better adopt one very soon, or they will face the exact problems that they would face with immediate withdrawal.

The bottom line is that our soldiers cannot handle this situation on their own, and fortunately they may not have to do so for years to come. There are far more institutions in the world today than there were in 1865 that can react and participate in developing an acceptable resolution in Iraq. Perhaps John Kerry's call for the use of multinational and U.N. peacekeepers isn't such a bad idea. It beats spending $100 billion a year on a war we are clearly unable to win.
We can no longer reject help from the United Nations and other countries for fear that they may reap some of the supposed benefits. If we simply leave Iraq all alone, there will be no benefits.

 We must watch Iraq externally, and prevent outside forces from moving across the border, but we need multinational peacekeepers to move in, so this isn't seen as an entirely American or Western industrialized effort. So, even if we pay for multinational troops this option will be far cheaper than "staying the course," as President Bush wants to do.

If the UN is in control of the occupation, it is no longer "US imperialism" supporting the new government, but a worldwide effort. The UN can be in places for years as peacekeepers, and so on, without rousing world or local anger. And through the UN, this force could be predominately Muslim (with obvious benefits to the overall situation, as well as limiting al Qaeda's appeal in keeping the situation untenable).

Unfortunately for American oil companies, they are going to need to move out if any success is to be achieved. Their presence garners hatred and violence that benefits no one, regardless of the profits they are reaping (and not sharing with the American or Iraqi public).

The more other nations are involved, the more resources are available and the more likely that the new government will be supported by the world. We failed to support the democracy process in the South one hundred and twenty years ago, and paid a great price for it in lost human dignity, lost lives, and allowing racism to flourish for many years afterward.

We now have another chance to support democracy, and, with the current world situation, our failure to do so may lead to not just a return to non-democratic Iraq, but a political disaster that has tremendous consequences for the future of the United States. Eventually we can withdraw our troops, but simply "bringing the troops home now" failed in 1876 and it will fail now. Let us for once learn a lesson from our own history, so we can actually make good use of the institutions we now criticize but which could actually help us. If we care about our soldiers, our country, and the world, we must utilize the resources they offer, and allow the institution we created for these types of problems to assist in the cause for a Democratic Iraq – the United Nations.

Setting the Stage

This essay was written at the height of the Obama health care debate. A far shorter version was eventually published, as a letter to the editor in the local major paper in Buffalo, New York. Here I essentially argue that at times, during intense negotiations that require eventual compromises, less public scrutiny during the process, is best. I look at how the media of today locks politicians into fixed positions in the public forum, often making compromises impossible. I review the process of the creation of the US Constitution and all the compromises that were needed to create that document, and wonder if such a process is possible today. I ask if we had the media of today, then, would we have a government or even a nation now.

Would We Have Our Constitution in the Age of Mass Media?

As we see this national debate on health care move into near-violent confrontations in town meetings (whether orchestrated or not), we need to see this process as part of democracy and part of the legislative process. However, what is "unfair" about the media's coverage of the current process is that the type of coverage we get from today's instant-gratification media, limits, not encourages, the very thing we need in this time of national crisis: free and open civil discussion. By focusing on the "media friendly" people aimed at showing outrage at the proposals being considered, and by trying to lock in the politicians into "unchangeable positions" early in the process of creating a law, and by spreading unsupported statements in a near-instant fashion, without challenge, the media limit the politicians' ability to actually do their job, which is to create a workable compromise on health care that will benefit as many Americans as possible.

This "rush to cover" and this "push to define a position" make the development of such compromises impossible; and it leads me to the question: would we have our Constitution, or even a nation, if the media of today existed in the late 19th century? After all, the development of the Constitution was actually an "extra-legal" event. The people who held the constitutional convention had no real authority to do so; the original purpose of the meeting was to settle trade disputes between some states. Imagine the media frenzy about the document on that point alone.

In addition, the debates in the meetings, over "the big states plan," "the small states plan," or how to address slavery, etc., were kept absolutely secret for some five months. Today, I am not sure something in D.C. can be kept secret for five seconds. How could compromise be reached if the members of the constitutional convention were forced into "locked in" positions early in the process, by media frenzy? We would never have reached the great compromises such as the "separation of powers" and the "people's House" and "state's Senate" under such pressure.

And what is not remembered is that when all the compromises were placed together and what we have now as a "Constitution" was presented to the public, it was a huge bomb, and nearly failed. We had then the equivalency of "town hall" debates across the country and extensive (for those days) media coverage and debate through a series of papers we now know as the "Federalist Papers." But less known today is that there was equally well-argued presentation against the proposed new "too much potential for government taking over our lives" constitution, now collectively called the "Anti-Federalist papers."

What we basically don't remember in our social history is that "Federalist" supporters of the proposed initial constitution, actually lost the public debate and the constitution was about to go down in flames, until the proponent agreed to a compromise of what we now call the "Bill of Rights" Imagine the wild arguments between pundits and just plain people over what was meant by "freedom of speech" or "right to bear arms," or what was in fact "cruel and unusual punishment" if we had the mass media of today back then. Imagine the talk shows we could have had on the radio or TV or discussion through Twitter on these points alone, with James Madison debating Sam Adams.

In fact, if we had to create a new Constitution today, or just pass the one we do have, the current state of the media would make it impossible. There could be no fair or clear debate, just media focus on anyone who was angry and a focus on those telling the greatest lies using the best (sound bite) rhetoric.

It is time that the media took a more constructive role in this health care debate by giving the public perspective and understanding, the sequence a great national debate needs to go through to reach a national consensus (through debate and compromise). The media should be supporting free and open discussions by helping people understand the nature of the debate, not by helping to close the process for good debate by focusing on the most extreme "photogenic" people. The media should be helping politicians to do their work, and therefore meet the needs of the people of this nation; the media should not to make it impossible to reach consensus.

Setting the Stage

We as a nation tend to over-react to events that seem to happen to us. As is the general theme of many of these essays, that over-reaction while in part normal on some physiological level, interferes with our abilities to work with other nations, or understand why we are either experiencing the events or the cause of these events, and perhaps worse; the consequences of our responses to these events.

This essay takes full aim at one of the more recent crisis in our history; that of the "economic melt-down" of 2008 or what was later called the "Great Recession." The purpose of this essay is not to look for the cause or the impacts politically or personal of the events, but to try and evaluate the crisis in terms of American and world history. It is an effort, to put the crisis and the response to the events, in perspective compared with other past occurrences, and perhaps more importantly, real disasters that have impacted most of the peoples of the world.

In order to attempt to do justice to this effort, I have to look at the concept of "American Exceptionalism" from a different view. Here in this essay, I use the term to show that much of America's abundance, and our traditions of democracy, is more based on the lack of "disasters" which have plagued the rest of the world, as opposed to something that was inherently present in the American culture from the beginning.

Yes, there is something different about Americans; we were fortunate to avoid a whole host of events that drove other cultures into ruin and despotism. We as a nation mostly avoided the issues discussed, and where we did not avoid them, the consequences were such that we appear like all the other peoples who experienced these disasters.

The primary example, although by far not the only, is the US South;

- Where the tradition of slavery was followed by the institutionalization of racism, and anti-democratic government (single party rule, with exclusion of minority voting rights) with a form of state terror (both legal through the police and semi-legal through the Klan.)

The traditional meaning and use of the term "American Exceptionalism" does not include this "South" and its "un-American activities." My effort to reframe its use, does so to a degree by asking what the US would truly be like if we had to deal with these disasters that other places were inflected by. My answer tends to be we would not be "exceptional" but more or less like all others who have faced them. Therefore the basic reason for this exceptionalism is that we were mostly free of the disasters.

However, again, the main goal of the essay is to show that without a foundation in a real understanding of history (both our own and the world's), and without skewed view of our exceptionalism our reactions to events are seen by other peoples of the world in a wide range of negativism. As I say, here, often we look like "a nation of wimps." Such a view cannot possible be to our advantage.

America in Time of Crisis – Or America Has No Sense of History

Part I - A Different View of Now

We, in the United States in the beginning of the second decade of the twenty-first century of the Common Era, are experiencing economic and political conflicts that seem to be overwhelming and perhaps irreversible. We look at record deficit spending and unstable housing and stock markets, as well as unprecedented numbers of homeowners facing bank foreclosure, and, of course, unaccustomedly high unemployment. Things seem very bad and, relative to the past half-century, they are very difficult indeed.

However, with a little evaluation we could really say that these times are not as difficult as:

- the period of "stagflation" of the late 1970s when we had roughly 15% inflation and 15% interest rates, or
- the Great Depression, which lasted almost a decade, and saw more than 1/3 of the workforce with sustained unemployment or
- the mid- to late-1960s where we had almost every major city erupting into riots during those "long hot summers" or
- the time of Jim Crow with one-quarter of the country overtly defying the Constitutional rights of minorities, and forcing one-third of its population to live in overt fear and abject poverty.

In addition the unemployment rates that scare us so much are lower than what is considered the norm for most of Europe.

Nor are we (any longer) living in a world where most of the people are controlled by horrid dictatorships, and we send seven million soldiers into harm's way to keep the Fascists and Militarists from taking over the rest of the world (even though in doing so we helped the colonialists maintain their empires for a while). Nor do we live in a MAD (mutually assured destruction) time, as we did while attempting to avoid a new general war as we waited for Communism to implode.

- Nor do we live in a world where we were the nation using weapons of mass destruction against defenseless cities and peoples (not just the A-Bomb, but firebombing in WWII and Viet Nam and poisonous defoliants in Viet Nam).

Today, in the face of this economic crisis, through our interventions and through abilities created by our wealth and institutions, we were able to avert the predicted collapse. It was frightening to watch, but the worst was avoided. We could and did forestall the "collapse" and therefore allowed "the market to correct itself."

In addition, unlike past "panics" and depressions, when a crisis would result in massive forced evictions that left millions of families without shelter and without any social services to support them (other than some religious efforts); where in this nation we saw real starvation and mass camp cities of the homeless; where our roads and railroads were filled with "Okies" and hobos, hopeless wanderers looking for any work, and our jails filled with the destitute, guilty of petty stealing just to try and survive; now there were hard times.

- Now, unlike the two hundred or so years prior to the Franklin Roosevelt administrations, we have unemployment, social security, welfare and dozens of other support methods to help keep families together and functioning during the economic hard times.

So even if the worst had come, it would not have resulted in the same deprivations as the "Great Depression."

In reality, no matter how hard it seems to get by in the United States, we as a nation and we as a people have tended to be far better off than most of the rest of the world, even in the worst of our times.

- Today, still about one third to one fifth (based on various estimates) of the world's population live on the equivalent of $1.00 a day.

Never mind looking at the world today; if we look at the people alive today and in the United States, and compare them to all other people who ever lived (about five billion people before this current time), even the worst off of us seem to be far better off than almost all who came before.

- This is a reality that Americans forget, or, perhaps better stated, just does not understand.

This is not to justify the economic disparity or unjustness that exists in the US now, or the corporate malfeasance and lack of government oversight that has led us to this point; it is intended as a simple statement of fact. It is trying to look at the current times not from the view of an individual but from the view of a people.

Virtually everyone in the US is far better off than those who ever lived before this time.

- This paper addresses only some of the political issues that are involved in this claim.
- The issues of technological differences and access to entertainment and work and travel, and the medical advancements, etc. that justify the claim of being so much better off, are just too obvious and will not be discussed here.

These amazing and rapid levels of technical advancements starting about 1900 have so changed the world; the discussion of this is simply not needed.

When we as a nation complain bitterly about our current crisis or project the potential of loss to the American standard of life, and through technology it is instantaneously heard by so many in the world whose lives would be so much better off by having "nothing" in America, compared to "nothing" in their land, we sound to the rest of the world as if we are a nation of wimps.

I understand many will not agree with this perspective. I know many think that this economic event is the worst event of their lives. And on the individual level, for many people alive today, who are not old enough to have personally experienced the events stated, this may be a true perspective. . However, we must learn to look beyond ourselves and our personal lives, to the greater perspective and ask:

- When we really consider all the things that have occurred to all people who have ever lived and all the people outside of the United States who are alive today, how does this economic event really fit into world history, or even American history?

Does the fact that this may indeed by the worst of times for some people, speak more to how "great" the times have been, rather than how bad the times actually are, when measured on some scale other than one's personal experience?

To fully do such an evaluation of the moment, we need to ask a series of questions about this crisis that simply cannot be answered here for lack of space and time, and of course the multiple answers possible for each of the questions. These questions include;

- What caused this event?
- Who benefited and how and why? and

- What can be done to try and avoid such things happening again?

Without the space and that perspective, what we are left with is asking the question:

- How bad is bad?

We can also speculate on the roots of the answer to this question, and the impact of our answers on not just ourselves but the world.

Of course the answer to "how bad is bad" is completely relative to individual experience and opinion; and of course knowledge of something other than your own life. . Here within this paper, I attempt to give a perspective based, not on the individual here and now, or even on a country's here and now, or on the collective short-term memory of the people of that country, but on the history of humankind.

Part II – No Sense of History

We in America today have such short and restrictive views of history, and in particular the history of the "common" person throughout time.

- We as a people, and we as a nation simply have no sense of history – our own and, even more so, the history of other peoples and other times.

We seem to judge each current crisis against the "norm" or, better said, the "myth" of the 1950s and therefore our evaluations of the issues and impact are all based on that "outlier" period of this nation's history.

Through the message of our media, and our own inability to see beyond ourselves and our time, we imagine that the American experience of the mythical 1950s is the true picture of all American's life for all of our history. We have also roughly judged that most of the rest of the "civilized" world was living a life something akin to the US, only a little more "primitive" or "quaint."

- As for the "uncivilized" sections of the world, we as a people historically cared little about them, except to keep them quiet and not communist.

There is not the space to justify the statement of the 1950s being an outlier period, but based on that premise:

- one of the basic laws of science is you should not generalize from the outliers.
- Therefore the general perceptions of Americans are flawed; through this view we assume so many false concepts.

Just a few of them include:

- the US and maybe Western Europe are always way ahead of the "savage" East and Africa.
- the West has always been the setter of culture, and
- the "others" always have wanted to take our things.

With no sense of history and holding these truly unsupported views, we are not only kept from making good decisions in the present, but we have a skewed view of such things as the current economic crisis and its impact.

The consequences of basing our current views on a myth are many, but to state the most obvious;

- we don't understand what is happening to us, and
- we don't understand how the rest of the world views not only what is happening to us, but how we are reacting to the event.

When we attempt to generalize from the outlying and when we also deny a people's history or simply are unwilling to learn their history, we cannot possibly understand their view of the world.

Part III - The Real American Exceptionalism

We often hear the term "American Exceptionalism" and think of it in terms of the US being a free nation, once independent, never subject to tyranny, and built on the rule of law. The term also refers to the idea of the freedoms which Americans have encoded into the rule of law. This exceptionalism is supposed to serve as a "shining city on a hill" to the rest of the world, or a "beacon of democracy."

I would offer that there is something more to this concept. We have been able, maybe as an accident of history, or maybe just as a matter of distance from other continents, to maintain this democracy and these freedoms mainly because we have also been free from the great "disasters" of the "old world." More than likely it is because we have not had these disasters that the other elements of our "exceptionalism" are possible.

Who can say what the US would be like if we had had just a few of these "old world disasters" as part of our history?

Judging from our response to 9/11 and this recent economic crisis, it's not hard to tell. We'd more than likely be close to a dictatorship and hardly be seen as an economic or social model. In fact we would be very similar to all the countries that did experience these disasters. (And the history of the US

South would be the more general history of the US – institutional racism, state terror on a major level and anti-democratic state with single party rule and minorities excluded.)

Where to begin in explaining these "disasters"?

I need to define my terms. This can perhaps best be started through an example explaining how we were first perceived by the rest of the world as a place where a person could come and be "better off."

The North American continent offered vast amounts of "empty" lands available due in large part to the die-off of the native peoples from war and the infections brought by the West.

- Therefore many of the "common people" coming to North America could and did have great economic success when compared to most of the people who remained in the "old world." The newly arriving person could have land in unimaginable amounts to those still in the "old world."

However, it was not just that there was land; it was land in which the common people could have ownership and mostly keep what they developed.

The first disaster that was avoided here, was the land was not gobbled up by "nobility" and churches, a practice that so dominated Europe. The common people, by coming here, could keep some 60% of the product of their efforts that went directly to the claims of the "church and state" in the old country.

Those (non-enslaved people that is) who came to America usually lived significantly better than their counterparts in other places in the world, because there was so much land to be had, and all the resources on the land (and under the land) was claimed by "common people."

The hand of government and church were distant and became more so as people moved west. Often there was simply no right of the nobles and church class to claim such taxes as those traditionally imposed on the old world peoples. And when they did try to tax, even on a mild level when compared to how others in the "old world were taxed the answer of the people was revolution.

This avoidance of "disaster" of consumption by the nobles and the church, helped to make people better off, but the real "disasters of the old world" that we, in what became the United States, mostly avoided were issues that really addressed life and death. This really did make "life" far better simply through the extension of life, and a relative sense that the extension of life was the norm.

Some of the other "life and death disasters" include:

- State-sponsored terror concerning religion and loyalty to the State
- Forced recruitment into armies,
- Mass devastations caused by wars,
- Famine, and
- Uncontrolled epidemics.

While the great powers did fight over North America, and there were wars with the native peoples, for the most part the major powers fought with armies in the field and not sacking towns (as was the custom in Europe), and the natives were never numerous or armed well enough to be a major threat.

Somewhat later, portions of the American south were devastated by the "total war" campaign in the later parts of the Civil War. And both North and South took relatively heavy losses. But this was more or less a single occurrence and relatively localized.

So while many newcomers to what became the US did not always advance economically that much, they primarily lived far better lives and longer lives because they were basically freed from tyrannical and uncaring governments (based in the concept of nobility), and now located in an area where the population density tended to limit or eliminate epidemics. In addition, while the immigrants could not always afford a great deal of food, there seemingly was almost always food available.

While subject in theory to a king, there was far too much land and food in the forests that, unlike in Europe, no king or noble could claim all the game of the forest as theirs.

In theory then, none in North America would go hungry if they had a rifle to hunt and access to the woods nearby. (For many, this was just in theory and many, far fewer than their counterparts did go hungry in the colonial period and beyond.)

- There is one story about Brazil that exemplifies the difference between the Old and New Worlds. There, where beef was so plentiful, beggars would curse those who gave them steaks rather than some cash.

These security items, freedom from state terror (including terror based in religious issues), freedom from the massive destruction from wars, freedom from extensive famine and epidemics may sound very common to those living in America today, since for the most part the people of the US have been free from these things, but these freedoms are very rare in world history.

Because of the freedom from these "old world disasters," unlike any other people in the present or in history, we as a people die in our own homes (or hospitals or "rest homes") or as a result of accidents or illness ... not in some massive "die-off" directly related to one of these "old world disasters."

- This is really the American exceptionalism. For the most part, we live lives relatively free of disasters. (And when disasters happen our government is there to help.)

While this freedom from major disasters is truly an exception in history (not quite unique to the US experience, but almost), we seem to have little understanding of or even empathy for these "disasters'" impacts on other peoples' history.

Without experiencing these things ourselves, we seem to have no sense of history and fail to understand how peoples whose histories are so filled with disasters act so differently than us.

We as a people are generous to others in the moment, in response to modern current events, such as famine or tsunami but fail to see how the past disasters continue to shape the cultures and needs of other nations.

Part IV - World History in Context

While the vast majority of Americans have no sense of history, or a sense of history warped by myths and right wing propaganda, we can safely say that the experiences of the people of the United States are so different than that of the rest of the world because of what we know from actual and provable history and can compare America's history to the history of others.

Let's point to the most obvious fact that proves this "American Exceptionalism":

- Some 80% of the deaths of all people who ever lived were "violent deaths" directly related to the "disasters of the old world" with these disasters being "exported" all over the globe.

Of course people can quibble over the meaning of "violent deaths," but in the case of this argument it simply means "premature" deaths cause in some form of "die-off" (either in a mass fashion or a slow rolling process based on continuing conditions).

Therefore, using this definition we can include deaths from:

- famine, or
- the result of a natural disaster, or
- war (including civil wars and internal revolts) or as a result of war, or
- state terror, or state-supported terror against its own people, or
- an epidemic (including drug addiction and its consequences) or,
- the impact of being enslaved and worked to death (slavery of all kinds, including serfs).

And in addition, the particular female-focused disasters of:

- death in the process of giving birth, due to lack sanitation for the procedure and other complications often due to multiple pregnancies (with no birth control available) and

- the custom of domestic violence which has (and does in some cultures still) allow men (husbands/fathers) to kill women (wives/daughters) without punishment; and
- rape and other forms of violent sexual assaults that can result in death; and
- consequences of the particular form of slavery now referred to as the "sex industry" or human trafficking; and
- the particular form of religious/state terror association with the accusation of witchcraft.

Using this list of causes, we can clearly say that "violent death" was the major cause of death of people for the whole history of the world. In fact we can say that four of the five billion people who ever lived prior to now, died "violent deaths."

- Obviously this cannot be said at all for people living in the United States today, or throughout its history.

These historical causes of most death are almost non-existent in our current society, with the exceptions of the AIDs epidemic, and the violence related to women. (But while the violence against women continues to exist, its status has shifted as social norms have changed dramatically.)

- While we did have slavery for much of our history, the slaves of North America were treated relatively better than the slaves in the rest of the Americas (where the life expectancy of a slave in the sugar areas, was about four years).
- The previous statement should not be seen as a justification or acceptance of slavery in any form, but should be seen as simply a statement of fact.

There are some new forms of violent death (auto and industrial accidents, gang warfare, assaults on the general public by "the lone nut" gunman, etc.), but they account for a relatively small number of deaths in the US. And the deaths from some of these things are relatively small when compared to relative issues from the past.

- The death rate in the US from drug addiction issues amounts to less than 1% over the last fifty years (not counting AIDS) compared to a comparable period in China during the "Opium Wars" period (say roughly 1815-65).
- It is estimated that at least fifty million Chinese were addicted to opium and at least ten million died as a direct impact of its use.

China, the rising power it is today, is a major competitor and partner for the US in this modern world.

It is important as we deal with China to understand that in a recent one hundred and fifty year time period (1830 – 1980), they had some 400 million violent deaths.

Today, we in the US tend to die from causes related to safety and abundance (heart attacks and diseases associated with both longevity and obesity). And despite occasional economic downturns, most Americans live relatively comfortable lives, especially when compared to at least four billion of the six billion people alive today and definitely compared to most of the five billion humans who lived up to this time.

- The American type of death and this level of comfort are completely unprecedented in world history.

Those people who lived before us really did have "hard times," and died in the most terrible of times and in terror.

Therefore, relatively speaking, the economic issues that we as Americans are living though today do not even reach the threshold of "real hard times" when compared to world history, and compared to the daily struggles of much of the world's population today.

With a real sense of history, we in this "time of troubles" would realize that our cities are not being burned and ransacked by alien armies; nor are our crops destroyed; nor are our own leaders torturing and murdered; nor are our people publically burned for non-belief in a certain religion.

And when we have issues and problems, we respond differently based on our exceptionalism.

So in recent times:

- We have had two major cities impacted by storms (Nashville and New Orleans), and several others in the past, but the people were not abandoned to starve, and insurance and governments have worked to help rebuild the places.

(And President Bush was severely hurt politically for seeming indifference to the destruction of New Orleans.)

- We face unemployment, but none have been forced into slavery based on their new unemployment status (with the exception of the sex slave world).
- We have a massive wave of new immigrants, but they come without weapons and are not destroying our armies and sacking our cities.
- We have an expanding government that to some seems too large and intrusive, but compared to the great tyrannies of the world, it comes nowhere close to ruling in an autocratic and violent manner.

It would seem that in comparison to the history of the world, Americans and those who live in America today are still living lives of security and abundance beyond the expectation of almost all who lived before.

Yes, we have troubles and need reforms on many levels. Yes, we have new rivals for lives of luxury and security (such as Scandinavia and the Gulf Emirates). Yes, we have new economic rivals (such as India and China).

But we need to see that:

Yes, we do live in wonderful times, when compared to all who have lived before.

To the rest of the world, who now hear all of our reactions to this economic crisis and the fact that so many of our people believe this is the "worst time ever," this overstatement of the crisis makes them see us as an ignorant and arrogant people.

- Our current obsession with zombie and movies about losing all of our power sources and returning us to a per-technological age; and the popularity of games that invite use to go to war with other developing cultures, is in fact based on our ignorance of what that type of disaster would mean to billions of humans who will die. What we have avoided we are seeking vicariously. Amazing!

And in this world, what "those people" think of us is highly important. We need to get them on "our side" through respecting them and their history and acknowledging the impact of the disasters of the past. And that starts with redefining American Exceptionalism as being lucky enough to have avoided so many of the "disasters" that they have gone through in the past.

We need to see that American Exceptionalism, the freedom from the disasters of the past, is truly a luxury that has enabled American wealth to develop as it has. Our goal as a nation is not to preach democracy per se but to work with peoples around the world to find a way to help spread the concept of avoiding "human-made disasters." This starts by learning their history and fully acknowledging their history of disaster.

We can't win them over by overstating our problems, but by stating that almost nothing we are going through comes close to what has happened in the past or is happening right now to most people. . We need to acknowledge their history as valid and then ask:

- do you really want to go through another series of disasters again?

We can gain their support through a united effort to avoid state terror, war, and all the other old disasters of the past. . We avoided them and came out wealthy. . If they can avoid them again, perhaps the real American Exceptionalism can be universalized and no longer be that exceptional.

Part V - Supporting Facts –Democide

Of course we cannot avoid all disasters, such as those caused by "nature." However, of all the great causes of mass die-offs of humans in history, as discussed in this paper, most are human made and most can be avoided; again these include:

- famine
- the result of a natural disaster
- death in war or as a result of war
- state terror against its own people
- an epidemic

- issues directly related to women
- enslavement.

Historically, the one that should be the most easily controlled and avoided is perhaps state terror.

However, again historically, it seems that state terror could account for perhaps the greatest number of "violent deaths" in human history. The impact of epidemics is most likely the greatest killer, when you take into account the die-offs from the great plagues of Europe and the impact on the Americas. However, if we are talking of deliberately planned and executed mass die offs, state terror is definitely the leading cause of deaths.

Of course the determination of the leading cause of mass deaths is in part based on the definition of terms. Somewhat recently a new term was developed that looks at all aspects of state terror, and by using this definition it becomes clear that state terror is the leading cause of mass die- offs in the world. This term is "Democide."

Democide is defined as

- "The murder of any person or people by a government (or institutions similar to governments such as a national church), including such acts as genocide, politicide and mass murder. For example, government-sponsored killings for political reasons would be considered Democide. Democide can also include deaths arising from "intentionally or knowingly reckless and depraved disregard for life."
http://en.wikipedia.org/wiki/Democide

The three acts of mass killings that come under Democide are labeled and defined as:

- Genocide: among other things, the killing of people by a government because of their indelible group membership (race, ethnicity, religion, language).
- Politicide: the murder of any person or people by a government because of their politics or for political purposes.
- Mass Murder: the indiscriminate killing of any person or people by a government.

http://www.hawaii.edu/powerkills/DBG.CHAP2.HTM

Examples of modern Democide include, besides the better known Nazi death camps include:

- The Great Purge and Gulag systems in Soviet Union under Stalin – untold millions died.
- The Congo Free State management in the late 1890-1910 (an estimated 10 million died in slave labor.
- China in the late 1950s with Mao's Great Leap Forward, which resulted in famine that killed millions of people.

See http://en.wikipedia.org/wiki/Democide

The developer of this new concept of organization of government terror and killing, Professor R. J. Rummel, claims that in the 20th Century (actually into the late 1980s when he wrote):

- the death toll from Democide is far greater than the death toll from war.

Rummel estimates that there have been 262 million victims of Democide in the last century. According to his figures, six times as many people have died from (state terror) than have died in battle.

Rummel also state that in the 20th century (up until 1987) there were:

- Fifteen mega-murderers—those states killing in cold blood, aside from warfare, 1,000,000 or more men, women, and children.

These fifteen mega-murderers have wiped out over 151,000,000 people, almost four times the nearly 38,500,000 battle-dead for all this century's international and civil wars up to 1987.

- The most "absolute power" states, that is the communist U.S.S.R., China and preceding-Mao guerrillas, Khmer Rouge Cambodia, Viet Nam, and Yugoslavia, as well as fascist Nazi Germany, account for near 128,000,000 of them, or 84 percent.

http://www.hawaii.edu/powerkills/DBG.CHAP1.HTM

Besides mega-murderers, he also classifies lesser mass killings as kilo-murderers, or those states that have killed innocents by the tens or hundreds of thousands.

- These and other kilo-murderers add almost 15,000,000 more people killed by Democide for this century.

http://www.hawaii.edu/powerkills/DBG.CHAP1.HTM

And the concept of Democide, while new, can now be applied to previous events in history. One of the more noted examples highlighted by this approach is the African slave trade.

- Overall, in five centuries, Europeans, Arabs, Asians, and African slave traders, possibly murdered nearly 17,000,000 Africans, perhaps even over 65,000,000.

http://www.hawaii.edu/powerkills/DBG.CHAP3.HTM

But prior to the 20th century the "honor" for the mega deaths of people went to the Mongols who, in some less than one hundred and fifty years of domination, killed in unbelievable, but validated, numbers (or as close to validated as we can determine).

- The Mongol khans and their successors and pretenders possibly slaughtered around 30,000,000 Persian, Arab, Hindu, Russian, Chinese, European, and other men, women, and children....
- According to a Chinese writer, "in gaining and maintaining his throne {Khubilai Khan} slaughtered more than 18,470,000" Chinese

http://www.hawaii.edu/powerkills/DBG.CHAP3.HTM

Although not competing in numbers with those massacred in Asia and the Americas, Europeans had their share of such genocidal massacres.

- An illustrative case is the St. Bartholomew massacre. On August 24th, 1572, [The Catholic French king] ... unleashed a slaughter of French Calvinists ... with estimates ... that 300,000 were killed; later estimates reduced this to 100,000, then 36,000.

http://www.hawaii.edu/powerkills/DBG.CHAP3.HTM

While the use of mass terror and Democide seems almost universal in human history, we can see from quick review of the Mongols and the other events described that Democide was in large part based in fear. Or perhaps the justifications for such acts were presented in forms of self-protection and in statements of fear of the "other."

For example, the Mongols killed in great numbers for two reasons. The Mongols were an invading force, conquering peoples with vastly greater numbers than themselves, therefore;

- they feared a mass resistance. To intimidate the next peoples in the line of march not to resist, they would slaughter whole cities as a warning; and
- they feared being overwhelmed by the newly subjected people; they often killed to eliminate the "surplus populations" that were too numerous for them to control or to govern.

The Christians in Europe stated that they killed for fear also. One of the major reasons for state terror in Europe was the fear that without religious conformity the wrath of God would return and punish them as He had punished the old kingdoms of Israel and Judah.

(And yes, there were political and economic issues as well, also based in fear, fear of peasant revolts, of neighboring peoples encroaching into their homelands, fear of commercial rivals and so on and so on.)

- For example, in Spain, the Catholic Monarchs, as they were labeled by the Popes, saw themselves surrounded by religious issues which caused them fear:
- fear of the Turks threatening Europe;
- fear of the heretics at home (secret Jews and Muslims, and backsliding conversos);
- fear of the "heretics" of the "reformed church" in their wide range of territories in Europe, and
- fear of the meaning of the heathens in the newly discovered lands of the Americas (resulting struggle over whether they had souls or not; whether to "save" them or enslave them).

The rulers of Spain believed that to not fight these forces of "evil" through creation of complete religious conformity in all the lands they now governed was tantamount to assuring destruction of themselves by God.

- In the eyes of Spain all actions to keep God happy were justified.

Some of the early efforts included extending the power of the Inquisition. Hundreds of thousands of Jews and Muslims and converts were killed or "cleansed" from their home land, all in the name of "state security," or as it was then called, the need for religious uniformity.

- The Spanish Inquisition established in 1480 …from 1483 to 1498 …may have burned to death as many as 10,220 heretics in total.
- Over the centuries in Spain, 125,000 persons possibly died from torture and privation in prison (due to charges based in religion).
- From 1480 to 1808 the "official count" of persons burned to death totaled 31,912. During the most intensive years of the Inquisition about 500 people per year also may have been burned to death in the New World (which could mean as many as 50,000 more persons).

http://www.hawaii.edu/powerkills/DBG.CHAP3.HTM

This review of Spanish state terror is by no means intended to say the Protestants did not quickly impose such tools, and, again, often based on their efforts to bring about "heaven on earth." The Protestants used tactics of Democide especially against women.

- The Catholic Church's attempt to purge heretics had its counterpart in the Reformation Protestant's campaign

against witches. Witches were believed to have sold their soul to the devil for magical powers.
- In some German cities historians estimate that as many as 900 "witches" in a year were killed, often after agonizing torture to force out confessions; in some villages, hardly a women was left alive.

In total, throughout Christendom more than 30,000 "witches" may have been killed. Taking into account the routine nature of these killings, the final figure may be around 100,000; it might even reach 500,000.
http://www.hawaii.edu/powerkills/DBG.CHAP3.HTM

Therefore using this concept of Democide, the efforts of the Church look relatively normal in the stream of world cultural history. And put in the context of world history, the attacks on non-believers or questionable converts may not match the "mega deaths" of the twentieth century, but were extensive and dominated the cultures of the time.

There is a need to say a bit more about Democide and slavery. We in America do not understand that in most places and in most times in history slavery was not based on color, or race; anyone could be a slave. And in some places almost everyone was a slave.

- A good third to a half of the population of the Roman Empire was classified as "slave."
- Serfs were in fact just another name for slaves bound to the land with no freedom. And for some five hundred years almost all non-nobles or military or church members in Europe were considered serfs, and therefore slave.

While there was a fading of that institution in Western Europe over time, in Russia this continued for millions of persons until about 1860.

Careful study of immigration into the "New World" over its first 350 years (from about 1500 to 1850) shows that some 87% of all people coming to all of the New World (not just what is now the US) were slaves or indentures. . Only 13% came as free people.

- Taken as a whole, the true picture of the New World for its first three hundred years or so was one of a massive slave death camp working to produce gold and sugar.

Once again, what was considered the waste lands that eventually became the United States (and Canada as well) was the exception.

It is clear that, for so many of the five billion who ever lived before this time, who managed to avoid a violent death from war or famine or plague, they lived out their lives as slaves, in dire conditions being worked to death, with little or no rights (and, for women, as absolute subjects to sexual desires of their masters).

In the eyes of the state and often the Church and even the reformed church, the slave was a non-person and, for the most part, not subject to any protections. We can therefore see the entire institution of slavery and all aspects of it as part of a process of Democide.

Part VI – Reconsidering Our Way of Looking at "Hard Times"

Compared to this… how do we assess states of mind or quality of life of various times and the sense of well-being of various cultures?

That is such a difficult question. Yes, the history of the world has been horrible. Yes, it is great that the people of the United States have mostly avoided the intense horrors of the past.

So, is it OK that we people of the United States don't know about or understand the horrors of the past? I obviously think not.

The American people, in order to make better choices about the present, truly need to know and understand the past. A perfect example of this poor understanding is our view of the current economic issues.

- The idea that our country is living through the "worst of times," or "the end days" in comparison to, not just the past of hundreds of years ago, but even the past of this last century, is, well, silly is perhaps the nicest word I can use; absurd is better.

Our self-absorbed and limited vision of these times actually can be seen as a national security issue, since our failure to understand what others have been through makes others hate us.

The old term, the "ugly American," was used to define a people ignorant of other's culture and history. That ignorance is no longer just the international jokes about Americans' lack of table manners or poor choice of wine, but potentially a source of international miscommunications and also potentially a tool for recruitment of terrorists.

In addition, that ignorance helps create a sense of fear at home. . This fear allows for the media and politicians of the Right Wing to continue to exploit people's ignorance, to build a false impression of the failure of America and the "crisis" that exists.

These are the fears that undermine what we can call the American Exceptionalism, and lead to the threat of state terror here at home. The drumbeat of the Right Wing media is this fear and the image of this being the "worst of times." Without this fear, what power would they have? Without this fear, where is the justification for war and state terror?

We need to inform and teach our people that where we live and when we live is so vastly different than our violent past. We need to show that, in just the last twenty-five years or so, we have, not just in the United States, but through American leadership throughout the world:

- Limited and controlled famine;
- Responded quickly to the result of a natural disaster;
- Stopped or at least limited the impacts of wars;
- Ended the state terror against its own people that existed in the Communist and Right Wing dictatorships in dozens of countries;
- Prevented massive die-off from epidemics;
- Introduced modern childbirth methods throughout most of the world;
- Stopped what remained of slavery in many areas of the world, and recognized and have taken steps against "debt slavery" in places such as India and the "human trafficking" of millions of women in what is politely called the "sex industry."

Today, none of what was once considered the norm or acceptable in these areas is now viewed as right or justified by "God's will" or to appease God, or, in fact, "right" in any fashion.

While some cling to these old concepts and see the impact of hurricanes as warnings against sin, most understand that it is more a natural "natural disaster." The responses to these events are no longer calls by the state and main religions to kill the non-believers and sinners among us, but to get aid and relief to the victims of the events.

Yes, Democides still continue, with recent ones in the Balkans, in several central African countries, in Sudan, Iraq, South Africa and the Russian state of Chechnya. Yet the responses to these have been vastly different than in the past.
There were international responses to most of them. Sudan was divided; Serbia was also divided, and South Africa peacefully transitioned to a more democratic state. Saddam Hussein overthrown (with great number of deaths not in the war to do so, but in the tragic aftermath with the US failing to deal with the struggle for power created by the ending of the dictatorship.)

Relatively speaking, the world no longer expects nor accepts Democide as the right of a state to control its own people, or a conquered people. Even the most limited acts of Democide are roundly condemned, and when possible are acted against.

Of course this new world view and the ending of these causes for mass die-offs have consequences that were foreseeable, but still not acted against. These issues, such as overpopulation; and global warming (in part brought on by providing the needs of the increased population, i.e. burning fossil fuels for seven billion people as opposed to the two billion population of a century ago), overuse of antibiotics, destruction of rain forests and so many more created new dangers for the world. . These new issues may lead to a new form of horrible die-offs. Our popular entertainment is filled with such predictions. Yet what is clear is that the old die-offs and their causes, and the potential new die-offs based on potential outcomes of new problems we face, all of these are far more horrific then the financial crisis we face now. Therefore:

- We are not currently living in horrible or even terrible times.

We have had a difficult financial event, in which actions were taken to lessen its impact, and the interventions seemed to have worked. (The car industry survived, Wall Street is rebounding, consumer confidence is rising, etc.)

For individuals with the direst impacts, there are safety nets in place that have prevented mass starvation and homelessness (which would have been common from a similar financial event in the past).

Many of the foreclosed homes were in fact second and third homes of well-off families. And the fact that so many people own their own home (most for the first time) is actually a sign of that wealth created by American Exceptionalism. Their loss of their homes is personally tragic, but not socially catastrophic. They have options that will allow them to find living situations that are still far better than perhaps 70% of the world's population.

Of course it is difficult when facing a personal problem to compare you to anyone else; especially to everyone who ever lived. . But we as a nation and we as a people cannot just look at things as if we are individuals. When issues such as the financial crisis occur, we need to face it and take steps to address the causes and impacts, but we must not overreact with spectacular rhetoric and claims of catastrophe, putting the event among the worst things that ever happened.

These responses show we simply have no sense of history and that we need a sense of fear to respond well.
The overblown responses show the rest of the world we are simply a people ignorant of the past and disrespectful of their histories. It also shows that we fail to understand how exceptional the United States really has been in world history.

As a modern nation, we should not require fear nor require overblown rhetoric to deal with a crisis. We need to assure our people that, in the light of things, this may be difficult but resolvable, and we will do so by not blaming others, and taking our fears out on the other, nor by resorting to war and repression, but by rational and real interventions and supports to our people to avoid traditional tragic events of past governments.

We must take advantage of our exceptionalism and not scare ourselves and alienate others when problems arise. These times are difficult but not a disaster.

Part VII - Addendum – The extent of mass death events during a relatively short time in Europe

This short overview is an adaptation of lists of events found at http://en.wikipedia.org/wiki/Centuries

With this list I try to offer an understanding of how many died violent deaths as a result of the other causes of major die-offs, this list only looks as some of the events that happened in the 14th to 17th centuries, mostly in Europe.

In the area of plagues and famines:

- As a result of the Little Ice Age, a massive famine hits Europe killing millions (known as the Great Famine of 1315-17)
- Black Death kills almost half the population of Europe (1347-1351). Russia descended into anarchy during the Time of Troubles (1598-1613): Millions die from starvation and plagues.
- As a result of "first contact" between "Old" and "New" world, with Christopher Columbus founding Spain's first New World colony on Hispaniola in 1492, over the next fifty years there is a 90% die off of Mesoamericans population. (Estimates range from 25 million to 100 million deaths of indigenous peoples.)

In the area of Church state terror:

- The Lollards heresy rises in England and meets with extensive repression.
- The Great Schism begins in 1378, eventually leading to three simultaneous popes. All peoples of Christendom are condemned by at least two popes at the same time. Each pope uses terror tactics to try and gain support from opposition.
- The Spanish Inquisition begins in 1481 (eventually publically burning or at least torturing tens of thousands).
- Jews are expelled from Spain in 1492, Moors in 1609, resulting in hundreds of thousands or religious refugees.
- Pompanio Algerio, a radical theologian, is publically executed in Rome by boiling in oil in 1556 as part of the ongoing Roman Inquisition.

In the area of a strong central state terror:

- In 1531-32 the king of England seizes control of most of England's Roman Church property and wealth, claims right of being the head of the Church. . Decades of state executions follow in the name of religion.
- To consolidate state power Catherine de'Medici instigates the St. Bartholomew Day massacre, which takes the lives of tens of thousands of Huguenots (Protestants). . The violence spreads from Paris to other cities and the countryside resulting in an extensive and prolonged French civil war (1585 to 1604), with the central French state becoming the power in the land.
- James the First in 1614 dissolves the Parliament, basically claiming absolute powers for the king.
- Cardinal Richelieu of France, in 1614 closes the French Parliament (the States-General) and claims absolute power for the King (Louis XIII).

In the area of "political" wars:

- The Hundred Years' War between England and France (with many other powers involved) starts in 1377.
- After the Great Plague, the Peasants Revolt followed.
- Extensive English civil war called War of the Roses rages off and on for thirty years (1455-85).
- Extensive Italian wars between city states lasting nearly sixty years leads to consolidations political and economic disaster (1494-1559).
- Spanish conquest of Mexico and Peru kills millions and creates a massive need for new labor to work the now near empty lands -- starting in 1519. . Soon the Spanish started "importing" slaves from Africa to solve labor shortages.

- Inspired by Luther, massive peasant uprisings in Central Europe result in tens of thousands of deaths (1524-25).
- Ottoman Turks overwhelm Christian forces to conquer Hungary and besiege Vienna, raid Italy ... many people feel that Rome will soon be taken (1526-1530).
- Dutch win independence from Spain after eighty year war (ending in 1648).
- Once allied against Spain, England and Holland engage in series of three wars – Holland wins and loses Brazil and loses their North American possessions (New Amsterdam, which becomes New York and New Jersey).
- Spain and England both fail in attacking each other with fleets of ships called Armada (1588-89).
- In the area of "religious" war
- First anti-Catholic state (Hussite) crushed in Bohemia (1420-34).
- Teutonic Knights who had conquered the Eastern Baltic and forced Catholic religion on the region defeated by recently converted Poland, losing territories including Prussia – 1454-66.
- German Catholic Holy Roman Emperor sacks Rome with utter devastation 1527.
- Pitting Catholic, Eastern Orthodox and Protestant armies against each other, Poland, Grand Principality of Lithuania, Sweden, Denmark and Russia fight the Livonian War over control of Eastern Baltic, leaving the region completely destroyed– 1558-83.
- France has thirty-seven year civil war between the Catholics and Huguenots (French Protestants) 1662-98.
- Second major religious war in Bohemia sparks the Thirty Years' War (1618-48).

Therefore, with this really incomplete listing of some of the horrors of the period, when we look at these times we see:

- famine killing millions and then,
- the Great (Black) Plague kills somewhere between one third to half of the population, and also
- war was almost constant, and,
- Governments and religious organizations were killing their own people in acts of state terror.
- We also see the advent of modern slavery.

How does the history of the US compare to these events?

Setting the Stage

In 2012, I was asked by some leaders in the modern peace movement to write an essay looking beyond the issue of drones and civil rights concerns to that of war and peace. I created an argument based on historical precedents that drones in the long run actually will, decrease the power of the United States and in fact create a huge risk for a new general war. Since I came at this piece in a non-biased approach towards war, and found the use of drones as a deficit to national security, neither the peace community nor drone supporters could really be happy with my approach, nor conclusions.

Drones and the Theories of General War
The Historical Pattern Associated with the Introduction of Drones

What tends to be left out of the discussion around drones is the real threat that drones bring to world security. What is missing from the current discussion is the basic question:

- In the future, will the widespread use of drones increase or decrease the likelihood of a general war?

And my answer, based on historical precedents, is drones significantly increase the likelihood of a new general war. Not because they give the US even greater dominance, but because the eventual spreading of drone capacities to nations great and small will actually decrease US military dominance.

This is not a statement of support or non-support of US dominance; it is meant simply as a statement of current status quo and historical patterns associated with when superpowers lose their military advantages.

History shows us that the longest periods of world peace have come when there are dominate superpowers that few would want to challenge in a general war.

The greatest periods of general war came when the superpowers were in decline and others were challenging to replace the declining force. Often, but clearly not always, the decline of the superpower comes when their main weapon arm, which at one point was without equal, becomes obsolete, based on technological changes.

Some caveats before I begin the argument in support of my premise.

- The approach of this essay is not intended to dismiss the other issues arising from the development of drones, only to add to the discussion.
- In limiting the size of the paper I am forced into great generalities to which exceptions can always be found; but exceptions do not eliminate the general rule.

In addition:

- I present this paper to a community that perhaps is repulsed by many of the concepts presented such as the need for "overwhelming force." I understand and can accept and even support these misgivings. But I approach this issue as a military historian, and I present this argument through this lens.

As a historian, I hate the idea of projecting into the future on almost any topic. On the issue of drones, however, I feel that there is extensive historical support to show drones fit the pattern of the past in which the widespread introduction of weapon systems that created a dramatic change in the balance of military power and greatly reduced the costs of weaponry, almost always led to massive increase in the number and intensities of wars. And it looks as if, in the future, drones will do exactly that: change the balance of power and lower costs.

Let me be a bit more-clear here: Any new technology that eliminates the current great powers' ability to be unchallenged in the area of military force leads to new conflicts. (Without putting values on the conflicts, so conflicts good, bad or indifferent, it does not matter - the issue is increasing the rate of conflicts and the intensity of these conflicts.)

The examples of the premise are proven time and time again throughout history; the (relatively) cheap modern cannon and Gatling gun and repeating rifles increased the rate of conflicts in the creation of the colonial empires and; the development of the cheap assault rifle and cheap plastic explosive and eventually Stinger and other cheap anti-aircraft missiles led to the massive increase in conflicts in anti-colonial warfare. In both cases, the conflicts (in these cases political opposites of each other) were made possible by the changes in technology and by the incredible decrease in costs of these weapons and, therefore, the massive increase of availability of the weapons. And, of course, with modern transportation systems comes an increase in the means of providing the weapons to one side or the other.

- However, the classic and best studied example of this premise is what happened with the introduction of the Dreadnought class of battleship (early in the twentieth century).

The Dreadnought was a revolution in fighting ships and made almost all other ships in existence virtually useless and obsolete. The general belief among most military historians is that the creation of this new type of battleship was the root cause that allowed World War I to start. Please notice I did not say the root cause of the war (which are many, and major points of contention among historians) but the root cause that allowed the war.

The premise of the "Dreadnought theory" goes back to the idea of "overwhelming force" being able to prevent wars (as well as giving great powers the ability to wage wars with relative assurance of success and therefore even limiting the scale of war). In this case, it was the overwhelming sea power of England that this new class of warship ended (even though the Dreadnought was in fact English), for we find that when England held exceptional sea power and overwhelming control of seas and the ability to transport soldiers and weaponry anywhere in the world unchallenged, no other power could realistically consider a major war against England or "against England's interest."

Such a premise held mainly true for a hundred years from the post Napoleonic period to the beginning of World War I, and no general war took place in Europe for that long period. While there were some wars in Europe during that period they were mainly limited, and, in addition many "disputes" that were growing towards war were "settled" by just the threat of English interference.

It was clear that when England used force it came as "shock and awe" to the world. In the 1850s the world stood in awe as the English were able to transport whole armies to the Crimea and shocked and defeated the Russian armies on their own territories. In addition, it was the English navy in its huge numbers which used "awe" often more than "shock" to create (almost unchallenged) arguably the world's largest empire, holding India and dominating China economically as well as beating her in wars.

The English had the ability to pay for the very expensive wooden ships (from the benefits of empire) that was the foundation of building and maintaining this empire. They held close to a 10 to 1 superiority in "battle ships" over most rivals and more than 4 to 1 over the closest potential rival (France). Most of the European rivals were envious of the empire and the influence of England, but could actually do little against it.

Then technology changed, and the balance of power changed. The iron and then steel ship replaced the wooden ships, the cannon ball was replaced by the shell, and the sail gave way to the engine. And the English near-monopoly of the seas was challengeable. And the rivals did just that; there was a rush to build the great new warships; it became a matter of "national pride" to create a new navy, especially Dreadnaught-type ships, in nations large and small.

- The superiority of ships for the English shrank to less than 2 to 1 in modern Dreadnought- type ships (with far greater geographic areas to protect than their rivals).

So in terms of history, relatively overnight most of the English fleet became ... obsolete. Soon nations no longer feared the long arm of the English navy or the idea of whole English armies being transported to their shore unmolested. Without those fears the rivals saw that the ability to challenge England around the world was possible.

And the challenges came quickly:

- Germany joining the scramble for Africa and the Pacific Islands.
- The US sending its White Fleet around the world and later seizing Spanish territories in the Pacific and Caribbean.

- Russia sending an entire fleet of "pre-Dreadnought" warships halfway around the world more or less without challenge from England, only to have the fleet wiped out by Japan and their modern ships during the Russo-Japanese War of 1905.

And realistically, without those fears a general war became more likely and in fact did occur, starting in 1914 --- ending Pax Britannia. With the voids created by the First World War, many other wars followed.

We can see some limits on wars with the creation of a new type of "overwhelming force concept." Both the US and the former USSR used new technologies of nuclear weapons to avoid general wars; the concept of Mutual Assured Destruction or MAD arguably prevented a new general war from the 1950s through the 1980s and in many ways still does (while many proxy wars took place). This is when we lived in a basically bi-nuclear world ... and the weapons were very expensive and very hard to produce. That world is rapidly fading.

Right now the "peace-maker" of overwhelming force in the world is essential air power (since nuclear weapons are not really able to be used in a "tactical fashion"). Air power in the sense of attack aircraft as well as cruise missiles and now drones is almost an exclusive domain of the US (and whomever it sells these weapon systems).

And like in the heyday of the English navy, all the arms of air power are relatively expensive, but can go almost anywhere unmolested and bring overwhelming force and fear to anywhere in the world. As long as the US maintains essentially uncontested overwhelming force in the air against any potential foe, the likelihood of general war is very limited. And as with the old English navy, both cruise missiles and attack aircraft are expensive to build and maintain and are vastly technologically more advanced than almost anything that could challenge them. And, currently, so are drones.

However, the cost of drones is changing quickly, and the technology needed to build and operate drones is also changing and becoming ever cheaper (one of the attractive elements for the military). Today any "technologically-advanced nation" could build drones and- if allied with one of the nations that has the satellite support systems (US, Russia, China, for sure), could actively deploy and use them. And soon, all too soon, drones will effectively eliminate the need for traditional very expensive (and ever-growing in cost) attack aircraft: How soon is debatable. However, the intention and direction for this transition to drones over attack aircraft is clear.

Therefore, based on the Dreadnaught theory, the general development of drone technology and its long-term projection on its use, in fact will, make a new general war more likely. And, the argument that the new technology will never be in the capacity of the "other" nations and therefore will increase US dominance - well tell that to the Russians, the English, the French, the Israelis, the Chinese, the Indians, the Pakistanis, the South Africans, the North Koreans and the several other nations who have or may soon have nuclear weapons. The US monopoly on the "bomb" lasted less than three years. What makes us think that the monopoly on drone technology will last much longer than that?

So as expensive wooden ships that were difficult to maintain gave way to metal ships that required smaller crews and did not rot, and delivered firepower never before imagined, so too are traditional attack airplanes about to give way in some fashion to drones.

And once the know-how to develop and use this far cheaper form of air power (that does not require highly trained pilots, and costly airships, and expensive highly trained ground crews and all these expenses go away), and the capacity to use airpower becomes vastly more accessible to nations large and small. With this leveling of field of combat weapons, historically, the likelihood of a general war greatly increases, just as it did when the English sea arm lost its near monopoly.

Again, let me close by saying historical projections are very impacted by variables unknown and unforeseen. So this essay does not declare that drones will cause a new general war, it only projects that based on historical precedent they greatly increase the likelihood of such a war. It also does not, per se, support any particular power or even the concept of superpowers, only states the obvious that these types of forces exist historically.

The essay also does not address the clearly practical argument of "can't put the genie back in the bottle"; drones are here and developing, and if we don't develop them someone else will. The purpose of the essay is to raise this issue of the Dreadnought Theory so as the debate on drones moves forward, we include a more global view of what the actual potentials are for this new weapons arm.

End note ... On Sept 30, 2012 CNN reports that seventy countries now have drone capacity

http://www.cnn.com/2012/10/01/opinion/bergen-world-of-drones/index.html?hpt=hp_c1

Glenn Young

Setting the Stage

In 2013, right after the bombing at the Boston Marathon, I was, as after most of the modern acts of terrorism, predictably dismayed at the "standard" type of coverage the media gave the events. We are fed the idea that this type of event is not just shocking and barbaric but more or less has been introduced by these "enemies of freedom." Here I attempt (in a relatively indirect approach) to show that the actions are neither new nor just a tool of the "enemies of freedom" but have been used for centuries to support one cause or another, and not just overseas, but right here in the US.

May Day, Boston and Our History of Terror

As the father of a daughter, and one who wanted her to share in a common culture, in her younger days I took her to a production of *Annie*. Much to my surprise the plot line of the play turned on a failed act of terrorism. As all of us who have seen the play know, here was the little cute orphan girl who is taken from dire poverty (or as a song title in the play *"It's a hard knock life for us"*) and inserted into the world of the over the top wealth of Daddy Warbucks, merely as a publicity stunt.

Despite all pleas of subordinates and the plucky behavior of the girl, the monopolist refused to keep her beyond the stunt, until her dog Sandy (arff) saves him from the bomb-throwing efforts of the dark and bearded anarchist lurking in the shadows. This prevention of the act of terror changes the heart of the wealthy Warbucks and enables the heroine to stay in the world of the modern American dreamland.

At the time I saw the play, it was amazing to me (as a historian with radical leanings) to see in this production one of the few then-current references to the incredible social conflicts that started some one-hundred years before I took my daughter to the play (the 1880s) and lasted till … well who can really say when it ended: at least in one phase until the 1950s or so. The *Annie* bomber was the stereotype of the revolutionary created after the Haymarket "event" of 1886, where during a labor rally a bomb blast in the Haymarket District of Chicago resulted in a police and labor battle in which several police and workers were killed.

The impact of the event created a social environment in which, for some fifty years on the labor union movement in the United States was associated with terrorists. While at the time massive debates raged over the person who really threw the bomb (anarchist, police, or police agent), now it's an event barely remembered in the US. However this one event, the Haymarket Riots, created the face of terrorism in this country for generations to come.

The "darkness" of the image of the 1880/90s bomber made the transference from one ethnic group to another easy enough, and soon the focus came to rest on Jewish anarchists from Russia (Emma Goldman and Alexander Berkman, etc.), with the Jews being the feared immigrant group of the moment. That round ball in hand, bearded bomber image lasted throughout the 1890s to the time of the Great Depression and the supposed timeframe of *Annie*.

Over this forty plus years the image was reinforced by the killing of a president (McKinley) by a self-proclaimed Anarchist; the corporate and government's attempt to crush the IWW (in part based on the bomb killing of a former governor of Idaho and the supposed multiple acts of sabotage that the IWW was accused of during their anti-World War I efforts), various later bombings in support of the pro-labor movements; and after the Russian Revolution, with so many Jews in leadership positions, the linking of communism to the

"Jew." (Of course the accusations abound with saying Marx was a "Jew" as well as Trotsky.)

- The medieval conception of a Jewish plot to destroy Christianity was revised in what became known as the "International Jewish Communist Conspiracy."

While, over a century, the old image of the crazed Rabbi looking like a bomber slowly faded, the fear of Jews as the "other" did not.

It took on the image of the Jewish intellectual, and the Rosenbergs and the Hollywood Ten, all in their own way out to destroy and betray America. With the Rosenbergs the threat changed from just a small round bomb in hand to THE BOMB.

- The same question was asked then as now. How could they (the other) come to America and find freedom and safety and still want to attack and kill and destroy us?

The question seemed to be asked most often and the loudest by those who themselves supported the most active terrorist group in the nation, the KKK. But since the KKK focused their attacks on the "other," few related them to the bomb-throwing anarchists of the time. The "right" of the time was not alone in accusing "the other" as so many of the "general population" lived in fear and wondered who were these Anarchists and Communists and Jews. (With the Tom Joad character of the *Grapes of Wrath* left to wonder about who were the Reds. (Copyright prevents direct quote)

Today, despite the decade-long war on terror, all that seems to be remembered in our culture of the longstanding fear of the "dark-haired wild Jewish/anarchist bomber" who was supposed to be around almost every corner, is this slight reference that was the plot-turner in this play designed mainly to appeal to young girls. We just have no cultural memory in this country.

In part, this fading of attention on the mad Jewish-type bomber was based on the success of Jews in the culture, and the demand for the end of stereotype-based attacks. It was also based on Jews becoming cultural heroes as targets of the Holocaust, the success-against-the-odds of Israel, and the massive support of Israel by the Christian Right (as needed for the Second Coming).

But also, in part, the ending of the image of the Jew as the mad-bomber happened when the attentions of the culture turned to the next "other," the next generation of "terrorists;" the Nazi's the Japs, the Italian gangsters and then the Black Panthers and the atheist children of those Jewish intellectuals who seemed to dominate the radical youth movement of the sixties.

- Now after a few more iterations of the "other," we have had for a decade or so -- radical Islam.

The Boston Marathon bombing should to quote an old labor song, "waive a flag" in our collective conscience. It should help us understand, we have all been here before, and been here in far more damaging and fearful ways before.

Unfortunately, we seem to have no memory of it. America has been racked by terror and terrorist events many times in the past. Oklahoma City, the World Trade Center (twice) and now Boston are only recent events that feel like new things, but that is only because we have no sense of history and no understanding of how we as a people got to where we are and stand for which we stand.

We also act as if this one or series of attacks are new and different and special because it's here in America. Again, not true ... we had attacks on US soil during both World Wars, and in the actual Civil War, and in the virtual civil wars of the labor movement.

Nor are US cities the only ones to experience bombings attacks. We only have to look at the terrorist campaign of the IRA against London that lasted decades, or the Palestinian efforts against Israel, the Chechen attack in Russia, or single attacks like Madrid or Mumbai or well ... all the way back to the group that were first called "the assassins" and their campaign of terror against the Crusader states and the apathetic Muslim rulers of the time to understand that terrorists are not about borders.

Most people have no frame of reference to the events I mentioned. And surely fewer still understand the connections between these previous acts of terror and the recent events in Boston. And, of course, fewer still know that the Haymarket bombing of 1886 is still remembered in some fashion throughout the world.

For the May Day (May First) celebrations of the Soviet Union and Communist China, which gave us such fear and continue to be held in so many democratic countries, are actually based on remembering (in part) the Haymarket events (of May 4th) as International Labor Day. Our "terrorists" became international heroes and the basis of world-wide celebrations every year. Here, without a sense of history, we recall the event slightly in *Annie*.

If we could only learn some of the past, we could perhaps put Boston and the other acts into the perspective of the risks involved in civilization and world culture. Terrorism has always been used and will always be used by a very few of those in dissent and is part of the price of being an open society.

If we only understood some history we would know that, in time, this particular reign of terror will also pass and become something that is only slightly remembered in some distant play. What history should teach us is that we, now, need to ensure that the "small" acts of terror are not the cause of major acts of terror by the state against its own people, even if at times some of our own people seem like "the other."

Circa 1900 image of Anarchist Bomber

http://www.google.com/imgres?imgurl=http://www.thirdwave-websites.com/blog/european-anarchist-bomber.jpg&imgrefurl=http://vannevar.blogspot.com/2009/07/anarchist-bomber-photos.html&h=341&w=335&sz=48&tbnid=Q4RzigS4moGvNM:&tbnh=89&tbnw=87&zoom=1&usg=__llpcPwhXAa8-t5LYDhqXMDYvBDI=&docid=BX4R-Ih_VKLJWM&sa=X&ei=h3wfUsmpIumciAKZrIGYCg&ved=0CDEQ9QEwAQ&dur=522

Making May Day the International Workers Holiday at the founding of the Second International

On July 14, 1889, the hundredth anniversary of the fall of the Bastille, there assembled in Paris leaders from organized revolutionary proletarian movements of many lands, to form once more an international organization of workers, patterned after the one formed twenty-five years earlier by their great teacher, Karl Marx. Those assembled at the foundation meeting of what was to become the Second International heard from the American delegates about the struggle in America for the 8-hour day during 1884-1886, and the recent rejuvenation of the movement. Inspired by the example of the American workers, the Paris Congress adopted the following resolution:

The Congress decides to organize a great international demonstration, so that in all countries and in all cities on one appointed day the toiling masses shall demand of the state authorities the legal reduction of the working day to eight hours, as well as the carrying out of other decisions of the Paris Congress. Since a similar demonstration has already been decided upon for May 1, 1890, by the American Federation of Labor at its Convention in St. Louis, December, 1888, this day is accepted for the international demonstration. The workers of the various countries must organize this demonstration according to conditions prevailing in each country.

See Alexander Trachtenberg. May Day Archive -- The History of May Day
http://www2.archivists.org/initiatives/mayday-saving-our-archives

Setting the Stage

I see the modern existence and the political positioning of religion as the greatest threat to individual freedom and to society's advancement. This perspective is a tough sell, based on how people view religion or spirituality for themselves. The general premise is less difficult when we see the organized religions of the world become a front for political power grabs or a front for sexual license (such as the priest abuse scandals in the West or the spreading of venereal disease throughout Central Asia by Buddhist monks).

However, this essay talks more about the political front and the reason why a return to control of the thoughts of society by religion is possible, if not likely. I attempt to approach this relatively simplistically, avoiding all issues of religious particulars and of conflicts far too often stated in the language of religion. I am attempting raw politics here.

Ten Things That I Learned about Religion:

This is obviously not a complete document of my journey to learn about religion, or better said, Western religion and in particular the religions that all claim Abraham as their origin. It is my evaluation not so much of the goals of a particular religion or the ideologies or dogmas of a given religion, but the general concepts of religion and its role in culture. This essay mainly recounts the findings of my search to understand what hold religion has on the minds of people and the future consequences of that hold.

As an atheist who has studied the roots of religions and the origins of certain of the religious concepts, I have reached some conclusions that should be stated, but are mostly not fully explored here. For this is a political essay, dealing with how religion has once again come to dominate much of the world, despite so much new information that contradicts the storylines of these religions.

Therefore no discussion in this essay of things I really do enjoy talking about (the common roots of religions and the variation of the stories that come out of these foundation myths). This is a discussion on why I see religion as the next cause of worldwide horror. This is not a discussion of the fine points of theology, but a look at how religion is back, and back once again, in all the negative ways it once was, as the driving force of culture and perhaps world history.

Needless to say, I am not a fan of this outcome, this shaping of the current world, but I understand why it has come about. Many writers and doubters and philosophers (not that I am any of these other than a doubter) before me have stated similar findings and definitely in in far more eloquent fashion than me, but these simply are my views and insights that I think may be considered useful to some.

I have shaped the approach in the modern parlance of a list, in this case as in so many others, my ten reasons. This list is in a logical order of why religion remains in the modern world at all, and why the modern world will really be overcome by religion. Logic and the Hegelian model that I agree with, show that religion, as it did with the ending of the Classical World, will overcome modern knowledge. The list shows how religion, once again, will establish the monopoly of thought by eliminating all the answers other than theirs.

As with all such lists, the concepts are truncated, the support limited and subtlety eliminated. We live in a world that has not time for details; victory comes to those with pat and quick answers. All too often these quick answers have a religious foundation. After all they have thousands of years of experience with the "quick answer."

The world seems to have not only forgotten H.L. Mencken, but perhaps his most important quote

"For every complex problem there is an answer that is clear, simple, and wrong."
http://www.brainyquote.com/quotes/quotes/h/hlmencke129796.html

This Mencken idea is never more-true when looking at the history of religious ideas. Ok - sometimes they have not always been clear or simple, but they have been wrong.

Wrong in the same way religions have twisted the basics of logic and understanding of the world, that being "correlation is not causation." Religious thinking throughout time has been and continues to be based in the opposite view; "correlation is causation." No wonder the modern world view and religion are in such conflict.

They forced their "wrong" view onto the West in the late 5th century CE, and maintained solid control of the thinking of the West for over 1,000 years. The fights with religion during the "Enlightenment," "Age of Reason," "Liberalism" and the "Communist era," never completed the task of elimination or even controlling religious thought in much of the West.

Now for the perhaps the first time since at least World War I, religion is making a huge comeback and once again may do as they did at the ending of the Classical age, take over society almost completely.

So here is my list of the ten steps and ten understandings that will lead to the end of our current world through religion triumphant once again.

Here is my logic:

1) **The primary purpose of religion has been and is to answer the unanswerable.**

Religion has simply lost the monopolistic powers it once had since being challenged by modern knowledge and new facts based in scientific research. Over time, as our knowledge of the facts of the universe has increased, and the hold of religion on the minds of people has decreased, the list of what was considered an unanswerable question has changed and, to the modern mind, greatly decreased. In the past, except during the "Classical age of thinking," religion was the definitive source for all things; now in the "modern world" of competing ideas, the areas in which the role of religion dominated thinking has been greatly limited.

In simple fact, the "modern" greatly decreased the need for religion. Therefore, by logic and reason, religion should be on the verge of ending, not increasing wildly as it has.

One key reason for the continuation of religion is that not all questions are answered by modernism.

2) **The key question unanswered – Is there life after death?**

This issue of "continued life" has, since the beginning of thought about religion, seemed to have been "a," if not "the," unanswerable question, far more important than why does it or does it not rain, what are the stars and what effect do they have on us, etc. The latter two have been answered to a large degree by those willing to accept modern thought, but not the first issue.

What happens to our loved ones, when death came so soon and frequently, was a burning issue to ancients. Of course at the core of this was a human emotion, love. We loved people and then, far too quickly, they were gone. There was and is a deep human need to know that there was a transition, and a hope of reuniting with the love one. This became a driving force for religion, and a question still unanswerable by the modern world.

Therefore, at its core, when stripped of foundation stories and myths and issues of power and control over daily activities: The authority of religion around the world seems to be based in having authority over what happens to a given person when existence in this reality ends:

- Will one or will one not reconnect with loved ones who no longer exist in this sense of reality.

Because the question cannot be answered, religion has that threat over all of us. Religion's power lies in the concept of "Do what we say and you will be treated well in the afterlife; don't do what we say and you will be … ," ; well, there are lots of options offered by lots of religions on what happens next.

Hellfire is most known in the West, but is actually a relatively recent development. The Jewish version of punishment for the wicked (since traditional Jewish thought did not have a concept of "hell") is roughly stated a bad seat in the afterworld "theater;" a placement very far from God. Coming back to this world as something far less than a human is the karmic-based religions view.

Religion's message has also come across as a protection racket. Do as we say, and your loved ones are happy in the next world; don't do as we say … well same format of horror is laid out them as well as for you.

No one can really prove or disprove the afterlife. That is why modernists do not try to state an answer one way or the other (except for atheists, who do so from logic and not proof). So religion has a free hand in this area, even as other areas of human concerns (Will the rains come? Will the sun rise?)… have been stripped away by modern discoveries.

Today, when given a chance people look to Agra-businesses for help with the crops, not the local priests.

Let's be clear; despite

- the endless reports of ghosts, zombies, ancestor sightings and reincarnated people in religious books, popular fiction and in a wide range of folk tales; and
- despite psychics and so many others who claim to talk to the dead (and claim that the dead talk back to them);
- over history there has never been a definitive finding of a dead person who returned from the dead; or a soul left in limbo; or
- any proof at all of an afterlife of any kind.

There are lots of tales and religious dogma, but no real scientific proof that meets modern standards of "proof."

Therefore:

- with what appears to be an almost universal concern of humanity is what happens after this existence, and
- with only religion in its many forms and many answers offering any direction in this question;

With this claim to control the afterlife comes the current basis of religion's power; it used to be just one of the many claims of power, but now, in the modern world, it is one of the key claims.

3) Besides answering the unanswerable, religion has served several other purposes in society, and often profits from this relationship.

This control over the issue of post-life is obviously not the only role that religion has played in society. Beyond the focus on the question of the soul, we see some of the roles of religion in society:

- As a support or challenge to the existing power structure
- As a means of giving a basis for controlling the daily behavior of people and controlling or encouraging their ambitions
- As a system that allows people to have hope for the current situation and for the future (and an answer to why it does or does not rain, and so on).

And

- In addition, religion has provided means for social coordination and a sense of community so strongly felt by most people; sometimes as being part of an existing society and sometimes as forming revolutionary activities against the current society.

In what can be described as modern society, all of these roles have been challenged if not replaced by modern thoughts and concepts created to operate in a non-religious-based world. "We hold these truths to be self-evident" or constitutional government, was one of many concepts created in the modern world to supplant the role that religion had in these areas.

The separation of church and state fostered by the Liberalism movement started much of this process, then Communism, Unionism, Socialism, Fascism, Liberalism, Republic-ism, Democracy, even Nobility and Monarchy (and on and on), are modern or relatively modern concepts designed to provide challenges to religion in the areas listed above. And while we often still see religion dominating these roles in certain cultures, those cultures where religion still takes on these roles are linked strongly to their traditions and, for the most part, have not transitioned fully into the modern world.

This is not to say that in the modern world religion does not want these areas of influence back under their domination. In fact much of the crisis we see in the current world is based on this new religious effort to keep or regain a wide range of social controls.

4) **Over history, religion has been flexible and Orwellian in its ability to rewrite itself when challenged and, at the same time inflexible as to the validity of its "core text."**

The study of religion shows how frequently the story changes, while the main core of the message and even some of the events stay the same. However:

Religion has shown much flexibility in allowing the setting, characters and timeframe of the stories that compose particular religions of the West to change as long as the essential elements of all Western religion stayed pretty much the same, with the core story dating back millennia.

Despite the claims of almost all religions to correctness and uniqueness, through stories of the gods, sons of gods and demigods and human heroes (kings, prophets, saints or "commoners touched by God"), the same message of social responsibility and hope for life after death have been told and retold in many ways. (The number of gods and the name of the entity sitting next to God for the purpose of post-death judgment have changed many times.)

- However, the overall goal of living a righteous life leading to post-death reward (however defined) and reuniting with lost loved ones remained pretty much constant since at least the religion of ancient Egypt, if not millennia before.

While the core messages of Abrahamic religions are more or less the same, the battle have become more over the legitimacy of one story or sacred text over another; which text is most "the word of god" and therefore definitive.

Now, as a result of competing "civilizations" and the rise of absolutist religions and the elimination of religious competition, the religious conflicts that remain are mainly reduced to a battle over the legitimacy of one or another particular story, verses, or sacred text.

These conflicts seem to boil down to the "means and methods" of salvation and reunification, and the means and methods of the objectives of a good life (social harmony and "post-life salvation," community, etc.). In other writings I would argue that what is really a stake is wealth and power in this world, but that is another subject.

Christians were quite remarkable in this functional flexibility, in modifying very ancient Egyptian stories to shape the images of both Jesus and Mary, and by taking the birth date and location of the birth of their son of God from the great religion called Mithraism, and, some 1000 years later, they adopted the Christmas tree from the pagan Germans. Muslims adopted many of the ideas and stories of the Christians and the Jews for the Koran, only with some modifications.

In addition, all the Abrahamic religions figured out a way around the sin of usury, to reject continuation of slavery, and condone the use of modern inventions never mentioned in their books. Yet they all still maintained the validity of themselves and their view of religion, based on a rigid view of their sacred text.

Societies used to be more accepting of the diversity of stories and looked upon all of these stories as sources of both insight and entertainment; the goals of the stories were considered far more important than the particular events. This changed with the rise of absolutist religions, and their efforts to supersede the state. (Once again, this area is a topic for a different paper.)

When the rigid and absolutist modern Christians first came to India to proselytize they were initially very hopeful as the Indians tended to want to hear the Bible "truths." They were later appalled when they realized that the Indians were just adding the Christ stories and the other Biblical stories to their vastly accepting pantheon; the Indians were acting like the majority of people over history, adding a good story to their sacred repertoire, cause a good story is valuable in itself.

However, now, in this modern age, stripped of almost all the issues where they were once dominant and challenged on all sides by modern options to their former monopoly of ideas, the legitimacy of their sacred books and the absolutism of their stories become more critical to any particular religions' very existence.

They need their book(s) to be absolutely correct, no matter how they have adopted it to meet modern times or other cultures, because if it is not divinely inspired, written, etc., then what basis do these obsolete stories of times long ago have to compete with the modern world?

5) Contrary to "current" folk culture, the relatively new concept of monotheism, or really the veneer of "monotheism," has actually been a cause of undercutting of human freedoms.

I often wondered why one god made more sense than two or more? The transition of monotheism is extremely interesting when you actually overlay the development of absolutist rule. So you will find that the Roman Republic had a concept of "heaven" or gods that mirrored what their government looked like: a bunch of squabbling entities with diverse powers. And the later empire switched to monotheism; the "One Emperor - One God" concept, again using religion to reflect what their government looked like. This view gives the statement "on Earth as it is in Heaven" a different meaning.

It occurred to me that freedom of thought, and in fact, freedom in general (at least up until the modern world), always appeared greater in polytheistic cultures or non-deity based cultures than in monotheistic cultures. We have seen monotheistic cultures demand conformity far more than non-monotheistic ones.

We find that as religions became more "monotheistic" (although all tend to maintain extensive aspects of polytheism with different names for what were previously called gods – demons, saints, angels, the devil) that the monotheistic religion's infrastructure demanded that the one god was responsible for all things, and therefore all occurrences were to due this god's choices.

- Therefore all obedience is due that god and that god alone.

This concept, and demand for adherence to this concept, eliminated the traditional exploration of knowledge that developed over time in the ancient/Classical world under the rubric of polytheistic religion. The attempts to understand the stars and the physical world, medicine, math and other sciences, each area with its "benefactor god" flourished in the more ancient/Classical world, and more or less ceased with the rise of absolutist monotheistic religions.

The idea of one god responsible for all things, with one sacred text responsible for the source of all knowledge of importance, often was used to stifled knowledge and exploration of ideas. Only with the breakdown of the absolutist religions did modern studies of these sciences redevelop. There are a few noted exceptions to this conclusion, with the most noted being the Arabic world of the 8th to the11th centuries.

However, for the most part the epochs of time where absolute monotheism has been the, or even "a" major power in society, have been times where the search for knowledge and the creation of new concepts have been most repressed. This truth goes contrary to the propaganda of Abrahamic religions, but not to the true evaluation of history.

And of course, what is well known is that the repression of ideas or exploration of ideas by the religion in power was often tied to the cries of "death for the infidel, heretic, non-believer, idolater, witch, sorcerer, devil worshiper" and on and on. And if death was not used to silence the opposition, then the weapons of isolation or expulsion or all kinds were used to keep the new ideas from being developed or heard.

Any idea that claims the absolute truth in all things is an idea that is against freedom. Monotheist religions claim to have the absolute truth and therefore they are really against freedom.

6) "Holy war" is one of the more powerful forces in history.

While not all wars were by any means based on religion, almost all wars had to be justified and sanctioned by religion. "God wills it" in monotheistic cultures, or something akin to that in polytheistic societies, was/is one of the major tools used to mobilize and justify the internal social processes needed to engage and carry on war.

The promise of "paradise" (under multiple names) as a reward for dying in a "holy war" led to the process by which millions of people died early deaths either from being a participant in these wars or from "collateral damage" of these wars. It could strongly be argued that without the sanction of and promises offered by religion most wars in the modern era could not have taken place.

World War II featured at least five powers that did not use the traditional appeals to deities (Nazi Germany, Soviet Russia, Fascist Italy, and non-Abrahamic based China and Japan), and shows that massive wars are not all religious-based. However, the exception does not prove or disprove the historical fact of the role that religion played in the West, including the horrors of the Thirty Years War and World War I. (The saying "there are no atheist in foxholes" was meant as a tribute to the power of God, or with some irony, the fear of men; but really only shows how the power of religion helped place that person in that foxhole.)

Today, as in the past, the intellectuals of the time attempt to disconnect the issues of God and war. However, if we look at relatively modern US history we see the stress of fighting the "godless" Communist for some fifty years in hot and cold wars, and the now ongoing struggles of the wars with Islamic

Fundamentalists places religion at the core of the struggles. In all cases the US executive has attempted to downplay the role of religion, while the Right in this country has continued to speak and to agitate over the need to protect our "Christian" way of life.

In the past, we can see some breakdown or even rejection of this religious connection to war and the requirements of people to support these wars based on religious grounds among intellectuals. In what, in its time, must be considered a revolutionary statement, in Shakespeare's "*Henry the V*", the king states on the eve of battle: "Every man's duty is to the King, but every man's soul is his own."

Such a thought in religiously dominated areas, where one must follow God's will or else your afterlife is at risk, an idea such as Shakespeare's would be sacrilege.

7) **The current revival of religion in the West mostly involves the greater role of religion as the challenger to the existing authorities.**

Something has happened in the last few years that has changed completely the role of religion in the world, and is bring about a highly unexpected rebound. Religion is no longer just attempting to answer the question of the afterlife; religion has occupied the void created by the collapse of socialism/communism/revolution/etc. and now is addressing those who are feeling lost and unsuccessful in the modern world. If Hegel was alive, he would say something like: "Yes, what did you expect?"

So now religion is gaining much power in its role as the Hegelian concept of "antithesis" to the current "thesis" that can best be labeled as "modernism." And as socialism attracted those not being successful in the new world order of "capitalism," so too does religion now attract those least successful in the modern world of technology and in the new economy of communications and technology rather than the "muscle economy."

The current justification of the glorification of "traditional values" either in war against modernism, or in political movements resisting non-religious changes, are revolts claiming to be based in "God's laws," again these laws being defined based in some sacred text or another.
So would-be revolutionaries of today study the Bible or the Koran, unlike those of the 19th and 20th centuries who studied Marx and Lenin; the goals of overthrowing the existing evil order remains the same, the justification rhetoric and the definition of evil differs.

In this current Hegelian manifestation of resistance to the dominant culture, the organizing language is not based in Marxian terminology or promises of social revolutions and redistribution of wealth, but in terms of the demands for a return to "God's law" (Biblical or Koranic law).

And the leaders of this movement project that wealth is not created by the investment of capital but by the blessing of God and his answer to individual prayer. And those who are failing in the economy, can claim the ability to feel superior to those who are succeeding, on the basis of seeing themselves as "saved" and can declare that the successful, those who are making it, are doing so by being seduced by evil. (This way of thinking is much like so many others who brand the successful as evil --- one of the more famous is when Mao use to call the successful, "Capitalist running dogs".)

The threat offered by the new antithesis is not the overthrow of the existing order and social revolution, but the return of God's wrath. In these days of God's return to power, or the son of

God return, based on which Abrahamic religion we are talking about, we will see justice being meted out and the righteous empowered in "the last days."

So now religion is attempting to reclaim an old area of control, through new tactics. They now are attempting to be the power of resistance against the powers that be (rather than what they had become, the partners of the power elite). Religion is taking up the mantle dropped by the "Left" of the last century, to answer the needs of the non-included, not through revolution promised by the old Left, but through God's gift and holy war. They are also reviving the concept that God's gift is not just for the afterlife, but for now.

- The ancient cry of "God wills it" is being heard all over the world, again.

Religion is now attempting to make the issues of social justice and inequality something that is an "unanswerable" by the modern world, and therefore once again the domain of religion. What should be noted is that the early stages of the Hegelian shifts are always marked by acts labeled as terrorism. And if Hegel was alive, he would still say something like "So, what did you expect?"

8) **Religion will remain a major part of society despite the technical challenges of the modern world because of the two main foci of religion: questions about afterlife and becoming the world leading opposition force, or the new antithesis in the Hegelian sense.**

If the religions of the world had maintained themselves as the tools of a dying power structure (as they had been since the decline of monarchy and authoritarian states), and were linked only to the question of life after death, religion may soon have faded away. So once again, religions are flexible to restate their inflexibility.

- The main religions of the world are now the main opponents of the modern world; resistance to imposition of modern concepts in wide areas of the world comes from Christians, Jews and Muslim fundamentalists, alike.
- Their justification for this flexible move is their undying allegiance to their inflexible devotion to their sacred text.

We see their leadership in both violent and non-violent actions.

- Bombings and other violence in the US were led by the Christian anti-abortion movements, and
- The Republican Party is acting as the "party of God" in state after state.
- The Catholic Church resists birth control and Gay rights.
- Islamist parties win popular elections (when they are allowed to run).

While many try to depict these events as disconnected and different from each other, some see these events as the world heading towards a new round of religious war. I see these events as very connected and a part of a predictable Hegelian event; in reality we seem to be heading towards a round of the new modernism being challenged by what appears to be those left behind or shut out by the modern world.

Some may not see the difference between a religious war and what I am saying, but I am stating that the struggle is not between religions, but between the modern relatively a-religious world and all the religions that resist modernism (or are speaking for those being left behind by modernism). Therefore as we have already seen, the next rounds of radicalism will be in religious terms.

9) **If allowed to, religion will again, as it did for close to 1500 years, eliminate independent and free thought and create the suppression of knowledge.**

Despite the great decline in the numbers of people who claim to be religious (some 18% of the world's population claim either to be agnostic or atheist), because of the new modern Hegelian role of religion, in the West, religion may now be on the verge of its second most powerful position of all history.

The debates of the world are now all being framed in religious terms. We see struggles in some areas over basic rights of women and in others over research into new medical interventions being framed in religious terms. We also see extensive resistance to everything from the understanding of the origins of all life on earth to efforts to stop elimination of life on earth (through either war or global warming) framed almost exclusively in religious terms.

While the Taliban and the Iranian and Saudi religious police are examples of modern efforts of religions to prevent social change and thought, the Christian religions have extensive examples of similar approaches ranging from the Inquisition to the widespread use of witch trials as a means of "state terror."

We now see the Republican Party in the US linked with the religious base. Once elected, the new "religious party" is not just eliminated women's rights in the area of abortion (and many other "right agenda items) but also attempting to control thought and knowledge of the future by inserting religious beliefs in public schools; this party is allowing public money to support fundamentalist Christian private schools (American Madrassas).

If we have learned anything in history we have learned that freedom and liberty of thought is an ephemeral thing. And freedoms do not fall right away in big bangs but are sliced away slowly, and then are fully taken when resistance is less unlikely.

The signs are all around, the history is predictive, we are about to slip again into an era of religious control of thought and progress. When such things happen, it has never been a time of freedom.

10) Religion is attempting to be the dominate class by comforting the poor.

Religion has provided a schizoid product to people, with one side trying to be the comforter and benefactor of the poor and oppressed, and at the same time also being the justification tool of the powerful and dominant classes.

For a while in certain places, religion managed to also become the dominant class: in Europe during the late Dark Ages, in Tibet in modern times, in India almost throughout Hindu domination. Now we see the Islamic Republic in Iran, Wahhabis in Arabia and, for a period, the Taliban in Afghanistan. Once again, and now world-wide even, we see the potential for religion to dominate as the elite class.

Religious rulers or potential rulers have over time figured out how and when to be flexible so they can position themselves for power. They have done a spectacular job of keeping the concepts of religion a moving target. As knowledge is developed to show that the dogmas of religion are false, religions have quickly moved to claim that they were not interpreted correctly.

The most obvious example of this is the locations of "heaven and hell." This issue is closely related to the issue of life after death, so it is very important to religion and its ability to be in power. We see how the location of these places went from being overhead and underfoot to some place in the realm of some other dimension very quickly.

When the first rocket went up and no deity yelled "ouch," heaven moved very quickly and so did the collective belief that it was right there above us. Now, to quote John Lennon, we all agree that "no hell below us, and above us only sky" ... but heaven and hell are still there somewhere for the believers.

Religion is flexible and inflexible and contradictory all the time, from defending the status quo to leading opposition to the status quo, they are nimble and stagnant. And now they quickly have gone from a fading remnant of the early Bronze Age to potentially the most powerful force on the planet. The afterlife is still theirs, but now the whole world of existence may also be theirs too.

Religion is able to do incorporate the contradictory based on some very simple and overt logic illustrated in this paper. To show this logic I come back full circle to the role of religion and the future of that role.

- Since the modernist has not answered the question of the afterlife, most people see the need for religion.
- Since modernists, with the relative failure of socialism, have not solved the problems of the poor and have not come up with a modernist alternative that attracts the poor, the poor and disconnected, look for an alternative to the modern.
- Since religion, and for now no other force, offers a vision of how the poor and disconnected should be treated, the poor become more attracted to religion.

- Since religion requires absolute acceptance of their sacred works, regardless how obsolete they are, those looking for social justice will be more attracted to religion, and forced to be completely accepting of the texts.
- Since absolute religions discourage independent thought and require absolute adherence to their worldview of everything, we now witness a massive upsurge in religious views fueled by those who oppose the modern world and have no other voice talking to them other than religion.
- Since we operate in relative republics … we in the West are on the verge of legal revolutions that will end freedom and create religious intolerant states.
- And of course, with the modern world being so self-absorbed in themselves and their own form of absolutist dogmas of modern capitalism and a modern variation of Social Darwinism, the modern world leaves the field to organize resistance to them to religion.

Therefore, the last thing I learned about religion is that:

- The current rise of religion around the world is the greatest threat to freedom and liberty since the rise of Fascism and must be resisted as such.
- And as the modern world ignored of placated the rise of Fascism then, it seems to do the same today by not challenging religion by working more effectively to end poverty in the world.

And of course the inherent contradiction of the modern world is that no politician in the modern US can run for office without adherence to religion and increasingly more so to fundamentalist religion. Therefore, there can and will not be resistance to this rise, until it is far too late. Thus a great irony:

through supporting freedom we will lose our freedom to think. What would Hegel say to that?

So it appears, talking of irony, that religion will once again dominate the world and may God/the gods/the force, etc. help us when it happens.

Setting the Stage

I had a thought that one of the problems with fighting Christian controls is that the Atheist offers no alternatives to the glories of afterlife (and such) offered by the religious. We do not try to offer a better alternative in a different existence, simply because we do not accept the concept of a life after death. Therefore, we have very hard time competing – do you want eternal happiness??? or, ... well, nothing. (This essay was obviously written prior to Pope Francis I announcing that Atheist could get into heaven. It seems that the Pope and I have similar thoughts, in at least a limited area.)

So I decided to try and turn the issue around a little, by asking if the religious view of heaven matches the political views of our nation. And the obvious conclusion is that it does not.

- Heaven in the eyes of the religions is gained by absolute adherence to a set creed; democracy is based on determining, through public debate, the direction of society, while avoiding the tyranny of the majority.

- In addition, heaven is based on following the dictates of an all-knowing and powerful being, again in opposition to the philosophy of democracy, which rejects the premise of anyone being all-knowing and always right.

Therefore, the way in this society to fight the religious is not to try and compete on the bennies of the future, since as Atheist we offer none, but to show how anti-democratic is the Christian view of heaven. Of course we cannot change the minds of the true believers but those who are Christian but also modernist and democratic at heart.

So this paper started out to be all too serious, giving the details of how authoritarian view heaven came about. And then I realized that there is another way to compete with the Christian view --- humorously.

We need to offer a vision of a heaven filled with SUVs and malls. How do we compete for the hearts and minds when we really have little to offer, other than the here and now? Make something up that is appealing to the here and now. It's been done before.

A Heaven for a Democracy

Part I – Introduction to the Afterlife

In the study of history of religion, at least Western religions, it's fairly clear that the concept of what heaven or the equivalent of heaven in a given culture pretty much models the conception of the lifestyles of the rich and the royal of the given time. One of the problems of modern day society, with its focus on the development of democracy and multiculturalism, is that many of the ancient views of heaven still exist; these being based on monarchy and absolutist styles of rule. Society has not caught up with itself and offered a modern view of heaven, one based on a society of choice and freedom, not one of totalitarianism and massive state control.

This essay attempts to show how the concept of heaven developed, and then evolved into an authoritarian model, and in the ends, offers a modern view of what heaven should be seen in our modern culture. The background offered in this paper is needed, but highly reduced. A new model of heaven is offered but is only a modest framework.

We need this new model primarily for a means of offering something different than the current totalitarian model. It is important in the current political and cultural world. While in much of the West religion is fading as a force, at least in the

United States and much of the developing world, it is still a major force of both politics and culture. In the area of afterlife and the joys of afterlife, the religions of the world hold a monopoly.

- They have always, and continue to do to this day, hold the model of heaven as the way life and order should be conducted in the pre-afterlife. The traditional saying of Christians is "on earth as it is in heaven."
- Without a non-authoritarian view of heaven, the current Christian model supports models of authoritarian rule, and is being used to support anti-authoritarian models one earth (On earth as it is in heaven.)

To truly create this new modern world, and need to compete with the current Christian views of heaven. We need to create a new view of heaven (for those who continue to the need religion) that is compatible with a world based on democratic principles rather than authoritarian rule. We need a heaven that is supportive of democratic principles, not absolutism and totalitarianism. We need a heaven as it is on earth.

- Can this melding of heaven and a democratic culture truly exist in a society?
- Can there really be a democratic afterlife for a democratic society?

Of course we can.

A study of history shows there has been frequent changing of the views of the afterlife, and on the mortals viewed the home of the gods, or God. In fact as we will see the early Christian view of heaven was at its time rather revolutionary and progressive. This study would show that these changes in the concept of heaven have mostly come about to satisfy political changes as society changed from migratory clans to civilizations to kingships. Now with the changes that are moving us towards a more democratic and free world, we simple need to change heaven again.

Unfortunately since this modernization of the world has come about relatively quickly, a view of heaven has not really evolved to meet a modern need. So we are now faced with a changing world trying to be based on freedom competing with a religious world still grounded in an authoritarian god governing in an absolutist heaven. And this view of heaven is often being used as a rallying point against efforts to make society even more progressive.

Therefore, asking to make a cultural change in the view of the afterlife is nothing new. For this this modern world, we need a modern view of heaven.

Part II - The Difference between Heaven and the Kingdom of Heaven

In this study of the past, we would find that heaven is an odd term to discuss, due to relatively modern use and understanding of the term differ greatly from the initial concept of the word. Historically, the term by its self mostly referred to the home of the gods or God, a place more or less reserved only for the gods (and their minions such as angels). However, modern use of the term (the place where good are reward) is in the view of the long history of civilization a relatively modern construct only something developed mainly with the rise of Christianity.

This concept of the place of ultimate reward was historically more closely connected to the term. While heaven was for the gods, other cultures did create a somewhat limited place of reward for worthy souls other than heaven itself. This place was more associated with the Christian concept of the "kingdom of heaven" rather than the actual term "heaven." Even the Christians initially restricted heaven to God and the "kingdom of heaven" as the place where souls would go after the return of Jesus (which always appeared imminent). Today, in modern Christianity, the two places are more or less seen as the same.

In fact, at the time Christians presented this new concept of merging heaven with the kingdom of heaven, it's was seen as "quite progressive." The idea of heaven being available to all good persons was one of Christianity's more attractive features as it tried to sell itself to the Classical world. Here was an innovation of Christianity that changed a view of heaven (though it arose in some sects of Judaism about the same time, if not earlier).

In a time when the Pax Romana was ending and civil wars and invasions were constant, and plagues became frequent, and life became far shorter and violent deaths more frequent, the idea that everyone can have a good afterlife, without an act of the Senate of Rome, was truly appeal of the peoples of the time. As the uncertainty of society rose, so did the early Christian movement.

However, before showing how the Christians stopped being progressive, we need to go further back in history to show the origins of heaven itself. The Christians actually were reviving a very ancient tradition (heaven for all) Prior to the rise of civilization, all the dead became the honored ancestors, and were worshiped as such. It appears that with the rise of civilizations, the control of the afterlife passed to the priest and the rulers of society compared.

With civilizations came kings and, while a family's dead relatives were still honored, the kings became more than honored dead and actually transitioned into gods often before death. They were superior on earth and they needed to be superior in the afterlife. Therefore, a different place, a better place for the god-kings and therefore the gods evolved to be heaven.

Soon much of the work of the masses in a given society was dedicated to preparing the ruler for that transition. The most noted obsessed society where extensive energies went towards preparing the king (and almost anyone who could afford it, for the afterlife was clearly in Egypt. However considering the great tombs of early Chinese emperors, Egypt was not alone in this obsession.

However, even in Egypt, eventually there was a form of democratization of the process, or a return to a more open heaven. Gradually, over thousands of years, we see (from the remaining copies of the Egyptian Book of the Dead) that the idea of judgment of individuals based on their right living becomes more universal and almost all people who "lived well" and could pass the tests of the transition process could determine a path to the afterlife (of course with the right resources and payment to the right priests).

But even if they did "not take the name of the gods in vain, did not steal, did not kill, did not commit adultery" (all requirements in the Book of the Dead long before the incident at Mt Sinai), the average Egyptian could not go to the same place as the Pharaohs, not to Heaven, but instead to something more akin to what became the Christian view of the "kingdom of heaven" - a good afterlife, but not one with the gods.

However, Egypt was less typical then most ancient societies of the West. As we see in Homer, for most of the Bronze Age cultures, the afterlife for the ancient Greeks was a place of shadowy existence with little joy or pleasure. Similar views were held by the Jews of the time who only talked about life after death as the "world to come" and never really explained more in their early writings.

In these societies, some kind of opening to a better place after death developed, mainly to encourage military enlistments and actions. Eventually, with the Greeks and the Romans and many other societies frequently engaged in war, the warrior classes were allowed a better place than this non-life afterlife (with the Elysian Fields and Valhalla being the most famous of the places of glory). These places were again not with the gods themselves but places where the warriors were rewarded for the valor and bravery, places more or less reserved for those brave fighters and their families.

- In their wars of national resistance to the Greeks and then Romans, the Jews created the concept of resurrection of the dead who fought bravely. Soon that concept was again democratized by the Christians to the resurrection of all the saved.

Over the more recent centuries, we have again seen somewhat a democratization of the idea of what happens in the afterlife as the traditional meaning of heaven has mostly came to be interchangeable with the meaning of the term early Christian concept of the "kingdom of heaven." This merging of the ideas of heaven and " the kingdom of heaven" now means that in a modern Christian view all the "saved" now have a chance to reside with God in heaven; the doors to the abode of the gods became unlocked by this Christian (and earlier Jewish) concept.

- This opening of heaven to all who are good can be seen as very progressive on the part the Christians when compared to the more ancient views of the separation between the abode of god or gods (Heaven) and where people go, if worthy, after death.

So with the study of ancient societies we can see how the concept of "heaven" and even "the kingdom of heaven" transitioned over time. Mostly we see that the transition involved some form of democratic struggle to recapture the ideal that seemed to have existed in the pre-civilization period where all persons could transition to some kind of positive afterworld, expanding access from only the elite being able to make that transition. While the later Classical and Iron Age civilized world still allowed for the elite to join the gods in heaven, soon "the kingdom of heaven" seemed to be open to all worthy souls.

However, even while this process of access to "the kingdom of heaven" opened, the view of heaven itself was also in transition. While the good afterlife was made more accessible, heaven itself moved more and more towards a realm of an absolutist god. So soon all good souls could get in, but into something that was something quite controlled and limited in options. How did this change in heaven come about?

Part III - The Roman Transitions

Our best view of this transition of the concept of heaven into a place of absolute rule is the Roman world. We see this cultural development over the course of some 2000 years from the founding of the Republic to the end of the Byzantine Empire: as this society transitioned from a republic to a dictatorship, so did the view of heaven change to meet the change in society.

Here we see a struggle over the idea of "on earth as it is in heaven" evolving from holding that view of heaven as one of "separation of powers" to one of a model of absolute power – One God- One Emperor. As the political struggle raged leading to the fall of the republican government to the development over time of an absolute emperor, so too did the idea of heaven change from a place of squabbling gods to a place of one absolute "perfect" and all knowing" God.

With Rome we see the period of the Republic (roughly 500 BCE to 50 BCE) as a time where the view of the realm of the gods (or heaven) is as a place filled with scheming beings in constant competition with one another and with gods having very set areas of authority.

In other words, the Roman Republic's concept of "heaven" matched the Senate and its way of operations. And like the times, only the gods resided in heaven, just as only the members of the Senatorial class could rule Rome. (And the human elite could be deified by the Senate and allowed to enter heaven upon death.)

During the Principate (or the transition period from the emperor being seen as first citizen to absolute dictator, roughly 50 BCE to 280 CE), where the emperors still competed with the Senate and there were still some checks on the power on the emperor, we see the political transition played out in the religious movements of the times as well. While the emperors moved to become more empowered, they sought to institute major religious changes including several efforts to impose a form of monotheism on the state. The senatorial classes clung to the old gods and their diversity of powers as they attempted to cling to their political powers in the face of the growing powers of the military-based emperors.

- The fight between what we now call paganism and Christianity can clearly be seen as a fight between the forces of republicanism and dictatorship, with the Christians clearly on the side of the dictators.

During the period of the Dominate, or the later Empire, with rule by close to an absolute emperor, the state did impose a state religion based on an absolute and single god, just as it had imposed the power of the emperor on the people as a single absolute ruler. As the emperors sought to destroy resistance to their will they also sought to destroy all resistance to their view of that one god.

- The details of this history are too complex to review in any detail. However, the general religious efforts of the emperors in the period of transition can be summed up in that one phrase of "One God /One Emperor."

Before the fall of the West, for nearly two centuries, several efforts were made by different emperors to create this new cult of one god. Different emperors offered up a particular god as the one and only true god (Baal, Sol Invictus, and Mithras.) Christianity and its one God, was only the last of this group of religions that potentially seemed to meet the needs of the emperors to impose their absolutist rule in a society.

During the transitional period to the absolute emperor, the particular efforts around a particular god only seemed to last as long as a particular emperor, and in the "Crisis of the Third Century," the emperors' came and went quite quickly. Therefore, while there clearly was a movement towards a single god during the third century CE, none of the options ever really got a foothold long enough to make a real impression, because few emperors lived long.

- The Emperor Aurelian came close to being able to establish Sol Invictus as the sole god of Rome, but was assassinated after six years of rule.

The Christian writers of the time were convinced that this was his intention and his early death was seen as the work of their god.

Despite Aurelian's death, Sol Invictus remained very popular with the ruling classes and the army of Rome and was the main, if not only, god of the Emperor Diocletian, who ended The Crisis of the Third Century and brought stability to the Empire for some twenty years.

- It is also true that Constantine supported Sol Invictus and over his life participated more in its rites than that of Christianity.
- While in present times Constantine is often referred to as the first Christian Emperor, the Christians of his time claim that Constantine was only baptized on his deathbed. They knew as they wrote that for his entire life Constantine was a supporter of the god Sol.

But as a ruler of an empire with much religious diversity and conflict, Constantine recognized the need to bring about internal harmony in the Empire and therefore promoted religious toleration (Edict of Milan, 310 CE) and supported all religious approaches, including Christians. He appears to be the first emperor to endow Christian organizations and build churches at state expense. However, Constantine did the same for several religious groups; his efforts towards the Christians may have been more of a way of buying off a very rowdy group that seemed to be constantly involved in internal riots.

- Constantine's effort with the Council of Nicaea was actually his effort stop the Christians from killing each other over disputes over dogma.

By the way, during this search for a "one god," the God of the Jews was never really considered as a serious contender by the Romans simply because of the great revolts by Jews. These revolts were seemingly never-ending and almost always very close to being successful. Despite the fact that during the early emperor period the Jews were close to 10% of the Roman population, they were seen as traitorous and dangerous people, too unwilling to accept Roman rule to have their God considered as the one true god by the Romans.

- The key ones being the revolt of 66-71 CE which resulted in the destruction of the great temple in Jerusalem, the "Revolt of the Diasporas" 117-120, in which Jews took over extensive control of Cyprus and Egypt as well as other places in the "East" and forced Trajan to retreat out of the newly conquered areas of Mesopotamia; and the great revolt of Bar Kokhba in the 130s CE, where millions were killed and enslaved; and the Jewish religion all but banned. There were also several other smaller but serious rebellions by the Jews during the time from about 50 BCE to 140 CE.

When the Empire actually became a dictatorship with a fully authoritarian ruler under Diocletian (about 280 CE), he took extensive steps to make the single emperor and single god concept more a reality; his choice for that god was Sol Invictus. And for some forty years (under Diocletian and Constantine)

- Rome was more or less, at least on the state level, a monotheistic state with Sol (the ever victorious Sun) as the one true god of the emperors.

It is in this time period we see that the image of heaven changes greatly, whether under Diocletian, Constantine or his Christian sons, and then later under the extensively pro-Christian Theodosius the Great, we begin to see the representation of heaven not as a bunch of equal gods fighting and arguing among one another, but as an abode of an all-powerful God sitting in court, in which all the "angels" constantly sing his praises: a God that is unquestioned in his power or wisdom or knowledge.

The god of heaven was represented as the emperors on the earth hoped to govern, as an unquestioned ruler. The emperors pushed to have "on earth as it is in heaven," once they redefined heaven to be an authoritarian state.

- The process of Roman society settling on Christianity is much less a story of divine recognition or some great religious truth than the emperors finding a religion that was very willing to accept the absolute earthly rule of a single authoritarian ruler. (Give unto Caesar ....)

As the world of Rome degenerated and the power shifted to the East, the emperors became even more authoritarian in power and the image of God and the heaven in which he ruled became more authoritarian in its representation. We today can see this representation in the preserved paintings of the Hagia Sophia in Istanbul (or what once was Constantinople).

- In the rump of the empire in the Eastern Empire, the effort to present "One Emperor- One God" was achieved through Christianity bending to the view of the emperor.

The struggle to maintain some form of democratic freedoms in the later Empire often appeared religious in nature. As late as 394, the Western Empire was in virtual revolt against Christian Eastern Emperor Theodosius the Great and his tyrannical rule.

The Roman Senators, without consent of Theodosius, elected the Emperor Eugenius as Emperor in the West, based on his pledge to re-establish all the traditional Roman "pagan" religious activities, including games and reopening the Altar of Victory (dedicated to Jupiter) and reinstating power sharing with the Senate.

After only two years of rule, in a massive battle in 394, Eugenius was killed and Christian absolutism was restored to the West, along with the absolute rule of the Emperor.

In the Eastern Empire, the Church became the tool of the emperor and the Church hierarchy accepted this new "One God One Emperor" view;

- The emperor was seen as having the same absolute authority on earth as God had in heaven.

The emperors supported the Church based on the church's support of the emperors' authoritarian power.

As long as the Eastern or Byzantine Empire existed, until 1453 CE, this view of absolutist earth and heaven was maintained in that ever shrinking state. This view of power and the relationship between emperor and God and the church transitioned into the view of heaven in the Slavic world of the Russian Empire, or the Third Rome as claimed by their rulers, where the Czar until 1917 CE claimed in absolute power based on God's powers, with the full support of the Church.

While in the West, after ending of the designation of an emperor in the West, the new crop of rules of the West still tried to claim this right to absolute power based on the model of heaven on earth passed on to them by the priests of the Western Church, and still maintained by the Eastern emperors.

In the West, with no recognized central state, the role of the emperor was seized by the leader of the Western Church, or what we today call the Pope. At first they seized one of the titles of the emperor under the "pagan" structure of state.

- The Pontifex Maximus (Latin, literally: "greatest pontiff") was the high priest of the College of Pontiffs

> (Collegium Pontificum) in ancient Rome. This was the most important position in the ancient Roman religion ...,, beginning with Augustus, it was subsumed into the Imperial office. ... The word "pontifex" later became a term used for Christian bishops, including the Bishop of Rome, and the title of "Pontifex Maximus" was applied within the Roman Catholic Church to the Pope. http://en.wikipedia.org/wiki/Pontifex_Maximus

Then the Church claimed earthly power as well. The Church, as emperors before them, was soon claiming all the successor states were directly under their dominion.

With that claim, for centuries there were extensive battles by the monarchs with the Western Church over who really had the absolute power based on modeling after heaven. With no gaps in power in the East, and then in Russia, such struggles never existed.

- When the West became centralized into kingdoms and then empires, over the centuries the more powerful earthly rulers were able to better control the Church and turned this model of "One God- One King" to their own advantage; they created the concept in the West of the "Divine Right of Kings."

Therefore, as the Church of the later united Roman Empire accepted and promulgated the view of heaven as being absolutist, for centuries to come the anti-democratic nature of the rule of the East and the West and their undemocratic view of heaven was supported by the Orthodox and Catholic Churches. While often at odds with each other in the West, the ideal of "One God-One Emperor" or "One King and One Pope," became mutually self-supporting.

And with the mutual control of earth and heaven any form of dissent or of community power based in the "will of the people," as opposed to the "will of God" could be and was condemned as both treason and heresy. With adoption of Christianity and the modification of Christianity to conform to the will of the emperors, Europe became dominated by absolutism and authoritarian rule for at the next millennia, and so did heaven.

The people who objected to this view were condemned as being similar to or supporting the only power that objected to the power and will of the god: the devil. The state and the church supported the notion that all dissent, political or religious, was alignment with the anti-god. And this anti-god soon became portrayed as the absolute ruler of an anti-heaven (Hell), and instead of reward for the believers, the dissenters were condemned to eternal damnation. But the model for heaven, earth and hell all were one of absolutism.

Part IV - The Fight against Absolutism and its Impact on Heaven

The effort to destroy this model of absolutist rule in the West has been long and torturous, lasting hundreds of years and vastly too great of a subject to be handled well here.

What needs to be said is that as with the later Roman period, for most of this time the fight against absolutism was put in religious rather than political terms. Therefore, as we look back on the political changes that began the decline of authoritarian rule:

- beginning with the Dutch ninety-year war of independence against Spain,
- the Protestant reforms
- the eventual rise of Liberalism and

- eventually the democracies of the United States and Revolutionary France

We find that all these movements had in common (among many things) the effort to change the view of heaven. For without a change in heaven, their new growing democratic view of the rights of people to determine the means to govern themselves seemed to be rebellion against heaven itself; for if heaven is the realm of an absolute god then what justified a democratic rule on earth?

Through the centuries long struggle (and even today in too many lands) the forces opposed to democracy continued to use the image of God in heaven as being the model and the justification for the continuation of the power of the authoritarianism (monarchs and other forms) on earth. Therefore the existing powers often called efforts for democratizing society as attacks on God and often, to avoid some civil reactions, brought the early agitators before religious courts of all kinds.

- Many people, who in today's language could be seen as freedom fighters, were burned in their time as heretics.

Over the centuries of struggle, various responses to this question of how to challenge the image of heaven arose from the "freedom fighters." First we see that the various movements claimed that God had been misrepresented; early on in the Protestant movement (and even pre-Protestant moments) the Pope was labeled as the "anti-Christ" and the existing church as representing the views of the Devil and not God.

- Some very early groups, such as the Cathars, even went so far as to claim that earth was really hell and the Pope really the Devil.

We then see in the Anabaptist 16th century revolts in the Low Countries and Germany, people trying to move away from the sticky point of redefining "heaven" to reviving the concept of the kingdom of heaven."

The leadership of the revolts tried to present a collectivist society, the shining city on the hill, on earth based on what they projected as the future home of the select in the "kingdom of heaven."

They saw "the kingdom of heaven" as all equals based on the common grace of Jesus. They attempted in their revolts to make heaven on earth; or, more correctly said, the "kingdom of heaven" on earth. These efforts quickly degenerated into authoritarian mini-states as one or more of the leaders claim divine right akin to the monarchs they so strongly opposed. They also imposed severe punishment on all those who did not see that their version of heaven on earth was the correct and only vision of heaven on earth. Without changing heaven, they only had the authoritarian model with which to work.

- Mostly people of this time could not really envision an alternative to the image of heaven with an absolutist "all knowing" and all-powerful God.

Starting roughly in the mid-17th century in England and France, as the movement away from the absolute monarchy grew the intellectual class began abandoning the concept of the Church and Christianity. (Cromwell, not one of these, claimed his actions were governed by God, and his view of the" kingdom of heaven" allowed him to kill a king and then to set up absolutist government with him as dictator, "Lord Protector.")

Some in the movement of that time claimed there was no God; others claimed some form of statement close to what much later was coined by Nietzsche; that "God is dead."

- Within these societies there were also more moderate efforts developed to keep religion, but to focus on the call for social justice and equality based on the direct teachings stated in the Bible. The Quakers, Unitarians and other "reformed" or "pilgrim" groups formed to seek reform without abandoning religion.

However, with the growth of science and logic, the pace of rethinking of God and heaven advanced quickly. We see the struggles in the writings of Voltaire and many others continuing to try to determine if God never existed or, if he had, was now dead. They needed the version of god they had been given by the Church and the kings to be gone, if they were to continue the trend to rid themselves of absolutism on earth.

As noted, since there was not quite yet a Marx, the writing on the subject often continued to seemed solely religious, since there was little other means to discuss the issues. However, as writers of the time expanded the concepts of Locke and others, a new type of language developed, and the discussion became more on the rights of man, with the responsibly to God limited, and the requirements of God's mandate reduced.

- "When in the course of human events …" was part of this new use of language to justify actions in the realm of earth, not as a mandate of heaven.

During the late 18th century the trend to eliminate the modeling of power on earth based on the totalitarian image of heaven split into two main trends, Liberal and Revolutionary.

The first was the American model, more or less the Liberal model, really first developed by English writers, but only adopted by the British after the Americans. This model called for the separation of the realm of religion from the realm of the state.

The separation of church and state basically declared that the state would not be modeled or based on a religious view or on an effort to replicate heaven (or the kingdom of heaven) on earth, but that the state will be created by the will of the people based on the needs of the people: "a government of the people, by the people, and for the people."

While intellectually Deists and lovers of rationalism, and mostly very opposed to organized religion, the US founding fathers did not want to impose any view of religion on a people, including no religion. They truly understood that many of the people who had initially created the colonies (becoming the states) came to the new lands to worship freely and not to have the state impose a national view of religion.

They understood that the people of the new nation would tolerate neither a state religion nor a state that banned religion.

- So the Americans simply divided the realms, each person could worship as they saw fit (or not), but the state would rule free of religious views and requirements.

In this Liberal approach, the question the design of heaven became one of no concern to the state, since the state did not govern by God's will but by the will of the people. Every religion could have their view of heaven and it would not impact the state at all.

France, on the other hand, chose the revolutionary option as far as God and religion. After centuries of absolutist rule and domination of an authoritarian church, when they had their revolution simply said enough is enough. The revolutionary government banned religion, confiscated the wealth and lands of the Church, reset time (declaring the new measurement of time the years would be based on the start of the Revolution), and officially declared for the worship of logic.

- As the Revolution descended into the Terror, then into Napoleon, and he into the Emperor, predictably religion returned, and for a brief time France again was a land where "One God one Emperor" became the dominant theme.

Liberalism had a far harder time in France than in the US or England, as kings and emperors with real power persisted in that country until the crushing defeats of the Prussian War of 1870.

While the revolutionary efforts of France collapsed, the liberals did not fair all that well either. From the American Revolution to prior to the collapse of most of the remaining absolutist monarchies with World War I, other efforts to establish a separation of Church and state were met with extensive bloodshed by the totalitarian states. The Carlist wars in Spain, the widespread revolts of 1848 and the Paris Commune all examples of defeat of the Liberal ideal of a non-religious based government.

And we truly need to reflect upon the fact that outside of a few places on the earth, the model of absolutism or modified absolutism continued until the horror of World War I, and then through the decades of Fascism and Communism (absolutism not based on God). For most of the world, we are less than twenty years into an epoch where absolutism was not the norm in most of the earth.

The eventual success of Liberalism or what can be called the American and British models, throughout the world has now put us in a position where, for the first time in history, the political structure of the world is vastly different than the image of heaven of the (Western) religious peoples of the world. There is for the first time ever a real mismatch between what is considered and ideal earth and an ideal heaven.

Part V - A Modern World, an Ancient Concept

As the concepts of freedom and democratic ideals took hold in the US, and later in some Western countries, religion has become less of a political factor. With this development the nature of heaven became less of a concern to the state, as the state justified its existence and design on the will of the people and not the will of the god. Public polling and votes replaced prayer and God's revealed word as the driving force for civil government action.

However, in the US and other lands frequent "revivals" swept through the "heartland" in which religious-based leaders came forth to call for the return of the people to the values of their religion.

These leaders claimed that the laws of God superseded the laws of man. Often these religious events had little impact on the state, but only on individual lives, and the balancing act between the new democracy and the tyranny of religious absolutism was maintained.

However, sometimes these revivals created demands for public actions, and forced the state to respond to the demands of the "people." In the US, over almost two-and-a-half centuries of existence we've seen various uses of this religion motivation, including the pressure for and against slavery, for and against welfare supports for the poor, for and against liquor and abortion and gay rights: and, unfortunately during the course of the nation's history, for and against civil rights and voting rights of minority peoples.

Through a good part of our history, a majority's vision of God and his abode (heaven) was a driving force behind racist and sexist norms of the time. While the non-democratic nature of God was not emphasized, throughout most of our history, God was declared to be white and male and in charge. Therefore even in the more democratic United States, the social pressures of the religious tried to continue the replication of heaven on earth by assuring that only (straight) white males, according to God's plan, were in charge.

Compromise was often sought by the state, such as allowing the invocation of God in schools (only to be struck down by the courts), and in the early 1950s adding God into the national pledge.

The largest victory of the Christian movements over time was clearly the Prohibition Amendment to the Constitution (looking at the Civil Rights movement as a social justice and not religiously based effort). The chaos and upsurge in crime and corruption that came about in trying to enforce the ban on alcohol led to a massive decrease in the influence of the revivalist reformers for nearly fifty years.

- However, since the 1970s, the religiously driven political forces have been on the constant rise.

Focusing on such issues as school prayer, creationism, abortion and gay rights, the Christians have won numerous elections based on the call for the nation to return to being something it never was intended to be; a Christian nation governed under Christian morals and rules (and looking towards and absolutist God for leadership and rules.

This movement has been extensively successful. Clearly, few if any candidates can be elected to office without an express statement in the belief in God and calling for that God's blessing on the people of the United States. Supporters of abortion rights are called murderers or gay rights as supporters of abomination by the Christian forces, with much success. The founding fathers would be horrified at the evolution.

Part VI - The Inherent Contradiction

A precept of the United States, and the premise by which we spread the new ideals of freedom and democracy throughout the world, is that no one person is divine nor has absolute knowledge; we call on a government of laws with clear checks and balances to protect the rise of dictatorial powers in any individual or group. We "preach" the need for all peoples to have a say in the government and avow that the rights of the minority must be protected against the potential tyranny of the majority. We also call on all groups to work together rather than fighting with each other, towards compromise and doable solutions.

However, in the form of Christianity that is dominant at the moment, a form which sees God's will as the only will and God's laws as the only laws (and declares there can be no compromise with God's laws or will) we see little room for compromise. This new political force is like so many older groups that desire to attempt to recreate heaven on earth (or at least the kingdom of heaven on earth), and can allow no compromise in this process. Here is simply a reshaping of the effort to crate absolutist rule and dictatorial power in the name of God.

We hear so much of the old language which declares that to go against God's will is to be condemned to hell, and denied the afterlife of heaven (or the kingdom of heaven).
This is not the language of our founding fathers but the language which they fought against. This is not the language of democracy but the language of tyranny and kings and emperors.

Yet in a "free" country which tries to separate the state from the religious, and allows for all advocating of all religion, the state cannot really take action against these religious advocates (except for the Timothy McVeigh's' of the world). As long as these new absolutists seek power through the tools of democracy, little can be done against them. (This Christian movement is following the same theory as Hitler's legitimate revolution of gaining power through legal means.)

And the more they gain power, the more they move to dismantle the presence of the separation of church and state. They dream of a return to a world based on god's will and law, they dream of authoritarianism, without an emperor perhaps, but an authoritarian state none the less. Democracy seems to be falling based on its own contradiction of allowing dissent.

Part VII - Is this a Possible Solution?

Logic and reasoning works little with people who deny logic and reasoning. The power of the new Christian message is that of absolutism and the call to replicate heaven on earth, or to prepare the way for the second coming, or prepare for participation in "the kingdom of heaven," after death or after the second coming or the idea of being superior by being saved. The basis for the call is the word of God, based on the Bible or the writings about the Bible. To so many, no other writings or logic or reasoning or science has any foundation other than the Bible, since they are convinced that that book is the revealed word of God and must be taken absolutely.

It matters little to them that the details of the Bible have been shown through logic and reason to be non-supportable. They deny logic and reasoning so that the belief in the "flood" or in Adam and Eve, or that the sun stood still, or that the world is only 6000 years old, or that Jesus was born of a virgin and that the temple was rocked with his crucifixion can be and must be maintained as absolute.

- Their logic goes that if any point is not true there is a foundation for all points to be not true, therefore all points must be true.

Traditional efforts to break this view fail continually; the non-believers are simply declared tools of the devil, and they will get their torment in the "end times" and be denied access to "the kingdom of heaven." The fundamentalist feel certain that the righteous will be saved and all others condemned.

And they are entitled to their right to think so.
Like so many of the intellectuals of the past I have no real solution. Most efforts to contain the power and growth of the Christian movement have focused more on logic and reason and criticism of their belief in the Bible as absolute. They seem to fail.
We are still faced with the same two options from before, eliminating religion or compromising with religion. One means of trying to eliminate religion is a campaign to show religion for what it is - a means towards totalitarianism.

- One possible way to do so is to actually create models of what life would be like based on all of the 613 commandments in the Bible. I think few modern people, except for the extreme Orthodox Jews would want to live in such a state.

Since elimination efforts do not work, I wish to offer a new way of compromising with religion. I offer this effort to try and contain their growing power by addressing the foundation of their demands: creating heaven on earth, or having earth as it is in heaven.

The compromise is we don't deny the concept of wanting to create heaven on earth; we just change the concepts of what heaven on earth would look like for a freedom-loving society. We offer another model for the "kingdom of heaven" for the afterlife. Therefore we create a new model of "on earth as it is in heaven."

- One again, since society has changed so much, we need to create an image of heaven that fits our society as was done so often in the past.

We need a heaven that is not designed to meet the earthly demands of absolutist emperors and popes but of democratic multi-cultural freedom loving and anti-authoritarian people. We need a heaven for a democratic society.

My post-life heaven would be where Mozart, Beethoven, Shakespeare, Jane Austin, Li Bai (or Bo or Po depending on translation) and Jim Morrison (as well as countless others from the East as well as the West), are still creating works of art. (So we don't just have to listen to *"Light My Fire"* or *the Ninth Symphony* over and over.) When we get there … well in my section of heaven there will be no re-runs (except for the ones I want of course).

And naturally we can exercise and eat to our no-longer-working-heart's content. We can travel the world, if not the universe, at will. Since this is heaven and heaven is each person's creation, in my heaven there is no money, or need for money, except in casinos where games of chance are still games of chance, with rewards for winning (and limits on losing). I can also have dinner with any of the great people of world history I want, and several at a time. .. Mr. Genghis Khan, meet President George Washington, and so on (like the frame work of an old Steve Allen show called *Meeting of the Minds*, which I loved).

Herein lies the dilemma in creating a broad model for a modern non-authoritarian heaven --- what I see as heavenly may not be so to another. So therefore, to paraphrase the Bible a little, John 14:2 precisely, "in my house there are many rooms."

- Heaven, in an anti-authoritarian model, is of one's choosing. What goes on in your room stays in your room, so to speak.

Based on the success of the Las Vegas add campaign, that actually should not be too hard to sell to the people of the modern world.

Just one last thing, in this new vision of heaven, if we based it on an American concept of freedom:

- There is no religious test to get in.

All people of faith or non-faith are welcome in, as are all people of all colors and backgrounds, and, of course, sexual orientation.

Other qualifications based on our culture's needs should be created to replace the old requirements fitting a much older time, replacing the demands of the Egyptian "Book of the

Dead," the Jewish "Ten Commandments.," and the requirements of Paul and Mohammad as laid out in their sacred books.

- This is not an effort to mimic such as Tolstoy, who sought to merge the great thinking of the past into a combined pacifist/anarchist Christian movement for his present (his modern); or his effort to create heaven on earth.

This is an effort trying to modernize the whole concept of heaven, for a modern people, so heaven reflects a modern earth.

Here's a quick list I would offer as a modern ten "social agreements" (as opposed to the authoritarian term "commandments".) These are offered as a starting point for suggestion that, in this modern world democratic would should be reviews, added to (nothing sacred about "ten" in this new world), or subtracted to, and of course we can wordsmith each item in committee to everyone's delight, or at least willingness through consensus.

- Winton Churchill, roughly quoting, called democracy the worst of all governments, except for all the others. Trying to achieve ten agreements for the modern world's qualifications for heaven could be a "worse process ... except for all the others," which of course would be based in authoritarianism.

Here are my ten as a starting point of discussion: Here I use the affirmation model of the Book of The Dead, rather than the authoritarian model of the Ten Commandments.

- I have honored the founding fathers by voting in all elections;

- I have attempted to purge myself of racism;
- I have attempted to purge myself of sexism;
- I have not abused fellow people either physically or mentally;
- I properly prepared myself for retirement;
- I supported my children and/or other children in their education;
- I have reduced my carbon footprint;
- I did not text, use my phone or drink while driving;
- I have coveted new things and bought them to support the economy;

And to restate an oldie but goodie …

- I have honored my father and mother to the point I can stand them, and then some.

And of course, over the gates of heaven there should be a sign that reads: "Give me your tired, your poor … (your rich and retired) all those yearning to be free …I lift my lamp beside the golden door."

Glenn Young

PART II –

THE PERSONAL AS HISTORICAL

Setting the Stage

The overall themes of the essays in the first section of this book have been the importance of history in understanding the present and the future. And so far, I have focused on mega-issues and avoided the personal. This and the following two essays look at how the personal is also impacted by history, and how history (a personal history, and a wider history) can impact major events, or just how a person reacts to a major event occurring around them.

For the first essay, here, I look at how action or non-action can lead to things happening or not. In the large picture, we operate with the understanding that we are all products of our times and social and economic environments. That being said, I have always (since consciously able to), fought against typecasting people based on their times and social and economic environments; capturing people in a cell of predestination.

People change, through all forms of experiences, good and bad. These changes impact how they act later on in their life, and what appears positive may be not so ... and of course what appears negative may not also be so. The experiences may likely change the destiny of people, and again without appearing too Zen, for the good or bad is never really know and often unclear at the time, or the near future after any given event.

Often ... far too often, the mega-moment in people's lives never happens. People may not recognize the moment, or if they do, cannot take the steps to make it happen. So of course we will never know if that moment would have really changed the person or the world. We just know it never happened.

This essay about a personal experience looks at the steps or non-steps people have to make to help bring about social change, or then again not bringing about social change. Opportunities missed or not missed change the world, including meetings taking place or not ... and this is a case in point ... in 2004 ...

(Also, obviously since this essay was first written the phone and tablet revolution has continued at what could be called warp speed. But at this time, it was happening with few foreseeing much of the total potential.)

How I Almost Met Bill Gates and Almost Changed the World

I was told he was in the room, Bill Gates that is. In the same room as I was, along with some 400 other bridge players. I was told he was in the far side of the room, just sitting at a table, just like all the other bridge players, trying to figure out the right bids and right sequence of card play to get the maximum outcomes of the hand, when compared with the 100 other tables of people playing bridge in this one section of the national bridge event taking place in Washington DC. And of course I had a very good reason to try and meet Mr. Gates. I had a great idea to pitch him.

Now, for the last two years, starting around 2002 or so, I've been thinking about and developing a new approach to adult literacy that could radically increase the capacity of millions of persons in the United States, if not the world, in a far, far more rapid timeframe than that offered in the current adult literacy system.

I've been calling the approach "virtual literacy," and it takes advantage of the extensive increase in technological tools that has made accessing knowledge through the internet on hand-held devices common place, and the fact that tools like the "Kindle" enable people to carry with them 1500 books on a device the size of a day planner. It also incorporates the new telephones that can take pictures of a written document and turn it into a text document almost instantaneously.

And all through this two-year process, of creating the concept and selling the idea to advocacy and service groups, of trying to get Congress and governmental agencies interested in this approach, one of my standard refrains to all I approached was, "If I could only get someone like Bill Gates to look at the concept, he would get it and support it right away."

And now here I was in the same room with Bill Gates, well, along with 400 others, and I think to myself, this is my chance to get to him with my idea, and well … change the world for the better. All I have to do is get to him and deliver my "elevator speech" and he'll love it. Here is another great chance for me to do what needs to be done and no one else seems to be able to do it.

I have had a few "great chances" in my past, and mostly I've succeeded in avoiding protocol and just "doing it," with positive results for my initial goals, but often with lots of problems for me, personally and professionally. I was generally "hell bent for leather" and disregarded what most people thought of me. In fact, since very early childhood I always thought that most people wouldn't like me anyway. So I turned that understanding into some kind of wearied benefit; I would do the things that needed to be done, regardless of what anyone would think, because no matter what I did they wouldn't like me … so I might as well "do the right thing," since they won't like me no matter what I do.

And I did that throughout many aspects of my so-called career, and it resulted in me being successful and hated at the same time. Without regard to wanting to be liked, I would speak truth to power, ask for money, organize protests, tell national organizations and governmental agencies that they were obsolete and hurting the people that it was their mission to help.

And in fact, most people I worked with or confronted tended to hate me, and my old nickname from high school, "Glenn the Obnoxious," still fits me well. But I also got things done, lots of things done that others wouldn't do for fear of offending.

Me, I had no such fear, since I knew I would tend to offend anyway. I focused on the endgame, not the cost to me. And, for decades, I got things done; from starting food co-ops and saving low-income housing and fighting against unjust wars, to development of civil rights coalitions, to creating the first validated screening tools in the nation for adults with learning disabilities, to raising gender bias issues concerning the identification of learning disabilities in females that led to changes in national and state welfare laws across the country. I also helped start and fund three major national research centers and served six years on the national board of the Learning Disabilities Association of America, testified in front of Congress and the Attorney General of the US and met with the President of the United States in the Oval Office.

Now I am focused on "modernizing the adult literacy world" through use of e-technology; no big thing, just trying to save the world again (or at least change it for the better). And now I'm in the room with Bill Gates, the guy who could actually help me bring about this change. And me, the man noted for no fear in approaching and confronting people, here I am ready to go.

For decades people have been covertly, overtly and in any other way telling me to change my tactics, that whole thing about getting more with honey, and so on. For the most part I've ignored them, partly because I did get so many things done that no others could do, so my act paid off for me on some levels, and partly because I am very ADHD and OCD (Obsessive Compulsive Disorder) along with my learning disabilities, so often I don't even know when I am offending or how I am offending, even when I'm on my meds.

The consultations and advisements of friends and co-workers (and bosses) and outright therapy of professionals has had some moderating impact over the years, but not as much as friends, co-workers, bosses and professional therapist have wished; I am still LD/ADHD/OCD and also highly focused on getting and keeping the eye on the prize and jumping when the chance arises.

At a bridge national event two years before in San Francisco, I met a friend of a head of a national foundation and through that meeting and a phone call the next morning, I came within an eyelash of getting funding for this project. It almost always seem to come down to the idea of it's not what you know it's who you know ... and you need to get to know the people that can make changes, through bridge or otherwise. So here's my chance to meet Bill.

My daughter went to a preschool run by the wife of one of the original owners of Starbucks, and when I was trying to save the Seattle Food Bank from collapse due to the Reagan cuts from social services, I was able to get to the president/owner of Starbucks and arrange for that company's first official corporate contribution. On my own it is very unlikely I could have made that connection. It's who you know, I know.

But, sometimes it's not who you know but what you're willing to do; and me, I'm usually willing to do a lot. So I was willing to "cold call" Apple to get them to "loan" me 50 Macs when they were first coming into the market, so I could run a fundraiser based on competition between investment houses using a simulated stock market game. And also "cold calling" the big stock brokers to sell them on the concept was something no one else I knew would do (at least in the fundraising world).

I researched and found that the stock brokers were the least likely of all groups to donate money to charities, so instead of going to the same wells for money, I designed an event specifically for the least likely to give. And with cold calling and no fear, it worked.

I was willing to cold call Coors Beer and ask them to loan me their corporate jet to get Greg Le Mond from Colorado Springs to Seattle for an event, just a few days after he first won the Tour de France. I was a "nobody" from a small private nonprofit in Seattle, but I called. The Coors people asked me if he would wear a Coors jacket when he got off the plane, and I told them if you gave him a jacket he'd wear it on his arrival to Seattle. Within ten minutes of a cold call from this nobody, I got a jet lent to me for free. Sometimes it's being able to ask, not just who you know.

Now here I was, ready to have no fear and to "cold call" Bill Gates at the national bridge event. And I was in the same room with him, so I decided to scope it out. During a break in the play I walked over to the other side of the room just to spot him, and to scope out how he looked and if he seemed "approachable."

When I walked over to look he was not at his assigned seat. I didn't know if he was off saving the economy or if he was just avoiding people or if I was being put on and he was not in the room. And as I turned around to go back to my seat, he rushed by, almost brushing me as he went. It was obvious to me, Bill Gates had to pee in the middle of the session, and he was rushing back to his seat after the long trek to the men's room from that location in the hotel (which all males in the event were complaining about).

As he went by I looked at him and my mindset shifted; he did not look like the multi- billionaire, first-, second- or third- richest man in the world, he just looked like the rest of us in the room: a poor schmuck trying to understand this card game that takes a few hours to learn and a lifetime to master.

OK, he plays with a professional bridge player, but here he was in what was considered a lowly little "side game" at the nationals, populated mostly by people who had failed in one of the "knockout" events played earlier in the week or day. (Well, there were mostly losers from other events; one of the top players in the world was sitting two tables away from me.) Bill was just another bridge player trying to have some fun and master each hand. I started to reconsider my approach.

I talked to a few of the "east/west" players coming to my "north/south" table and they told me that almost everyone coming to his north/south table was "hitting on him" for something, ranging from ideas for new products to complaints about Vista to requests for pictures and autographs, and how he was clearly polite about it, but clearly hated it.

OK I decided to wait a bit after the event to see if a crowd formed around him. If not, I would approach in a very apologetic fashion, maintaining my disdain for all the others who had approached him, but stating that my "thing" was too good not to "seize the time" and give him my pitch.

But when the event was over, I had to make that long trek to the men's room, and when I came back … poof he was gone, and so was my chance I thought. But again, a few minutes later, there he was, just like so many others, hanging out in the bar going over the bridge hands, trying to understand why he didn't come in first, or even in the "money."

Actually in bridge, it's not money, but master points that are awarded for each event. You need to gain at least 300 master points to obtain the status of life master, but at least 25 points need to be won at a national event (gold points) or at sectional or regional events (silver points). Me I have well over 1,000 points (actually very low in high-level competition) and long since a life master, so I give little concern to these things. However, I heard that Bill has enough points but lacks some gold points, and therefore is still considered less than a life master in bridge … the richest man in the world and not a life master yet. I was developing a great deal of empathy for this guy.

In an open section of the bar he was talking to his hired gun and going over hand after hand from the sheet provide by event. He sipped his beer and occasionally slapped his head as if to say "how could I be that dumb." Far too often people interrupted him for a photo or a handshake, and, while very polite about it all, I could clearly see all he really wanted was to be like all of us lower-level bridge people and understand what he (I) did wrong … and we always do so many things wrong. He was relaxing and having fun and being … well, not Bill Gates the richest man in the world (depending upon the day), but Bill Gates, bridge player, trying to get those few points needed to become a life master. He wasn't someone at the top of the world, but someone … well, pretty near the bottom of this world of bridge.

So I got even more concerned, and I guess conflicted. Should I just go up and shake his hand, give him my card and my elevator speech? Should I wait to see if there was some kind of break in the discussion? Who was I, "Glenn the Obnoxious" or the Glenn with lots of therapy and finally listening to the consults of others to be polite; should I push or not?

Actually I knew that you had to be uncommon, as I have always been. And if many are coming up to him to give him ideas and he clearly did not like it much, no matter how polite he was being, my pitch would not work. It was too common at that point in time. So it wasn't that Glenn the Obnoxious was being controlled, or that the veteran of therapy Glenn was being let out, it's that Glenn the knowledgeable fundraiser was in charge … I think this was the good old conflict of the id, ego and superego, and my superego started taking over.

And I saw my chance when Bill needed to go pee again, or perhaps make a phone call or something. Regardless he got up and walked away. I saw my chance and swooped in. I sat down next to his pro and started talking to him.

I expressed my understanding that Bill was just trying to learn from him, and I didn't want to interrupt that process, but I had this great idea that Bill would like. And he said everyone seemed to … and I gently protested that this was about education and technology, an area that Bill is very interested in. I tried to present a compromise to the pro. I gave him my card and said that when he was done going over the hands, he could say to Bill that this guy wanted to talk to him, and I was waiting close by. And I was being polite and supportive by not intervening in their discussions but hoped to get a minute or two. The pro said that could maybe work and took my card.

For the next ten minutes or so, I stood about ten feet from the two of them, hovering but being polite, talking to friends.

We were betting on if I would get my face time, or not, or if I could stand it or not, if "Glenn the Obnoxious" would win out or not. And during that time, the pro held my card in his hand and used my card as a pointer… showing the richest man in the world the errors of his ways, in bridge.

For the ten minutes I was in near pain as my card passed in front of Bill Gates face, time after time. My friends laughed at me as, with each passing, I was saying things like "so close, so very close." And saying I wish the pro would just drop the card and Bill would pick it up… but no. Nothing happened.

Bill soon got up, shook hands with the pro and walked off. I didn't follow. I decided to let Bill Gates be just another bridge player, and not get assaulted by just another guy with a great idea. I let Bill Gates be a human being for a little while, not a walking god. Maybe all that therapy and the work of friends and family went too far. How could I do it, let Bill Gates go by, and not make a run at him to change the world together?

I went back to the pro who promised to give him the card the next day. And of course this was my last day at the national event. If he did or did not, I don't know. I just know Bill has not called me yet.

Of course there is some satisfaction that I acted less like "Glenn the Obnoxious" than in the past.

There is also some satisfaction in knowing that in all likelihood making a run at him would not have worked, since on that night he wanted above all just to be Bill Gates, another struggling low- level bridge player. So, I didn't get to meet Bill Gates, and I didn't get to change the world again (yet). But, perhaps the biggest satisfaction was that on that night, with a "pick up partner" that I had never meet or played bridge with before, on that night my partner and I in this low level "side game" got a better score than Bill Gates and his hired pro. And, while I missed a chance to change the world, on that night I could have even helped Bill Gates.

Setting the Stage

My life in the US was not the prototype of "normal," or perhaps, with real research, it was closer to normal than most want to project. However, it was not considered "standard." So, my views of events and people and history and relationships are not and were not "standard" as evidenced by the insights presented in this book.

In this nonstandard fashion, how I met the Pope and our reactions to each other were not standard either.

This essay incorporates my views on religion, cultural dominance, chauvinism, and all the other themes and how they all came together as a result of a brief interchange with perhaps one of the most popular people of the 20th century, Pope John Paul II.

The Pope and the Great American Bird

There I was, just four feet from the Pope. And between him and me, well there was just air; and that half-inch of bulletproof plastic that surrounded him, part of his famous "pope-mobile." I turned around and there he was in his full regalia, John Paul II, and he looked right at me.

I know he did since I was standing all by myself, at least three feet from anyone else, so I know he looked at me directly, and he smiled and raised his hand and gave that sign, the sign of the cross and a papal blessing, directed exclusively at me.

I know it was to me since I was standing there alone, in that space between him and the tens of thousands that lined the streets of Los Angeles who had all come to see him and, if possible, be blessed by the Pope directly. And while the "masses" could guess if the blessing being thrown out was for them, I knew I was getting one directed at me.

So it wasn't a guessing game, one that would be argued amongst the onlookers of whether the Pope really looked at them and blessed them directly. I knew he did to me.

I was there in that space away from everyone in the crowd, with space between me and the crowd and me and the Pope, because I was there doing what so many good Americans try to do at "events"; I was there making money. I was part of the subculture that has existed for almost all time, but has truly become a lifestyle in America, of vendors who travel from event to event to sell "things."

I was there alone, in the street, because I had a cart filled with Pope "paraphernalia" that I was busy trying to sell to all those tens of thousands behind the ropes. I had the Pope-does-Mass records (in English, Spanish, Polish and Latin), I had papal flags, framed pictures of the Pope, and little funny Papal hats, and lots of other American crap that we got handed to us by our bosses (as well as bottles of water and soda). My favorite was "Pope on a rope" ... soap with the image of the pope impressed in it, with a cord of rope through it so you could hang it in your shower.

We work around the edges of the mainstream culture, or perhaps it better to say we live off the mainstream culture. As the "mainstream people" of America seek entertainment at sporting events, you'll find us there selling programs, hats and food, and that all-encompassing term "souvenirs." At street fairs, county fairs, community parades, we're there selling whatever the event requires and is focused upon, balloons, toys, hats, food, programs, on and on. So as the Pope passed by, I was there selling, along with lots of other venders, and part of a specific crew.

Our year actually has a pattern that begins at the end of the "mainstream" year. We make most of our money at all the football bowl games (colleges, and pro), and then we move on to the final four of college basketball in March.
Between those events we have Mardi Gras in New Orleans for a month; some of us then split off to work in steady vending jobs at the six-month long baseball seasons at stadiums around the country.

Some find this too dull and constraining and follow the community parades that exist throughout the year throughout the South, but most famously in Texas. We even have our own "busman's holiday," as many of us convene on the Reno Rodeo each year to sell beer to cowboys during the day and gamble away all the profits all night. There are enough of these events to keep us busy most of the year and to pretty much keep us spread out over the country and out of one another's way or off each other's turf.

And then there are those "once in a lifetime events," such as the Olympics or the visit of the Pope to "your town." Then we all converge on the place, and try to find a way to get our "piece of the action" and still stay out of one another's way.

With the Olympics, there is so much to do and sell we can all seem to find a niche, and make the money. In '84, in LA, I was able to have a "piece" of a stand selling "official Olympic ceramics," as well as work in the Coliseum for ten days straight selling soda to the track and field fans.

Prior to the games actually starting, I was with a crew that followed the Olympic torch all around Southern California, selling little American flags, trying to stay less than a mile ahead of the runners carrying the torch. We made a mint doing this; we bought the flags from our handlers for fifty cents and sold them for two dollars.

Our biggest problem was finding product. When our handlers ran out we ended up "raiding Wal-Mart." We had to pay the retail price of 75 cents each in the stores, so we upped our prices to three dollars. It didn't matter. We sold them all; it seemed that ever "mainstream" person wanted to be able to wave the flag as the torch went by.

Another problem at these types of one-time events was the amount of cash we always seemed to have on us ... there was no place to put it. With our work hours we couldn't go to banks, and this was a time before ATMs. We were living out of a van, eating at I-Hops and Burger King, there wasn't even a hotel room to stash money (if you wanted to trust the hotel room). So while following the torch, every night I had to "face" this massive mess of one dollar bills and bundle them into packets of fifty and stash them somewhere safe.

It was not easy; sometimes the money went in the wheel wells and other places in the van. Often it just went into long plastic bags down my pants. Eventually our handlers would exchange these bundles for twenties and hundreds, but it could be a week or so walking around with all this cash to worry about.

In '84, I also had my own little venture going, trading Olympic pins. These pins were where most of the "action was," the Olympics for the true entrepreneurs. Having the right pin to sell was the entry to meeting the "right people" at the games, and getting into parties, and making a lot of money. Near the end of the Olympics in LA, I was in a tent where the pin sellers had about $3.8 million in front of them in cash, from that week sales of pins. That was just from the cheap "official pin stores -"the real money" was in the corporate pins.

In Atlanta in '96, two pins I was given and later sold ended up paying the cost of my entire Olympic trip (as a mainstream person, not as a vendor): tickets, food, housing, very expensive Olympic clothing, etc., all of the costs for both me and my girlfriend. They were just the "hot pin" of the moment; the corporate pins of the Piggly Wiggly stores. I sold them for the price of my trip as we were leaving town, to a pin trader, who, within ten minutes, had sold the pins for a good $250 profit each.

At the Olympics it's a momentary monetary economy driven clearly by irrationalism. I tried to explain to my educated friends that there was a formula for this "once in a lifetime event" economy that went something like this: the value of a given item is greatly reduced in proportion to the time and distance from the given event, with the converse also being true.

Also, besides watching the sporting events, and trying to meet athletes, pin trading was the major pastime of most of the people there. In LA, one of the largest buildings created for the event was the pin trading center. It was truly a world right out of the ancient Mideast, including a little old woman who was the "expert" appraiser. She sat in a little booth with her products, but mainly made her money by settling arguments; she was the final arbiter on the price of any pin. In 1990, I ran the pin center at the Seattle Good Will Games (Ted Turner's attempt to compete with the Olympics). At that event, I was the "little old lady"; it was sure fun and profitable.

In LA I got started with the pins when I met a pretty young woman from NBC, who, after flirting a bit with each other, invited me over … not to her place, but to her place of work. I was not after her body, I was after her pins. Before the games, as we were doing the set up, I had seen people wearing them and got curious. When I met this woman she was doing a story about the Olympic park and all the booths; she had a few pins on her.

She interviewed me as a vendor in the park, and afterwards I asked if I could have a few of the NBC pins. That's when she invited me over and I went to the NBC offices and she gave me a handful of NBC Olympic pins and even an NBC Olympic golf shirt. From that point on, I was a going concern of my own. For the next three weeks, while I was not "manning" our booth, or selling soda, I was trading and selling pins.

While other "pinheads" walked around with photo albums crammed full with pins from the present and past Olympics, I used my baseball cap as my showroom, letting people know what I had at their own convenience. It was a conversation-starter with all kinds of people, but also a source of some quick sales.

The most stupid of which happened when I was confronted by the most cliché of all people I think I have ever encountered; he must have been about six foot six, wearing cowboy boots and a "ten gallon hat" and a sports coat with those metal endings on the lapels.

He literally was looking down upon me as he talked in that heavy Texas accent. "Are they them Olympic pins I've been hearin all about? How about you all sellin me four? I'll give you one hundred dollars right now for four good ones." In no time I gave him four shitty ones for which I had many duplicates. He walked away smiling saying ... yes he actually said it "Much ahbliged."

OK what is clear is that we vendors seem superfluous to the mainstream, but we are always there. When we are seen, we are acknowledged only if we are in the process of the exchange of money for goods. It is assumed we have ripped the mainstream person off and we are an inconvenience, but that we got the thing that is wanted and no competition so ... we got to be dealt with, and be paid the over price.

To the mainstream, we look tired (which we almost always are, since we work for hours in advance to blow up balloons and vinyl toys, and then march around for hours up and down the streets trying to get the sales done before the parade goes by).

We look dirty (try sweating for hours as you run up and down parade routes or yell "cold lemonade" or "get your cotton candy," or hawk tee shirts or whatever we're selling that day for hours on end). And we look like bums.

I admit vending is not the chosen profession of college educated, and people with permanent homes or "wives and children" or health care or needed skills. But the money that is made for the time put in far, far outdoes working in most of the other options available; it sure beats vision offered in Jim Croce song; Working in the Car Wash Blues. (Copyright laws prevent the direct quote of the line about depression associated with that type of job.)

It's also not really a "babe-catcher" among "mainstream women." When I became divorced I started dating again, sometimes through the "want ads." When many women found out what I did for a living, they started looking at their watches ... a sure sign that not only would there be no sex that night, (not such a long shot on a first date in the pre-AIDS wild 80's) but the date was really over before even the soup was served.

But I was so much closer to mainstream than most. I was actually one of the few of the crew, of that whole subculture, with any kind of education and that worked, and had a "permanent address" and, before the divorce, actually a wife and daughter. And I am one of the few who actually made it out of the life to become "mainstream" myself.

But I am dyslexic and also have ADHD and a few other things that made it difficult for me to reach that level of mainstream for a long time. Yet this family I had also kept me from the "main cycle" of the road that most of the vendors kept. I couldn't really afford to be gone for a month at a time to Mardi Gras or something, and keep the love of my wife and daughter. I kept working in one area (Seattle,) and I only ventured out a few times a year for a few days at a time away from my family. So, I was seen by the real "vagabonds" only as a semi-guy, one of the crew, but still not truly bought-in completely to the "life."

But the "real crew" of vendors took advantage of my place; when they came through Seattle there was a home for them to crash in, a home-cooked meal to enjoy and a kid to play with. My daughter had lots of "road uncles" who would show up for a few days and take advantage of me and my being part of that "mainstream" culture. She had more vinyl toys and stuffed animals then anyone around, thanks to her "uncles."

Among vendors, like Bedouin, or any wandering people, hospitality was important, since no one seemed to want to offer us any other than ourselves.
We were below the mainstream in so many ways. In Marxian terms perhaps we are the "Lumpenproletariat," people who work "below" legitimate jobs, who functioned only in the "unofficial economy." Marx and most "revolutionaries," except for Huey P. Newton of Black Panther fame, saw us, this breed of people, as not to be trusted, people who were bound to become counter-revolutionaries because we were so used to selling to anyone.

Newton saw that almost the whole Black community was Lumpenproletariat and wanted to base the whole revolution on that population (like Mao wanted to base in peasants, while Marx and Lenin hated peasants).

Me, I knew different. As an American-bred radical, I knew that we vendors were really just capitalists and, like the concepts of capitalism say, we will work in our own best interest. And with the money we made, this vending gig was clearly in our best interest. And in America we could make a great living at it, since there were just so many events that needed us to provide our services, selling crap and souvenirs. I told college-educated ex-radical friends who just didn't understand why I was doing this gig, that by doing this I was "making lawyer wages."

But big events, like the visit of the Pope, were hard work and filled with lots of "free labor" (the term used in the vendor world was "Chinese," which I hated as racist). This free labor can get pretty horrid and utterly depressing. One time I pulled a sixteen-hour stint blowing up balloons getting ready for the "Rose Parade" in Portland Oregon.

The endless screams of the helium leaving the canisters and entering the balloon was enough to drive anyone to "action." My "mate" for the prep work turned out to be the ex-wife of Andre the Giant of wrestling fame. She and I got so bored that we started joking around that we vendors needed union protection, and, with my radical past and my understanding for the need for "direct action," there and then we became the founding (and I think only) members of MIGWA (Militant Inert Gas Workers of America).

Word of this silliness spread by word of mouth and seemed to catch on with as lease a few. For years at some vendor parties the chant of "MIGWA, MIGWA" could be heard among drunken people, or occasionally from a vendor in the streets in need of help or protection from a "union brother."

Later, at a party I had for my graduation from a Master's program, in which all the strange elements of my life, from "my radical days, from my vendor days, and now, from my entre into the intellectual elite," converged together, my MIGWA mate showed up with a present of a MIGWA tee shirt, complete with tie-dyed images of balloons all over the shirt.

One of my most uptight professors, who had distained to show up at my party at all, spent the early part of the evening coming up to me saying "you really know Andre the Giant's ex-wife." I finally said to him, yes, and now you can know her too. They spent much of the rest of the evening chatting. She frequently gave me a look of "come rescue me," but I had many other people, vendors, PhD's, politicians, social service agencies, people with disabilities, and just families and friends, to integrate.

My life had been complex and diverse. And as part of that diversity, I was also born Jewish. I didn't practice it much but I still claimed throughout all my days to be an apostate Jew, one who had fallen away, but still held to some of its concepts. I based in my radicalism (and still do) my hated all religions (opium of the masses and all that), but I loved the Jewish concepts of freedom and the celebrations of liberation from tyranny and slavery (Hanukah and Passover).

My Seders that I held were overtly political and used left-wing Haggadahs. I thought they were quite fun ("Oy, meetings upon meetings, debates upon debates, the brick makers union is questioning if Moses is leading us the right way," etc.).

The Seders, with the right people there, more than anything else became political critics of the Left and debates of "right action" concerning the events of the time, We seldom finished the Seder service, but made sure we drank all four glasses of wine ... they were fun events.

And my studies of history only reinforced my hatred of religions and how the religions were portrayed over time and in the present. My view of this has been greatly shaped by being an American, and an American radical and an American radical who was born and raised Jewish, and an American radical who was born Jewish and was also not part of the mainstream, or at least not for a good while. I often thought while I was vending that I was like so many other poor Jews who had their "pushcarts" on Hester Street in New York or on so many other streets in America and in Russia: the rag man or the fruit seller, me vending crap at the Pope; I was really being quite traditional- the Jewish rag man.

And at one point during the Pope's visit he performed a Mass for 90,000 people in the LA Coliseum. When he was there, there was no way the vendors could keep out of one another's way, he was where the action was and we were all there. When I got to the place with my cart, the Coliseum looked like an old walled city under siege, with all the vendors around the outside of the walls of the coliseum with their little booths and lights.

I knew I couldn't sell much in this "mass" of other venders during the blow off (vender language for the exiting crowd) ... just too much competition. I ventured away from the crowd of vendors to a parking lot where I wasn't supposed to be, but got there just as the Mass ended. The parking lot turned out to be reserved for the 9000 priests and nuns who had attended the Mass. The gates opened and they came rushing out, and I looked at them and them me and I just did my thing – I started yelling and selling. And they bought. They just about bought me out, and I was the only vendor there; I had the monopoly and these holy men and women wanted their souvenirs.

All the while I was huffing and puffing during this "priestly blow off," stuffing dollars in my apron and where ever else I could, I noticed two little "classic" nuns, still in the full habit dress, off to the side quietly laughing. As the blow off ended and I was starting to catch my breath again, they approached me and said they wanted to ask me a question.

And I started showing them what scraps I had left and asking what they were interested in ... and they said, no, no, we just want to ask you something.... And I said, what is that? One of them said; "are you Jewish?"

And I said, "of course," with as much of a straight face as I could muster ... "of course." They said, "We thought so," and laughed again and just walked off. I chuckled as I started to try and bring some order to the massive amount of cash I had just made off the Mass. It would be a long night facing the money ... but I had gotten it.

(None of my fellow vendors who had stayed in the "siege" area did anywhere as well as me. I had sold almost everything, they almost nothing. Some times ... "Ya got to go where they ain"t.)

Like an American I had gotten it, and like my old Jewish ancestors, I had made that money. And in my study of religions and history I studied a lot about my ancestors, the Jews, and why so often they were required to become "rag man," their history of transitions and expulsions throughout the world. And how they came by the millions to America, including my grandparents, driven out of Russia by the Czar's policy to "end the Jewish Problem" by one/third conversion, one/third expulsion and one/third extermination (some fifty years before Hitler's final solution). For them coming to

America was to worship free of popes and czars and, of course, to make money.

But I also knew that the Jews, my ancestors, had been driven from place to place by the Catholics and other Christians of the West long before the Czars came into existence. And how when the Pope called for the Crusades, the Catholics killed every Jew they could find along the way (throughout England France, Germany, etc.); and that the Jews were not just kicked out of Spain in 1492 (by the most Catholic of Kings and Queens), but from England and France hundreds of years earlier.

And no matter where they went, except into Muslim lands, the Catholics followed with their "inquisitions" and Auto de Fe, which tortured hundreds of thousands and killed tens of thousands with the consent of the popes of the past. Even when there were the "good popes," that on occasion were willing to "protect the Jews," they created the "ghetto" as the safe place for them to live, but the popes also created the ghetto as the only place where the Jews could live. The czars had the Pale, the popes the Ghetto; both designed to restrict my ancestors, restricted in options and opportunity in education and work, restricted often to the level of "rag man," with their little carts.

And I know that today the popes were nothing like before, even this one, John Paul II, who some eight years after this trip would claim that he ended the Communist Empire. (I think it was more Steve Jobs or Ronald Reagan, or, actually come to think about it, the Russian people themselves, or maybe John, Paul, George and Ringo; the school is still out on the real reason, but this Pope claimed it.) And they've not been much of a real-world player ever since Stalin asked how many tanks the Pope had. And this Pope was trying to "build bridges" between the religions and all that, but he still was the Pope.

No Sense of History

And I know in my study that so many fled to the new world to be free of the religion of the popes, or, on the other hand, to be free to worship the religion of the popes; both were true. And people also fled to be free from kings and queens and dukes and barons and such (as well as cardinals and bishops), who all in one way or another restricted people from progress and opportunity.

But mostly they came in hope of making money. We all know that America's myth was that the nation was founded by people seeking to avoid the tyranny of state religions (only to impose their own tyranny here). But really, most came, if they were not brought in chains, to make more money than they had before, to have 160 acres of land rather than a quarter-acre, and to give less of that money to the support of the rulers (nobles or religions) of the land.

And America truly is the land that has been the most free from religious control, where people could be religious or not or free to change their religions or not; and also free to make money in so many ways, legal and not, formal economy or not.

And I knew this stuff when I went down to LA ... about my hatred for religion and my radical worldview and my disgust at the treatment of Jews by Catholics throughout history, when I went to LA to "do the Pope." My friends thought it bizarre that I'd go at all. But I went there for the most American of all reasons, to make money. I was not there to be in awe of anything or anyone. I didn't go to see the representative of "Christ on Earth", which I thought was a myth upon myth. I went there to make money, from all those who were silly enough to think they were seeing "Christ's representative upon Earth."

And so there I was, in the street within four feet of this guy, this direct descendant, in name at least, of Peter, the rock, supposed to be one of the best Popes of all time, but still without tanks, John Paul II, looking right at me and blessing me. And as I was stuffing more dollars in my apron and I looked right at him, a thought rushed into my head, of a scene from a really bad Jack Palance movie where he played Attila the Hun.

In that movie Jack (Attila) told some Catholic priests who were crossing themselves something like "take your magic spells away from me, holy man."

And that's the thought I had as I was making money and stuffing dollars in my apron and selling crap and the Pope looked at me and blessed me, I thought ... "take your magic spells away from me, holy man," and then I did what I think in the end almost every Jew in history, since the development of the popes, would have loved to do and to be able to get away with it.

I gave the Pope the bird, the most American of all symbols. I flipped him off. I gave him the finger, the great American bird ....

And I could give him the finger without fear of being taken away and burned or tortured or beaten or, in fact, I could give him the finger without fear at all. And I did, I gave him the finger without fear, but I think I got to be representative for all those who for centuries had lived in fear of the pope and couldn't do what I had just done ... "take your magic spells away from me ... and by the way here's my spell right back at you baby ..."

And I know he saw me do it. I could see him look back at me with a very confused face, something between, "Hey, I'm the Pope ... a good pope ... everyone loves me and; so what just happened?" and "Shit, I can't give him one back, I'm in public"

His pope mobile just keep rolling slowly by … and I looked to see if he's look back again … and he did …. And he stared at me for a moment … but his hands kept doing that holy magic finger crossing thing to the front.

He looked back at me, but he couldn't return the American bird salute to me. I'm sure he had the same question in his head that the little old nuns had had: "Are you Jewish?"

And I chuckled some and kept selling, and I sold through the blow off, and I made more money selling crap. Later that night, I told the story to my crew who just were amazed that I actually got to flip the bird to the Pope… and even though I was only a semi-guy, that night I was more than treated as one of the culture, not someone near at all to the mainstream. All my beers were paid for by others…and we all chanted MIGWA, MIGWA several times that night.

Glenn Young

Setting the Stage

This is a piece that started off as an effort to express an experience that should be common to everyone, though the particulars of this story are mine. All of us experience reflections about (quoting the Bible and not the song "a time to embrace [the past] and a time to refrain from embracing" ... [what has been]. We are all conflicted by this need to move forward and put our wilder days behind us. For a historian that seems like a contradiction.

I close this set of essays with something that is personal, and reflective, and in many ways says all that is trying to be said in all the other essays. We must remember the past both on a personal level and in a social and political level. Without knowing the ancient and recent the past, we miss the meaning of existence and how to *Carry On*.

Now that is how it started, this essay that is, but that is not all it has become. When I wrote the essay as a personal thing and not intended for publication, I was free to quote lyrics from the songs noted. In fact to make the piece work I had to quote these songs.

But when I decided to add this essay to the book, I found that with the current copyright laws of today, I was not free to use these quotes. Yes, I can use lyrics with permission from the current owners of the lyrics (who are now some major corporation rather than the songwriters themselves.) However, based on the information in several self-publishing web sites, the process of gaining such permission is extremely slow, often costly and in the end usually denied. All the sites advised against using any lyric from songs published since the 1930's. Song titles are OK but not quotes from those very songs.

No Sense of History

Therefore after being confronted by the reality of the moment I was left with the options of cutting the essay, re-writing it to remove the quotes, or using this as a moment point out the absurdity of the times, at least for *My Generation* in trying to write about my times and life without making direct references through quotes of the music of my times and life.

I grew up with the music of the times, and at some points in my life it seemed that all I did was to quote Dylan for almost every occasion and for every intellectual need of mine. To write what I have done without quoting the songs of my time is … *Crazy* (or a title of a song slightly out of my interest.)

Since protest has been part of my nature for most of my life, my choice became obvious. I have now designed the essay in such a fashion as to look like a censored version of books and letters in some not to recent totalitarian country. Perhaps this way of presenting the essay fits better into the overall tone of the book.

I could say something more about not backing down, or hoping the times will change, or not caring about what others say, or imagining that we could actually quote our songs of our times, but in doing so, I would most likely fall back on the words of the poets of my generation and come close to breaking copyright laws. So I am almost held *Helpless*.

Almost Cut My Hair Reprise – Censored version

"▮▮▮▮▮▮▮▮▮▮▮▮▮▮▮▮▮▮▮▮▮▮▮ … So, there I was looking in the mirror and thinking my hair was just a bit too shabby. "▮▮▮." Not having much hair any more it's hard to tell. But I figured I needed to look a little clean, even though there are few around me these days, and no real reason

to be much concerned about how my hair looks since I no longer work and am alone. *Carry On* ... So what once was important seems, well, less so, since I have no one to please any more: "███████████████████████████████████████
████████████████████████████████" I was just having some of the problems of being an older man alone ████████████████████████████████

So while my house ███████████████████" there is no one to light the fire, and I'm allergic to cats. So, no one to tell me it's time to get a haircut. "█████████████████████████
█████████████

Then as I stared into this device that reveals that I am no longer who I would want to be, I remember: I can't get a haircut today. I was going to see a concert with Graham Nash and David Crosby that very night. And, since one of Crosby's more memorable songs, at least for me, is one called *I Almost Cut My Hair,* out of respect to the man and my youth, well I just wouldn't do it. Just couldn't do it. I owed it to David, or maybe myself, to hold off one more day. ████████████████". Ok, I am now 61 and not 16, but the idea of cutting my hair on the day of this concert just struck me as too odd. And I started humming the song as I went on with my day, just kind of "████████████████ a little once again. "██████████████
██
█████████

My days, these days, are more limited than I ever hoped, and most of my entertainment comes at the casino in Niagara Falls, where I tend to win at poker and lose on the table games. And of all things odd, the casino was also where the concert was being held."████████████████████" So I spent a few hours in the poker room with some 200 others playing cards and telling some that I was going to the concert. Most had no interest; the younger people had no idea of who I was talking about.

No Sense of History

One couple, who were also going to the concert and because they gambled so much were invited to a pre-event party with the band, actually pulled out of a bag a forty-three year old original vinyl of the first *Crosby, Stills and Nash* album. I opened it up to look at the liner notes and received an incredible hit of mildew. The record may not have been open in well, maybe forty years, ok, maybe thirty ▮▮▮▮▮▮▮▮▮▮▮▮▮▮▮▮▮▮▮▮▮▮▮▮▮

I learned that this couple who claimed to be big fans had never even heard of the song, *I Almost Cut My Hair*, after I told them of my non-activity on this day. One of the dealers joked with us by singing the first few words. I was impressed that a younger person even knew as much of the song as she did, but then in our conversation she showed she had no idea of the meaning of the song, and didn't know many lines other than the first ("I ▮▮▮▮▮▮▮▮▮▮▮▮▮▮▮▮▮▮ After I sang some more of the song, she wondered what a freak flag was. I suggested that I give her ▮▮ ▮▮▮▮▮▮▮▮▮▮▮▮▮▮▮▮▮, and she again had no idea of my reference. ▮▮▮▮▮▮▮▮▮ other things in common, we didn't share all of the music of my youth. She did, however, deal me a winning hand … ▮▮▮▮▮▮▮▮▮▮▮▮▮▮▮▮▮▮▮▮▮▮▮

I had no idea why I was really going to the concert; kind of *Helplessly Hoping* to relive my youth a little. Between the ages of fifteen and eighteen, while living in San Francisco, I went to so many concerts, I guess I kind of burned out on them long ago; and besides, they all became super commercial and expensive.

Back in my day (Oy, I'm saying that?), at the Fillmore or the Avalon ballrooms, we saw three bands, each doing two sets a night, for three dollars. I often went multiple times a weekend, but then after leaving San Francisco I mostly stopped. But in that time, I saw every group from that period, as well as all the old blues singers and jazz bands that came through San Francisco, and "███████████████████████████████" Then purple berries had multiple meanings.

In those years, *the Byrds* were my favorite group (David Crosby's second group), and later I was somewhat less impressed than many around me at that time with *Crosby, Stills and Nash*, for their seeming lack of politics. I was more impressed with them when Neil Young joined the group, and they started singing about "███████████████" and the trials of the Chicago Eight (then Seven). And, I've always been a fan of words in music, and felt, despite their lack of political songs, that *Crosby, Stills and Nash* were more a band of poets rather than musicians searching for some words to go with the voids between guitar riffs. So my initial opinion changed, but I still liked their later stuff more than their first big hit album. I guess I can say that in their time they were among the most interesting bands around, and their time was a time of my early adulthood.

When I was nineteen I myself staged a few rock concerts to raise money for activities of my lefty political collective. We ended up naming the coffee shop we opened (with the intention of it being the lefty political center for Hartford, Connecticut), *Wooden Ships,* over my objections (I wanted a more overt political name).

However, I guess all I'm trying to say is that I suspected there was something about this concert more for me than for most going. "██ ██████ But I was still reluctant, not wanting to be just an old man trying to seem *Younger then Yesterday.*

Up until the day before, I couldn't decide to go or not. I checked and there were still tickets, and not too costly. But I was still undecided, not really thinking that there was a

No Sense of History

purpose for me in going. "█████████████████████████████████?" So while sitting at a poker table I said to a dealer "put me on a rush and if you do, I'll buy a ticket to the concert."

No sooner said then I won five out of the next six hands, winning some $700, so the choice had been made. I started to ████████████████████████████████ After all, "████ ██ ████████████████" One moment I was excited and the next I thought this concert was no big deal, but I had set the ground rules of the poker rush, so I was not committed.

So, I started to go to the concert venue and took the escalator that traveled less than *Eight Miles High*. I sailed away into the room sitting two thousand with no *Wooden Ships* anywhere, just straight-back folding chairs. All around me were people who seemed far too straight or less involved in their youth or just now looking far too old or too young to understand what they were about to see. "████████████████████████████ ████████████"

It seemed most of the people there were there since there was little else to do in Buffalo and the concert was cheap and they may have heard a song some time before. But, my vibe was that they had not lived the songs the way I did. I'm sure there were some, but most, well .... "████████████████████████ ██ ██

Then, right at eight o'clock the "████████████████" and the ██ ████████████. For the next two hours, I was caught up in that past.

Glenn Young

Every song I knew on the first note played (except for the two new ones they added). They began the set with my favorite song from when I was sixteen (*Eight Miles High*) and worked their way through Nash's pop-like songs (*Marrakesh Express*) and Crosby's "strange shit," as Nash called them (*Déjà vu*, "*Guinevere*).

The band was tight and they used minimal lighting effects. They looked like and acted like the bands of my youth, almost unscripted (or at least making it feel that way), appearing to jam on several songs, taking requests from the crowd and saying that they would deviate from their planned set to meet the requests. In other words, they were having fun playing, and I was having fun listening.

I tried successfully to blot out the limited environment and lack of dance space, and the mostly flat reception from what appeared to be more than half the crowd. To me, every cord, every note, every minute of the event (ok except for the few new ones), helped me to recall moments of joy and pain and success and failures that I lived through, but it helped me recall things I mostly don't choose to remember since it was so long ago and far away, and so different than most others.

I sat in my straight chair and rocked in both my head and body. I felt like, as I imagined my own actions and looked occasionally at the inactions of those around me, I was still looking at the " ▇▇▇▇▇▇▇▇▇▇▇▇▇▇▇▇▇▇▇▇▇▇▇▇ . I listened and was moved and did remember that I had fought the *Military Madness* that had ruined my country and that I had seen " ▇▇▇▇▇▇▇▇▇▇▇▇▇▇▇▇▇▇▇▇▇▇ and I remembered the " ▇▇▇▇▇▇▇▇▇▇▇▇▇▇▇▇▇▇▇▇▇ " and I got "

354

No Sense of History

▇▇▇▇▇▇▇▇▇▇▇▇▇▇▇▇▇▇▇▇▇▇▇▇▇▇ and became myself, with "▇▇▇▇▇▇▇▇▇▇▇▇▇

And it's funny that with all their hits, the centerpiece of the concert was David Crosby belting out a very bluesy version of *I Almost Cut My Hair*. There he was at almost seventy, hitting every high note and carrying on the note as if he knew where he would be tomorrow. He looked great and sounded great and made remarks throughout the concert that he had finally found some peace and some inner light. It did make me ▇▇▇▇▇▇▇▇▇▇▇▇▇▇▇▇▇▇▇▇▇▇▇▇▇▇▇▇▇▇▇▇▇▇▇ ▇▇▇..

But the concert ended with *Wooden Ships* and an encore of *Teach Your Children Well* that was mainly sung by the audience. And I floated back to a packed poker room where few cared or were interested in my moment of pleasure. I was back in my limited world, and I guess I'll cut my hair tomorrow. Or, maybe not, since, for me, I was reminded that there is still time and still a chance to be like my long-term musical idol … and *Carry On*. After all

Glenn Young

Setting the Stage

I was a community organizer in a very poor neighborhood in Seattle for some six years. We were doing many good things and word got around and we attracted many people to come and work with us. At one point we managed to have nearly fifty people on some kind of payroll or stipend. We had a community center, senior center, a health clinic and a food coop. We also ran the local park and the community garden area. We had the form but not always the structures that were expected. Our strength came from our people, and there were so many of them, who came and went. Collectively they all added things both positive and negative that for a while made the whole place seem successful.

This poem was written after hearing of the death of one of those who passed through though for a while. He later went on to become one of the leading naturopathic therapists in the United Kingdom, but in those days, we all were well ... not where we were all going. We were all there, in Cascade Community, and our value was seen in what we gave there.

When he died, those of us still around and in contact with each other remembered him for what he was then.

The poem is specifically designed to discuss the feels and the experience of being with people in any place any time, where things felt good. It is general so all who have had that place, can relate to the concept, rather than writing about the particulars

Learning of the Passing of a Comrade

He was there for a while
In that place, in that time, for a while
Where we all felt connected

No Sense of History

Where we all felt that we did things and
It is that place and that time we still always seem to keep
Warm in our hearts; forever.

He was there and I was there for a while
And we did things that seemed to be important
We talked of things that seemed important
And we did things with people that made us
All feel connected, that made us all feel like
Well ... comrades

It was that place and time, like no other
That always seems to be remembered as that time, that place
Where for a while we were connected and no matter what
    happened later
No matter all the new places and new connections
It was that time and place that was always
    binding forever
The place where we all felt like
Well ... comrades.

He was there in that place for a while and then
well he was gone
We were all soon gone from that place, that time
Either by ourselves or in pairs, soon in other lives
Away from that place and time and that connectivity
Where we all felt like we did things, important things
Where we all were
Well ... Comrades

I saw him so much later far away from there, that place
In his new place far away from me
I went there to that new place not to see him but for me
I was there involved in a new connectivity but

Glenn Young

I saw him in that new place, far from that other place
Where we had been, for a while
Well ... Comrades

We talked at each other
About our new places, our new connections
And then we talked with each other
About that place, that time and all the people
About all the connectivity and then it was like it was
For a while like that other place where we were for a while
Well ... comrades

Then I was gone from his new place
Gone to so many other places
Looking for a means to feel that feeling again
That feeling I had for such a short time with him, with others
That feeling of connectivity of doing things important
And talking about things that seemed important with
Well ... comrades

Now I learn that his is gone, from his new place
In fact he is gone from all places
No longer is there hope of regaining that
    connectivity with him
That promise of doing things that seem important with him
No longer will we talk with understanding that can only be
    understood
By those who had been in that place in that time
    where we did things
And talked of things that seemed to have meaning
    and importance
And where we all were for a while
Well ... comrades.

Made in the USA
Columbia, SC
19 November 2022